Business Policy and Strategic Management

Business Policy and Strategic Management

Ravikant Mukherjee

ADHYAYAN

ADHYAYAN PUBLISHERS & DISTRIBUTORS
New Delhi-110002

Published by
ADHYAYAN PUBLISHERS & DISTRIBUTORS
4378/4B, 105, J.M.D. House, Murari Lal Street
Ansari Road, Darya Ganj, New Delhi - 110002
Ph.: 011-23263018, 011-23277156, Fax: 011-23280028
Email: adhyayanpublishers@yahoo.com

Business Policy and Strategic Management

Edition 2010
ISBN 978-81-8435-181-1

Printed in India

Published by Harish Chandra Yadav for Adhyayan Publishers & Distributors, Delhi. Laser Typesetting at V. M. Graphics and Printed at Tarun Offset Printers, Delhi

Preface

Strategic management is the conduct of drafting, implementing and evaluating cross-functional decisions that will enable an organisation to achieve its long-term objectives. It is the process of specifying the organisation's mission, vision and objectives, developing policies and plans, often in terms of projects and programs, which are designed to achieve these objectives, and then allocating resources to implement the policies and plans, projects and programs. A balanced scorecard is often used to evaluate the overall performance of the business and its progress towards objectives.

The business policy is a guide that stipulates rules, regulations and objectives, and may be used in the managers' decision-making. It can be used to determine mission, vision, values, goals, objectives, roles and responsibilities, timelines, etc. Policy planning is a disciplined effort to produce fundamental decisions and actions that shape and guide what an organisation is, what it does, and why it does it, with a focus on the future.

This book is designed for students of strategic management and business policy. It contains the latest research and examples of well-known and not-so-well known companies dealing with complicated strategic issues. It offers an engaging look into new and traditional strategic management topics. Its thorough coverage helps readers develop an understanding of the wide range of theories and research available in this field. Integration of international issues throughout provides an essential understanding of global economics and its impact on business activities in any location. Besides students, directors of strategic planning, competitive intelligence analysts, and strategic planners will also will find this book of utmost use.

Ravikant Mukherjee

Contents

1

Introduction to Strategic Management

Strategic management is the highest level of managerial activity. Strategies are typically planned, crafted or guided by the Chief Executive Officer, approved or authorised by the Board of directors, and then implemented under the supervision of the organisation's top management team or senior executives.

Strategic management provides overall direction to the enterprise and is closely related to the field of Organisation Studies. In the field of business administration it is useful to talk about "strategic alignment" between the organisation and its environment or "strategic consistency". According to Arieu "there is strategic consistency when the actions of an organisation are consistent with the expectations of management, and these in turn are with the market and the context."

> "Strategic management is an ongoing process that evaluates and controls the business and the industries in which the company is involved; assesses its competitors and sets goals and strategies to meet all existing and potential competitors; and then reassesses each strategy annually or quarterly to determine how it has been implemented and whether it has succeeded or needs replacement by a new strategy to meet changed circumstances, new technology, new competitors, a new economic environment., or a new social, financial, or political environment."

Strategic Management Processes

Strategic management is a combination of three main processes which are as follows.

Strategy Formulation

— Performing a situation analysis, self-evaluation and competitor analysis: both internal and external; both micro-environmental and macro-environmental.

— Concurrent with this assessment, objectives are set. These objectives should be parallel to a timeline; some are in the short-term and others on the long-term. This involves crafting vision statements (long term view of a possible future), mission statements (the role that the organisation gives itself in society), overall corporate objectives (both financial and strategic), strategic business unit objectives (both financial and strategic), and tactical objectives.

— These objectives should, in the light of the situation analysis, suggest a strategic plan. The plan provides the details of how to achieve these objectives.

This three-step strategy formulation process is sometimes referred to as determining where you are now, determining where you want to go, and then determining how to get there. These three questions are the essence of strategic planning. I/O Economics for the external factors and RBV for the internal factors.

Strategy Implementation

— Allocation and management of sufficient resources (financial, personnel, time, technology support)

— Establishing a chain of command or some alternative structure (such as cross functional teams)

— Assigning responsibility of specific tasks or processes to specific individuals or groups

— It also involves managing the process. This includes monitoring results, comparing to benchmarks and best practices, evaluating the efficacy and efficiency of the process, controlling for variances, and making adjustments to the process as necessary.

— When implementing specific programmes, this involves acquiring the requisite resources, developing the process, training, process testing, documentation, and integration with (and/or conversion from) legacy processes.

Thus this type of problem can occur in strategy. In order for a policy to work, there must be a level of consistency from every person in an organisation, including from the management. This is what needs to occur on thc tactical level of management as well as strategic.

Strategy Evaluation

Measuring the effectiveness of the organisational strategy. It's extremely important to conduct a SWOT analysis to figure out the strengths, weaknesses, opportunities and threats (both internal and external) of the entity in question. This may require to take certain precautionary measures or even to change the entire strategy.

In corporate strategy, Johnson and Scholes present a model in which strategic options are evaluated against three key success criteria:

- Suitability (would it work?)
- Feasibility (can it be made to work?)
- Acceptability (will they work it?)

Suitability

Suitability deals with the overall rationale of the strategy. The key point to consider is whether the strategy would address the key strategic issues underlined by the organisation's strategic position.

- Does it make economic sense?
- Would the organisation obtain economies of scale, economies of scope or experience economy?
- Would it be suitable in terms of environment and capabilities?

Tools that can be used to evaluate suitability include:

- Ranking strategic options
- Decision trees
- What-if analysis

Feasibility

Feasibility is concerned with the resources required to implement the strategy are available, can be developed or obtained. Resources include funding, people, time and information. Tools that can be used to evaluate feasibility include:

— cash flow analysis and forecasting
— break-even analysis
— resource deployment analysis

Acceptability

Acceptability is concerned with the expectations of the identified stakeholders (mainly shareholders, employees and customers) with the expected performance outcomes, which can be return, risk and stakeholder reactions.

— Return deals with the benefits expected by the stakeholders (financial and non-financial). For example, shareholders would expect the increase of their wealth, employees would expect improvement in their careers and customers would expect better value for money.
— Risk deals with the probability and consequences of failure of a strategy (financial and non-financial).
— Stakeholder reactions deals with anticipating the likely reaction of stakeholders. Shareholders could oppose the issuing of new shares, employees and unions could oppose outsourcing for fear of losing their jobs, customers could have concerns over a merger with regards to quality and support.

Tools that can be used to evaluate acceptability include:

— what-if analysis
— stakeholder mapping

General Approaches

In general terms, there are two main approaches, which are opposite but complement each other in some ways, to strategic management:

— The Industrial Organisational Approach
    — based on economic theory—deals with issues like competitive rivalry, resource allocation, economies of scale

    — assumptions—rationality, self discipline behaviour, profit maximisation
- — The Sociological Approach
    — deals primarily with human interactions
    — assumptions—bounded rationality, satisfying behaviour, profit sub-optimality. An example of a company that currently operates this way is Google

Strategic management techniques can be viewed as bottom-up, top-down, or collaborative processes. In the bottom-up approach, employees submit proposals to their managers who, in turn, funnel the best ideas further up the organisation. This is often accomplished by a capital budgeting process. Proposals are assessed using financial criteria such as return on investment or cost-benefit analysis. Cost underestimation and benefit overestimation are major sources of error.

The proposals that are approved form the substance of a new strategy, all of which is done without a grand strategic design or a strategic architect. The top-down approach is the most common by far. In it, the CEO, possibly with the assistance of a strategic planning team, decides on the overall direction the company should take. Some organisations are starting to experiment with collaborative strategic planning techniques that recognise the emergent nature of strategic decisions.

Strategy Hierarchy

In most (large) corporations there are several levels of management. Strategic management is the highest of these levels in the sense that it is the broadest—applying to all parts of the firm—while also incorporating the longest time horizon. It gives direction to corporate values, corporate culture, corporate goals, and corporate missions. Under this broad corporate strategy there are typically business-level competitive strategies and functional unit strategies.

Corporate strategy refers to the overarching strategy of the diversified firm. Such a corporate strategy answers the questions of "in which businesses should we compete?" and "how does being in these business create synergy and/or add to the competitive advantage of the corporation as a whole?"

Business strategy refers to the aggregated strategies of single business firm or a strategic business unit (SBU) in a diversified corporation. According to Michael Porter, a firm must formulate a business strategy that incorporates either cost leadership, differentiation or focus in order to achieve a sustainable competitive advantage and long-term success in its chosen arenas or industries.

Functional strategies include marketing strategies, new product development strategies, human resource strategies, financial strategies, legal strategies, supply-chain strategies, and information technology management strategies. The emphasis is on short and medium term plans and is limited to the domain of each department's functional responsibility. Each functional department attempts to do its part in meeting overall corporate objectives, and hence to some extent their strategies are derived from broader corporate strategies.

Many companies feel that a functional organisational structure is not an efficient way to organise activities so they have reengineered according to processes or SBUs. A strategic business unit is a semi-autonomous unit that is usually responsible for its own budgeting, new product decisions, hiring decisions, and price setting. An SBU is treated as an internal profit centre by corporate headquarters.

An additional level of strategy called operational strategy was encouraged by Peter Drucker in his theory of management by objectives (MBO). It is very narrow in focus and deals with day-to-day operational activities such as scheduling criteria. It must operate within a budget but is not at liberty to adjust or create that budget. Operational level strategies are informed by business level strategies which, in turn, are informed by corporate level strategies.

Since the turn of the millennium, some firms have reverted to a simpler strategic structure driven by advances in information technology. It is felt that knowledge management systems should be used to share information and create common goals. Strategic divisions are thought to hamper this process. This notion of strategy has been captured under the rubric of dynamic strategy, popularised by Carpenter and Sanders's textbook.

This work builds on that of Brown and Eisenhart as well as Christensen and portrays firm strategy, both business and corporate, as necessarily embracing ongoing strategic change, and the seamless integration of strategy formulation and implementation. Such change and implementation are usually built into the strategy through the staging and pacing facets.

HISTORICAL DEVELOPMENT

Origin

Strategic management as a discipline originated in the 1950s and 60s. Although there were numerous early contributors to the literature, the most influential pioneers were Alfred D. Chandler, Jr., Philip Selznick, Igor Ansoff, and Peter Drucker. Alfred Chandler recognised the importance of coordinating the various aspects of management under one all-encompassing strategy. Prior to this time the various functions of management were separate with little overall coordination or strategy.

Interactions between functions or between departments were typically handled by a boundary position, that is, there were one or two managers that relayed information back and forth between two departments. Chandler also stressed the importance of taking a long term perspective when looking to the future. In his 1962 groundbreaking work Strategy and Structure, Chandler showed that a long-term coordinated strategy was necessary to give a company structure, direction, and focus. He says it concisely, "structure follows strategy."

In 1957, Philip Selznick introduced the idea of matching the organisation's internal factors with external environmental circumstances. This core idea was developed into what we now call SWOT analysis by Learned, Andrews, and others at the Harvard Business School General Management Group. Strengths and weaknesses of the firm are assessed in light of the opportunities and threats from the business environment.

Igor Ansoff built on Chandler's work by adding a range of strategic concepts and inventing a whole new vocabulary. He developed a strategy grid that compared market penetration strategies, product development strategies, market development strategies and horizontal and vertical integration and diversification strategies. He felt that management could use these strategies to systematically prepare for future opportunities and challenges. In his 1965 classic Corporate Strategy, he developed the gap analysis still used today in which we must understand the gap between where we are currently and where we would like to be, then develop what he called "gap reducing actions".

Peter Drucker was a prolific strategy theorist, author of dozens of management books, with a career spanning five decades. His contributions to strategic management were many but two are most important. Firstly, he stressed the importance of objectives. An organisation without clear objectives is like a ship without a rudder. As early as 1954 he was developing a theory of management based on objectives. This evolved into his theory of management by objectives (MBO).

According to Drucker, the procedure of setting objectives and monitoring your progress towards them should permeate the entire organisation, top to bottom. His other seminal contribution was in predicting the importance of what today we would call intellectual capital. He predicted the rise of what he called the "knowledge worker" and explained the consequences of this for management. He said that knowledge work is non-hierarchical. Work would be carried out in teams with the person most knowledgeable in the task at hand being the temporary leader.

In 1985, Ellen-Earle Chaffee summarised what she thought were the main elements of strategic management theory by the 1970s:

— Strategic management involves adapting the organisation to its business environment.

— Strategic management is fluid and complex. Change creates novel combinations of circumstances requiring unstructured non-repetitive responses.

— Strategic management affects the entire organisation by providing direction.

— Strategic management involves both strategy formation (she called it content) and also strategy implementation (she called it process).

— Strategic management is partially planned and partially unplanned.

— Strategic management is done at several levels: overall corporate strategy, and individual business strategies.

— Strategic management involves both conceptual and analytical thought processes.

Growth and Portfolio Theory

In the 1970s much of strategic management dealt with size, growth, and portfolio theory. The PIMS study was a long term study, started in the 1960s and lasted for 19 years, that attempted to understand the Profit Impact of Marketing Strategies (PIMS), particularly the effect of market share. Started at General Electric, moved to Harvard in the early 1970s, and then moved to the Strategic Planning Institute in the late 1970s, it now contains decades of information on the relationship between profitability and strategy.

Their initial conclusion was unambiguous: The greater a company's market share, the greater will be their rate of profit. The high market share provides volume and economies of scale. It also provides experience and learning curve advantages. The combined effect is increased profits. The studies conclusions continue to be drawn on by academics and companies today: "PIMS provides compelling quantitative evidence as to which business strategies work and don't work"—Tom Peters.

The benefits of high market share naturally lead to an interest in growth strategies. The relative advantages of horizontal integration, vertical integration, diversification, franchises, mergers and acquisitions, joint ventures, and organic growth were discussed. The most appropriate market dominance strategies were assessed given the competitive and regulatory environment. There was also research that indicated that a low market share strategy could also be very profitable. Schumacher, Woo and Cooper, Levenson, and later Traverso showed how smaller niche players obtained very high returns.

By the early 1980s the paradoxical conclusion was that high market share and low market share companies were often very profitable but most of the companies in between were not. This was sometimes called the "hole in the middle" problem. This anomaly would be explained by Michael Porter in the 1980s.

The management of diversified organisations required new techniques and new ways of thinking. The first CEO to address the problem of a multi-divisional company was Alfred Sloan at General Motors. GM was decentralised into semi-autonomous "strategic business units" (SBU's), but with centralised support functions.

One of the most valuable concepts in the strategic management of multi-divisional companies was portfolio theory. In the previous decade Harry Markowitz and other financial theorists developed the theory of portfolio analysis. It was concluded that a broad portfolio of financial assets could reduce specific risk. In the 1970s marketers extended the theory to product portfolio decisions and managerial strategists extended it to operating division portfolios.

Each of a company's operating divisions were seen as an element in the corporate portfolio. Each operating division (also called strategic business units) was treated as a semi-independent profit centre with its own revenues, costs, objectives, and strategies. Several techniques were developed to analyse the relationships between elements in a portfolio. B.C.G. Analysis, for example, was developed by the Boston Consulting Group in the early 1970s. This was the theory that gave us the wonderful image of a CEO sitting on a stool milking a cash cow.

Shortly after that the G.E. multi factoral model was developed by General Electric. Companies continued to diversify until the 1980s when it was realised that in many cases a portfolio of operating divisions was worth more as separate completely independent companies.

Marketing Revolution

The 1970s also saw the rise of the marketing oriented firm. From the beginnings of capitalism it was assumed that the key requirement of business success was a product of high technical quality. If you produced a product that worked well and was durable, it was assumed you would have no difficulty selling them at a profit. This was called the production orientation and it was generally true that good products could be sold without effort, encapsulated in the saying "Build a better mousetrap and the world will beat a path to your door." This was largely due to the growing numbers of affluent and middle class people that capitalism had created.

But after the untapped demand caused by the second world war was saturated in the 1950s it became obvious that products were not selling as easily as they had been. The answer was to concentrate on selling. The 1950s and 1960s is known as the sales era and the guiding philosophy of business of the time is today called the sales orientation. In the early 1970s Theodore Levitt and others at Harvard argued that the sales orientation had things backward.

They claimed that instead of producing products then trying to sell them to the customer, businesses should start with the customer, find out what they wanted, and then produce it for them. The customer became the driving force behind all strategic business decisions. This marketing orientation, in the decades since its introduction, has been reformulated and repackaged under numerous names including customer orientation, marketing philosophy, customer intimacy, customer focus, customer driven, and market focused.

Japanese Challenge

By the late 70s people had started to notice how successful Japanese industry had become. In industry after industry, including steel, watches, ship building, cameras, autos, and electronics, the Japanese were surpassing American and European companies. Westerners wanted to know why. Numerous theories purported to explain the Japanese success including:

— Higher employee morale, dedication, and loyalty;
— Lower cost structure, including wages;
— Effective government industrial policy;
— Modernisation after WWII leading to high capital intensity and productivity;
— Economies of scale associated with increased exporting;
— Relatively low value of the Yen leading to low interest rates and capital costs, low dividend expectations, and inexpensive exports;
— Superior quality control techniques such as Total Quality

Management and other systems introduced by W. Edwards Deming in the 1950s and 60s.

Although there was some truth to all these potential explanations, there was clearly something missing. In fact by 1980 the Japanese cost structure was higher than the American. And post WWII reconstruction was nearly 40 years in the past. The first management theorist to suggest an explanation was Richard Pascale. In 1981 Richard Pascale and Anthony Athos in The Art of Japanese Management claimed that the main reason for Japanese success was their superior management techniques.

They divided management into 7 aspects (which are also known as McKinsey 7S Framework): Strategy, Structure, Systems, Skills, Staff, Style, and Supraordinate goals (which we would now call shared values). The first three of the 7 S's were called hard factors and this is where American companies excelled. The remaining four factors (skills, staff, style, and shared values) were called soft factors and were not well understood by American businesses of the time Americans did not yet place great value on corporate culture, shared values and beliefs, and social cohesion in the workplace.

In Japan the task of management was seen as managing the whole complex of human needs, economic, social, psychological, and spiritual. In America work was seen as something that was separate from the rest of one's life. It was quite common for Americans to exhibit a very different personality at work compared to the rest of their lives. Pascale also highlighted the difference between decision making styles; hierarchical in America, and consensus in Japan. He also claimed that American business lacked long term vision, preferring instead to apply management fads and theories in a piecemeal fashion.

One year later The Mind of the Strategist was released in America by Kenichi Ohmae, the head of McKinsey & Co.'s Tokyo office. He claimed that strategy in America was too analytical. Strategy should be a creative art: It is a frame of mind that requires intuition and intellectual flexibility. He claimed that Americans constrained their strategic options by thinking in terms of analytical techniques, rote formula, and step-by-step processes. He compared the culture of Japan in which vagueness, ambiguity, and tentative decisions were acceptable, to American culture that valued fast decisions.

Also in 1982 Tom Peters and Robert Waterman released a study that would respond to the Japanese challenge head on. Peters and Waterman, who had several years earlier collaborated with Pascale and Athos at McKinsey & Co. asked "What makes an excellent company?". They looked at 62 companies that they thought were fairly successful. Each was subject to six performance criteria. To be classified as an excellent company, it had to be above the 50th percentile in 4 of the 6 performance metrics for 20 consecutive years.

Forty-three companies passed the test. They then studied these successful companies and interviewed key executives. They concluded in In Search of Excellence that there were 8 keys to excellence that were shared by all 43 firms. They are:

— A bias for action - Do it. Try it. Don't waste time studying it with multiple reports and committees.

— Customer focus - Get close to the customer. Know your customer.

— Entrepreneurship - Even big companies act and think small by giving people the authority to take initiatives.

— Productivity through people - Treat your people with respect and they will reward you with productivity.

— Value-oriented CEOs - The CEO should actively propagate corporate values throughout the organisation.

— Stick to the knitting - Do what you know well.

— Keep things simple and lean - Complexity encourages waste and confusion.

— Simultaneously centralised and decentralised - Have tight centralised control while also allowing maximum individual autonomy.

The basic blueprint on how to compete against the Japanese had been drawn. But as J.E. Rehfeld explains it is not a straight forward task due to differences in culture. A certain type of alchemy was required to transform knowledge from various cultures into a management style that allows a specific company to compete in a globally diverse world. He says, for example, that Japanese style kaizen (continuous improvement) techniques, although suitable for people socialised in Japanese culture, have not been successful when implemented in the U.S. unless they are modified significantly.

Competitive Advantage

The Japanese challenge shook the confidence of the western business elite, but detailed comparisons of the two management styles and examinations of successful businesses convinced Westerners that they could overcome the challenge. The 1980s and early 1990s saw a plethora of theories explaining exactly how this could be done. They cannot all be detailed here, but some of the more important strategic advances of the decade are explained below.

Gary Hamel and C. K. Prahalad declared that strategy needs to be more active and interactive; less "arm-chair planning" was needed. They introduced terms like strategic intent and strategic architecture. Their most well known advance was the idea of core competency. They showed how important it was to know the one or two key things that your company does better than the competition.

Active strategic management required active information gathering and active problem solving. In the early days of Hewlett-Packard (H-P), Dave Packard and Bill Hewlett devised an active management style that they called Management By Walking Around (MBWA). Senior H-P managers were seldom at their desks. They spent most of their days visiting employees, customers, and suppliers. This direct contact with key people provided them with a solid grounding from which viable strategies could be crafted.

The MBWA concept was popularised in 1985 by a book by Tom Peters and Nancy Austin. Japanese managers employ a similar system, which originated at Honda, and is sometimes called the 3 G's (Genba, Genbutsu, and Genjitsu, which translate into "actual place", "actual thing", and "actual situation"). Probably the most influential strategist of the decade was Michael Porter. He introduced many new concepts including; 5 forces analysis, generic strategies, the value chain, strategic groups, and clusters.

In 5 forces analysis he identifies the forces that shape a firm's strategic environment. It is like a SWOT analysis with structure and purpose. It shows how a firm can use these forces to obtain a sustainable competitive advantage. Porter modifies Chandler's dictum about structure following strategy by introducing a second level of structure: Organisational structure follows strategy, which in turn follows industry structure. Porter's generic strategies detail the interaction between cost minimization strategies, product differentiation strategies, and market focus strategies.

Although he did not introduce these terms, he showed the importance of choosing one of them rather than trying to position your company between them. He also challenged managers to see their industry in terms of a value chain. A firm will be successful only to the extent that it contributes to the industry's value chain. This forced management to look at its operations from the customer's point of view. Every operation should be examined in terms of what value it adds in the eyes of the final customer.

In 1993, John Kay took the idea of the value chain to a financial level claiming " Adding value is the central purpose of business activity", where adding value is defined as the difference between the market value of outputs and the cost of inputs including capital, all divided by the firm's net output. Borrowing from Gary Hamel and Michael Porter, Kay claims that the role of strategic management is to identify your core competencies, and then assemble a collection of assets that will increase value added and provide a competitive advantage. He claims that there are 3 types of capabilities that can do this; innovation, reputation, and organisational structure.

The 1980s also saw the widespread acceptance of positioning theory. Although the theory originated with Jack Trout in 1969, it didn't gain wide acceptance until Al Ries and Jack Trout wrote their classic book "Positioning: The Battle For Your Mind". The basic premise is that a strategy should not be judged by internal company factors but by the way customers see it relative to the competition. Crafting and implementing a strategy involves creating a position in the mind of the collective consumer.

Several techniques were applied to positioning theory, some newly invented but most borrowed from other disciplines. Perceptual mapping for example, creates visual displays of the relationships between positions. Multidimensional scaling, discriminant analysis, factor analysis, and conjoint analysis are mathematical techniques used to determine the most relevant characteristics upon which positions should be based. Preference regression can be used to determine vectors of ideal positions and cluster analysis can identify clusters of positions.

Others felt that internal company resources were the key. In 1992, Jay Barney, for example, saw strategy as assembling the optimum mix of resources, including human, technology, and suppliers, and then configure them in unique and sustainable ways. Michael Hammer and James Champy felt that these resources needed to be restructured.

This process, that they labelled reengineering, involved organising a firm's assets around whole processes rather than tasks. In this way a team of people saw a project through, from inception to completion. This avoided functional silos where isolated departments seldom talked to each other. It also eliminated waste due to functional overlap and interdepartmental communications. In 1989 Richard Lester and the researchers at the MIT Industrial Performance Centre identified seven best practices and concluded that firms must accelerate the shift away from the mass production of low cost standardised products. The seven areas of best practice were:

- Simultaneous continuous improvement in cost, quality, service, and product innovation
- Breaking down organisational barriers between departments
- Eliminating layers of management creating flatter organisational hierarchies.
- Closer relationships with customers and suppliers
- Intelligent use of new technology
- Global focus
- Improving human resource skills

The search for "best practices" is also called benchmarking. This involves determining where you need to improve, finding an organisation that is exceptional in this area, then studying the company and applying its best practices in your firm. A large group of theorists felt the area where western business was most lacking was product quality. People like W. Edwards Deming, Joseph M. Juran, A. Kearney, Philip Crosby, and Armand Feignbaum suggested quality improvement techniques like Total Quality Management (TQM), continuous improvement, lean manufacturing, Six Sigma, and Return on Quality (ROQ).

An equally large group of theorists felt that poor customer service was the problem. People like James Heskett, Earl Sasser, William Davidow, Len Schlesinger, A. Paraurgman, Len Berry, Jane Kingman-Brundage, Christopher Hart, and Christopher Lovelock, gave us fishbone diagramming, service charting, Total Customer Service (TCS), the service profit chain, service gaps analysis, the service encounter, strategic service vision, service mapping, and service teams.

Their underlying assumption was that there is no better source of competitive advantage than a continuous stream of delighted customers. Process management uses some of the techniques from product quality management and some of the techniques from customer service management. It looks at an activity as a sequential process. The objective is to find inefficiencies and make the process more effective.

Although the procedures have a long history, dating back to Taylorism, the scope of their applicability has been greatly widened, leaving no aspect of the firm free from potential process improvements. Because of the broad applicability of process management techniques, they can be used as a basis for competitive advantage. Some realised that businesses were spending much more on acquiring new customers than on retaining current ones. Carl Sewell, Frederick F. Reichheld, C. Gronroos, and Earl Sasser showed us how a competitive advantage could be found in ensuring that customers returned again and again.

This has come to be known as the loyalty effect after Reicheld's book of the same name in which he broadens the concept to include employee loyalty, supplier loyalty, distributor loyalty, and shareholder loyalty. They also developed techniques for estimating the lifetime value of a loyal customer, called customer lifetime value (CLV). A significant movement started that attempted to recast selling and marketing techniques into a long term endeavor that created a sustained relationship with customers (called relationship selling, relationship marketing, and customer relationship management). Customer relationship management (CRM) software (and its many variants) became an integral tool that sustained this trend.

James Gilmore and Joseph Pine found competitive advantage in mass customisation. Flexible manufacturing techniques allowed businesses to individualise products for each customer without losing economies of scale. This effectively turned the product into a service. They also realised that if a service is mass customised by creating a "performance" for each individual client, that service would be transformed into an "experience". Their book, The Experience Economy, along with the work of Bernd Schmitt convinced many to see service provision as a form of theatre. This school of thought is sometimes referred to as customer experience management (CEM).

Like Peters and Waterman a decade earlier, James Collins and Jerry Porras spent years conducting empirical research on what makes great companies. Six years of research uncovered a key underlying principle behind the 19 successful companies that they studied: They all encourage and preserve a core ideology that nurtures the company. Even though strategy and tactics change daily, the companies, nevertheless, were able to maintain a core set of values.

These core values encourage employees to build an organisation that lasts. In Built To Last they claim that short term profit goals, cost cutting, and restructuring will not stimulate dedicated employees to build a great company that will endure. In 2000 Collins coined the term "built to flip" to describe the prevailing business attitudes in Silicon Valley. It describes a business culture where technological change inhibits a long term focus. He also popularised the concept of the BHAG (Big Hairy Audacious Goal).

Arie de Geus undertook a similar study and obtained similar results. He identified four key traits of companies that had prospered for 50 years or more. They are:

— Sensitivity to the business environment - the ability to learn and adjust
— Cohesion and identity - the ability to build a community with personality, vision, and purpose
— Tolerance and decentralisation - the ability to build relationships
— Conservative financing

A company with these key characteristics he called a living company because it is able to perpetuate itself. If a company emphasizes knowledge rather than finance, and sees itself as an ongoing community of human beings, it has the potential to become great and endure for decades. Such an organisation is an organic entity capable of learning (he called it a "learning organisation") and capable of creating its own processes, goals, and persona.

Military Theorists

In the 1980s some business strategists realised that there was a vast knowledge base stretching back thousands of years that they had barely examined. They turned to military strategy for guidance. Military strategy books such as The Art of War by Sun Tzu, On War by von Clausewitz, and The Red Book by Mao Zedong became instant business classics. From Sun Tzu they learned the tactical side of military strategy and specific tactical prescriptions. From Von Clausewitz they learned the dynamic and unpredictable nature of military strategy. From Mao Zedong they learned the principles of guerrilla warfare. The main marketing warfare books were:

— Business War Games by Barrie James, 1984

— Marketing Warfare by Al Ries and Jack Trout, 1986

— Leadership Secrets of Attila the Hun by Wess Roberts, 1987

Philip Kotler was a well-known proponent of marketing warfare strategy. There were generally thought to be four types of business warfare theories. They are:

— Offensive marketing warfare strategies

— Defensive marketing warfare strategies

— Flanking marketing warfare strategies

— Guerrilla marketing warfare strategies

The marketing warfare literature also examined leadership and motivation, intelligence gathering, types of marketing weapons, logistics, and communications. By the turn of the century marketing warfare strategies had gone out of favour. It was felt that they were limiting. There were many situations in which non-confrontational approaches were more appropriate. The "Strategy of the Dolphin" was developed in the mid 1990s to give guidance as to when to use aggressive strategies and when to use passive strategies.

A variety of aggressiveness strategies were developed. In 1993, J. Moore used a similar metaphor. Instead of using military terms, he created an ecological theory of predators and prey, a sort of Darwinian management strategy in which market interactions mimic long term ecological stability.

Strategic Change

In 1970, Alvin Toffler in Future Shock described a trend towards accelerating rates of change. He illustrated how social and technological norms had shorter lifespans with each generation, and he questioned society's ability to cope with the resulting turmoil and anxiety. In past generations periods of change were always punctuated with times of stability. This allowed society to assimilate the change and deal with it before the next change arrived. But these periods of stability are getting shorter and by the late 20th century had all but disappeared.

In 1980 in The Third Wave, Toffler characterised this shift to relentless change as the defining feature of the third phase of civilisation (the first two phases being the agricultural and industrial waves). He claimed that the dawn of this new phase will cause great anxiety for those that grew up in the previous phases, and will cause much conflict and opportunity in the business world. Hundreds of authors, particularly since the early 1990s, have attempted to explain what this means for business strategy.

In 1997, Watts Waker and Jim Taylor called this upheaval a "500 year delta." They claimed these major upheavals occur every 5 centuries. They said we are currently making the transition from the "Age of Reason" to a new chaotic Age of Access. Jeremy Rifkin popularised and expanded this term, "age of access" three years later in his book of the same name.

In 1968, Peter Drucker coined the phrase Age of Discontinuity to describe the way change forces disruptions into the continuity of the lives. In an age of continuity attempts to predict the future by extrapolating from the past can be somewhat accurate. But according to Drucker, we are now in an age of discontinuity and extrapolating from the past is hopelessly ineffective. We cannot assume that trends that exist today will continue into the future. He identifies four sources of discontinuity: new technologies, globalisation, cultural pluralism, and knowledge capital.

In 2000, Gary Hamel discussed strategic decay, the notion that the value of all strategies, no matter how brilliant, decays over time. In 1978, Dereck Abell described strategic windows and stressed the importance of the timing (both entrance and exit) of any given strategy. This has led some strategic planners to build planned obsolescence into their strategies.

In 1989, Charles Handy identified two types of change. Strategic drift is a gradual change that occurs so subtly that it is not noticed until it is too late. By contrast, transformational change is sudden and radical. It is typically caused by discontinuities (or exogenous shocks) in the business environment. The point where a new trend is initiated is called a strategic inflection point by Andy Grove. Inflection points can be subtle or radical. In 2000, Malcolm Gladwell discussed the importance of the tipping point, that point where a trend or fad acquires critical mass and takes off.

In 1983, Noel Tichy recognised that because we are all beings of habit we tend to repeat what we are comfortable with. He wrote that this is a trap that constrains the creativity, prevents us from exploring new ideas, and hampers the dealing with the full complexity of new issues. He developed a systematic method of dealing with change that involved looking at any new issue from three angles: technical and production, political and resource allocation, and corporate culture.

In 1990, Richard Pascale wrote that relentless change requires that businesses continuously reinvent themselves. His famous maxim is "Nothing fails like success" by which he means that what was a strength yesterday becomes the root of weakness today, We tend to depend on what worked yesterday and refuse to let go of what worked so well for us in the past. Prevailing strategies become self-confirming. In order to avoid this trap, businesses must stimulate a spirit of inquiry and healthy debate. They must encourage a creative process of self renewal based on constructive conflict.

In 1996, Art Kleiner claimed that to foster a corporate culture that embraces change, you have to hire the right people; heretics, heroes, outlaws, and visionaries. The conservative bureaucrat that made such a good middle manager in yesterday's hierarchical organisations is of little use today. A decade earlier Peters and Austin had stressed the importance of nurturing champions and heroes. They said we have a tendency to dismiss new ideas, so to overcome this, we should support those few people in the organisation that have the courage to put their career and reputation on the line for an unproven idea.

In 1996, Adrian Slywotsky showed how changes in the business environment are reflected in value migrations between industries, between companies, and within companies. He claimed that recognising the patterns behind these value migrations is necessary if we wish to understand the world of chaotic change. In "Profit Patterns" he described businesses as being in a state of strategic anticipation as they try to spot emerging patterns. Slywotsky and his team identified 30 patterns that have transformed industry after industry.

In 1997, Clayton Christensen took the position that great companies can fail precisely because they do everything right since the capabilities of the organisation also defines its disabilities. Christensen's thesis is that outstanding companies lose their market leadership when confronted with disruptive technology. He called the approach to discovering the emerging markets for disruptive technologies agnostic marketing, i.e., marketing under the implicit assumption that no one—not the company, not the customers—can know how or in what quantities a disruptive product can or will be used before they have experience using it.

A number of strategists use scenario planning techniques to deal with change. Kees van der Heijden, for example, says that change and uncertainty make "optimum strategy" determination impossible. We have neither the time nor the information required for such a calculation. The best we can hope for is what he calls "the most skilful process". The way Peter Schwartz put it in 1991 is that strategic outcomes cannot be known in advance so the sources of competitive advantage cannot be predetermined.

The fast changing business environment is too uncertain for us to find sustainable value in formulas of excellence or competitive advantage. Instead, scenario planning is a technique in which multiple outcomes can be developed, their implications assessed, and their likeliness of occurrence evaluated. According to Pierre Wack, scenario planning is about insight, complexity, and subtlety, not about formal analysis and numbers.

In 1988, Henry Mintzberg looked at the changing world around him and decided it was time to reexamine how strategic management was done. He examined the strategic process and concluded it was much more fluid and unpredictable than people had thought. Because of this, he could not point to one process that could be called strategic planning. Instead he concludes that there are five types of strategies. They are:

— Strategy as plan - a direction, guide, course of action - intention rather than actual

— Strategy as ploy - a maneuver intended to outwit a competitor

— Strategy as pattern - a consistent pattern of past behaviour - realised rather than intended

— Strategy as position - locating of brands, products, or companies within the conceptual framework of consumers or other stakeholders - strategy determined primarily by factors outside the firm

— Strategy as perspective - strategy determined primarily by a master strategist

In 1998, Mintzberg developed these five types of management strategy into 10 "schools of thought". These 10 schools are grouped into three categories.

— The first group is prescriptive or normative. It consists of the informal design and conception school, the formal planning school, and the analytical positioning school.

— The second group, consisting of six schools, is more concerned with how strategic management is actually done, rather than prescribing optimal plans or positions. The six schools are the entrepreneurial, visionary, or great leader school, the cognitive or mental process school, the learning, adaptive, or emergent process school, the power or negotiation school, the corporate culture or collective process school, and the business environment or reactive school.

— The third and final group consists of one school, the configuration or transformation school, an hybrid of the other schools organised into stages, organisational life cycles, or "episodes".

In 1999, Constantinos Markides also wanted to reexamine the nature of strategic planning itself. He describes strategy formation and implementation as an on-going, never-ending, integrated process requiring continuous reassessment and reformation. Strategic management is planned and emergent, dynamic, and interactive. J. Moncrieff also stresses strategy dynamics. He recognised that strategy is partially deliberate and partially unplanned.

The unplanned element comes from two sources: emergent strategies (result from the emergence of opportunities and threats in the environment) and Strategies in action (ad hoc actions by many people from all parts of the organisation). Some business planners are starting to use a complexity theory approach to strategy. Complexity can be thought of as chaos with a dash of order. Chaos theory deals with turbulent systems that rapidly become disordered.

Complexity is not quite so unpredictable. It involves multiple agents interacting in such a way that a glimpse of structure may appear. Axelrod, R., Holland, J., and Kelly, S. and Allison, M.A., call these systems of multiple actions and reactions complex adaptive systems. Axelrod asserts that rather than fear complexity, business should harness it. He says this can best be done when "there are many participants, numerous interactions, much trial and error learning, and abundant attempts to imitate each others' successes". In 2000, E. Dudik wrote that an organisation must develop a mechanism for understanding the source and level of complexity it will face in the future and then transform itself into a complex adaptive system in order to deal with it.

Information and Technology Driven Strategy

Peter Drucker had theorised the rise of the "knowledge worker" back in the 1950s. He described how fewer workers would be doing physical labour, and more would be applying their minds. In 1984, John Nesbitt theorised that the future would be driven largely by information: companies that managed information well could obtain an advantage, however the profitability of what he calls the "information float" would all but disappear as inexpensive computers made information more accessible.

Daniel Bell examined the sociological consequences of information technology, while Gloria Schuck and Shoshana Suboff looked at psychological factors. Zuboff, in her five year study of eight pioneering corporations made the important distinction between "automating technologies" and "infomating technologies". She studied the effect that both had on individual workers, managers, and organisational structures. She largely confirmed Peter Drucker's predictions three decades earlier, about the importance of flexible decentralised structure, work teams, knowledge sharing, and the central role of the knowledge worker. Zuboff also detected a new basis for managerial authority, based not on position or hierarchy, but on knowledge which she called "participative management".

In 1990, Peter Senge, who had collaborated with Arie de Geus at Dutch Shell, borrowed de Geus' notion of the learning organisation, expanded it, and popularised it. The underlying theory is that a company's ability to gather, analyse, and use information is a necessary requirement for business success in the information age. In order to do this, Senge claimed that an organisation would need to be structured such that:

— People can continuously expand their capacity to learn and be productive,

— New patterns of thinking are nurtured,

— Collective aspirations are encouraged, and

— People are encouraged to see the "whole picture" together.

Senge identified five components of a learning organisation. They are:

— Personal responsibility, self reliance, and mastery—We accept that we are the masters of the own destiny. We make decisions and live with the consequences of them. When a problem needs to be fixed, or an opportunity exploited, we take the initiative to learn the required skills to get it done.

— Mental models - We need to explore the personal mental models to understand the subtle effect they have on the behaviour.

— Shared vision - The vision of where we want to be in the future is discussed and communicated to all. It provides guidance and energy for the journey ahead.

— Team learning - We learn together in teams. This involves a shift from "a spirit of advocacy to a spirit of enquiry".

— Systems thinking - We look at the whole rather than the parts. This is what Senge calls the "Fifth discipline". It is the glue that integrates the other four into a coherent strategy. For an alternative approach to the "learning organisation".

Since 1990 many theorists have written on the strategic importance of information, including J.B. Quinn, J. Carlos Jarillo, D.L. Barton, Manuel Castells, J.P. Lieleskin, Thomas Stewart, K.E. Sveiby, Gilbert J. Probst, and Shapiro and Varian to name just a few. Thomas A. Stewart, for example, uses the term intellectual capital to describe the investment an organisation makes in knowledge. It is comprised of human capital (the knowledge inside the heads of employees), customer capital, and structural capital.

Manuel Castells, describes a network society characterised by: globalisation, organisations structured as a network, instability of employment, and a social divide between those with access to information technology and those without. Stan Davis and Christopher Meyer have combined three variables to define what they call the BLUR equation. The speed of change, Internet connectivity, and intangible knowledge value, when multiplied together yields a society's rate of BLUR. The three variables interact and reinforce each other making this relationship highly non-linear.

Regis McKenna posits that life in the high tech information age is what he called a "real time experience". Events occur in real time. To ever more demanding customers "now" is what matters. Pricing will more and more become variable pricing changing with each transaction, often exhibiting first degree price discrimination. Customers expect immediate service, customised to their needs, and will be prepared to pay a premium price for it. He claimed that the new basis for competition will be time based competition.

Geoffrey Moore and R. Frank and P. Cook also detected a shift in the nature of competition. In industries with high technology content, technical standards become established and this gives the dominant firm a near monopoly. The same is true of networked industries in which interoperability requires compatibility between users. An example is word processor documents.

Once a product has gained market dominance, other products, even far superior products, cannot compete. Moore showed how firms could attain this enviable position by using E.M. Rogers five stage adoption process and focusing on one group of customers at a time, using each group as a base for marketing to the next group. The most difficult step is making the transition between visionaries and pragmatists. If successful a firm can create a bandwagon effect in which the momentum builds and your product becomes a de facto standard.

Evans and Wurster describe how industries with a high information component are being transformed. They cite Encarta's demolition of the Encyclopedia Britannica (whose sales have plummeted 80% since their peak of $650 million in 1990). Many speculate that Encarta's reign will be short-lived, eclipsed by collaborative encyclopedias like Wikipedia that can operate at very low marginal costs. Evans also mentions the music industry which is desperately looking for a new business model.

The upstart information savvy firms, unburdened by cumbersome physical assets, are changing the competitive landscape, redefining market segments, and disintermediating some channels. One manifestation of this is personalised marketing. Information technology allows marketers to treat each individual as its own market, a market of one. Traditional ideas of market segments will no longer be relevant if personalised marketing is successful.

The technology sector has provided some strategies directly. For example, from the software development industry agile software development provides a model for shared development processes. Access to information systems have allowed senior managers to take a much more comprehensive view of strategic management than ever before. The most notable of the comprehensive systems is the balanced scorecard approach developed in the early 1990s by Drs. Robert S. Kaplan and David Norton. It measures several factors financial, marketing, production, organisational development, and new product development in order to achieve a 'balanced' perspective.

Psychology of Strategic Management

Several psychologists have conducted studies to determine the psychological patterns involved in strategic management. Typically senior managers have been asked how they go about making strategic decisions. A 1938 treatise by Chester Barnard, that was based on his own experience as a business executive, sees the process as informal, intuitive, non-routinised, and involving primarily oral, 2-way communications.

Bernard says "The process is the sensing of the organisation as a whole and the total situation relevant to it. It transcends the capacity of merely intellectual methods, and the techniques of discriminating the factors of the situation. The terms pertinent to it are "feeling", "judgement", "sense", "proportion", "balance", "appropriateness". It is a matter of art rather than science."

In 1973, Henry Mintzberg found that senior managers typically deal with unpredictable situations so they strategise in ad hoc, flexible, dynamic, and implicit ways. He says, "The job breeds adaptive information-manipulators who prefer the live concrete situation. The manager works in an environment of stimulous-response, and he develops in his work a clear preference for live action."

In 1982, John Kotter studied the daily activities of 15 executives and concluded that they spent most of their time developing and working a network of relationships from which they gained general insights and specific details to be used in making strategic decisions. They tended to use "mental road maps" rather than systematic planning techniques. Daniel Isenberg's 1984 study of senior managers found that their decisions were highly intuitive. Executives often sensed what they were going to do before they could explain why. He claimed in 1986 that one of the reasons for this is the complexity of strategic decisions and the resultant information uncertainty.

Shoshana Zuboff claims that information technology is widening the divide between senior managers (who typically make strategic decisions) and operational level managers (who typically make routine decisions). She claims that prior to the widespread use of computer systems, managers, even at the most senior level, engaged in both strategic decisions and routine administration, but as computers facilitated (She called it "deskilled") routine processes, these activities were moved further down the hierarchy, leaving senior management free for strategic decions making.

In 1977, Abraham Zaleznik identified a difference between leaders and managers. He describes leadershipleaders as visionaries who inspire. They care about substance. Whereas managers are claimed to care about process, plans, and form. He also claimed in 1989 that the rise of the manager was the main factor that caused the decline of American business in the 1970s and 80s. Lack of leadership is most damaging at the level of strategic management where it can paralyse an entire organisation.

According to Corner, Kinichi, and Keats, strategic decision making in organisations occurs at two levels: individual and aggregate. They have developed a model of parallel strategic decision making. The model identifies two parallel processes both of which involve getting attention, encoding information, storage and retrieval of information, strategic choice, strategic outcome, and feedback. The individual and organisational processes are not independent however. They interact at each stage of the process.

Reasons why Strategic Plans Fail

There are many reasons why strategic plans fail, especially:

- Failure to understand the customer
  - Why do they buy
  - Is there a real need for the product
  - inadequate or incorrect marketing research
- Inability to predict environmental reaction
  - What will competitors do
- Fighting brands
- Price wars
  - Will government intervene
- Overestimation of resource competence
    - Can the staff, equipment, and processes handle the new strategy
    - Failure to develop new employee and management skills

- Failure to coordinate
    - Reporting and control relationships not adequate
    - Organisational structure not flexible enough
- Failure to obtain senior management commitment
    - Failure to get management involved right from the start
    - Failure to obtain sufficient company resources to accomplish task
- Failure to obtain employee commitment
    - New strategy not well explained to employees
    - No incentives given to workers to embrace the new strategy
- Under-estimation of time requirements
    - No critical path analysis done
- Failure to follow the plan
    - No follow through after initial planning
    - No tracking of progress against plan
    - No consequences for above
- Failure to manage change
    - Inadequate understanding of the internal resistance to change
    - Lack of vision on the relationships between processes, technology and organisation
- Poor communications
    - Insufficient information sharing among stakeholders
    - Exclusion of stakeholders and delegates

Limitations of Strategic Management

Although a sense of direction is important, it can also stifle creativity, especially if it is rigidly enforced. In an uncertain and ambiguous world, fluidity can be more important than a finely tuned strategic compass. When a strategy becomes internalised into a corporate culture, it can lead to group think. It can also cause an organisation to define itself too narrowly. An example of this is marketing myopia.

Many theories of strategic management tend to undergo only brief periods of popularity. A summary of these theories thus inevitably exhibits survivorship bias (itself an area of research in strategic management).

Many theories tend either to be too narrow in focus to build a complete corporate strategy on, or too general and abstract to be applicable to specific situations. Populism or faddishness can have an impact on a particular theory's life cycle and may see application in inappropriate circumstances.

In 2000, Gary Hamel coined the term strategic convergence to explain the limited scope of the strategies being used by rivals in greatly differing circumstances. He lamented that strategies converge more than they should, because the more successful ones get imitated by firms that do not understand that the strategic process involves designing a custom strategy for the specifics of each situation. Ram Charan, aligning with a popular marketing tagline, believes that strategic planning must not dominate action. "Just do it!", while not quite what he meant, is a phrase that nevertheless comes to mind when combatting analysis paralysis.

Linearity Trap

It is tempting to think that the elements of strategic management -

(i) reaching consensus on corporate objectives;

(ii) developing a plan for achieving the objecti es; and

(iii) marshalling and allocating the resources required to implement the plan - can be approached sequentially.

It would be convenient, in other words, if one could deal first with the noble question of ends, and then address the mundane question of means. But in the world in which strategies have to be implemented, the three elements are interdependent. Means are as likely to determine ends as ends are to determine means. The objectives that an organisation might wish to pursue are limited by the range of feasible approaches to implementation. In turn, the range of feasible implementation approaches is determined by the availability of resources.

And so, although participants in a typical "strategy session" may be asked to do "blue sky" thinking where they pretend that the usual constraints—resources, acceptability to stakeholders, administrative feasibility—have been lifted, the fact is that it rarely makes sense to divorce oneself from the environment in which a strategy will have to be implemented. It's probably impossible to think in any meaningful way about strategy in an unconstrained environment.

Our brains can't process "boundless possibilities", and the very idea of strategy only has meaning in the context of challenges or obstacles to be overcome. It's at least as plausible to argue that acute awareness of constraints is the very thing that stimulates creativity by forcing us to constantly reassess both means and ends in light of circumstances. The key question, then, is, "How can individuals, organisations and societies cope as well as possible with... issues too complex to be fully understood, given the fact that actions initiated on the basis of inadequate understanding may lead to significant regret?"

The answer is that the process of developing organisational strategy must be iterative. It involves toggling back and forth between questions about objectives, implementation planning and resources. An initial idea about corporate objectives may have to be altered if there is no feasible implementation plan that will meet with a sufficient level of acceptance among the full range of stakeholders, or because the necessary resources are not available, or both.

Even the most talented manager would no doubt agree that "comprehensive analysis is impossible" for complex problems. Formulation and implementation of strategy must thus occur side-by-side rather than sequentially, because strategies are built on assumptions which, in the absence of perfect knowledge, will never be perfectly correct. Strategic management is necessarily a "repetitive learning cycle [rather than] a linear progression towards a clearly defined final destination."

While assumptions can and should be tested in advance, the ultimate test is implementation. You will inevitably need to adjust corporate objectives and/or your approach to pursuing outcomes and/ or assumptions about required resources. Thus a strategy will get remade during implementation because "humans rarely can proceed satisfactorily except by learning from experience; and modest probes, serially modified on the basis of feedback, usually are the best method for such learning."

It serves little purpose to pretend to anticipate every possible consequence of a corporate decision, every possible constraining or enabling factor, and every possible point of view. At the end of the day, what matters for the purposes of strategic management is having a clear view—based on the best available evidence and on defensible assumptions—of what it seems possible to accomplish within the constraints of a given set of circumstances.

As the situation changes, some opportunities for pursuing objectives will disappear and others arise. Some implementation approaches will become impossible, while others, previously impossible or unimagined, will become viable. The essence of being "strategic" thus lies in a capacity for "intelligent trial-and error" rather than linear adherence to finally honed and detailed strategic plans. Strategic management will add little value—indeed, it may well do harm—if organisational strategies are designed to be used as a detailed blueprints for managers.

Strategy should be seen, rather, as laying out the general path—but not the precise steps—by which an organisation intends to create value. Strategic management is a question of interpreting, and continuously reinterpreting, the possibilities presented by shifting circumstances for advancing an organisation's objectives. Doing so requires strategists to think simultaneously about desired objectives, the best approach for achieving them, and the resources implied by the chosen approach. It requires a frame of mind that admits of no boundary between means and ends.

References

Barney, J., "Firm Resources and Sustainable Competitive Advantage", *Journal of Management*, vol 17, no 1, 1991.

Chaffee, E., "Three models of strategy", *Academy of Management Review*, vol 10, no. 1, 1985.

David, F., *Strategic Management*, Columbus:Merrill Publishing Company, 1989.

Drucker, Peter., *The Practice of Management*, Harper and Row, New York, 1954.

Hamel, G. & Prahalad, C.K., "Strategic Intent", *Harvard Business Review*, May-June 1989.

Hammer, M. and Champy, J., *Reengineering the Corporation*, Harper Business, New York, 1993.

Lamb, Robert, *Boyden Competitive strategic management*, Englewood Cliffs, NJ: Prentice-Hall, 1984.

Levinson, J.C., *Guerrilla Marketing, Secrets for making big profits from your small business*, Houghton Muffin Co. New York, 1984.

Ohmae, K., *The Mind of the Strategist McGraw Hill*, New York, 1982.

Pascale, R. and Athos, A., *The Art of Japanese Management*, Penguin, London, 1981.

Peters, T. and Waterman, R., *In Search of Excellence*, HarperCollins, New york, 1982.

Rehfeld, J.E., *Alchemy of a Leader: Combining Western and Japanese Management skills to transform your company*, John Whily & Sons, New York, 1994.

Schonberger, R., *Japanese Manufacturing Techniques*, The Free Press, New York, 1982.

Woo, C. and Cooper, A., "The surprising case for low market share", *Harvard Business Review*, pg 106-113, November-December 1982.

2

Approaches to Strategic Management

Strategic management teams develop strategies. The process for large organisations is very complex and it cannot effectively take place unless people at various levels are made to participate to arrive at meaningful conclusions. Lets put five benefits of working in a team: Similarly, the team consists of managers from all the levels viz. corporate, business, and functional level.

In addition to the data from external sources, the data from within the organisation is generated through participation of company planning staff and lower levels viz. Junior managers, supervisors, and workers as the data generated for implementation of strategies is very vital for any company. The CEO of the company has to be essentially present including his team of other directors, business unit heads and heads, of functional groups.

The strategic decisions taken by the company are key to its survival and progress, and make a tremendous impact on the company and need widespread and large commitments of resources of the company; hence the presence of top managers in these teams is necessary. These persons are often designated as General Manager, Managing Directors, Presidents, VicePresidents, and Executive VicePresident etc.

The traditional view of the General Manager is that he is a reflective thinker who maps strategy, creates design of an organisation and roles for people through the tactical plans to achieve the goals, using his vast experience, knowledge and insight, and sets goals. He is considered to be a strategist, planner, leader, and is aware of various human, technical, economic, and political needs of the environment of the organisation. He has to fit various units into a jigsaw puszle through everchanging circumstances.

The experience shows that CEOs have to simultaneously handle several factors, activities etc., on a schedule that rarely give him time to contemplate. Now put down at least five roles which the CEO of the company performs: The process of intuition and judgment, depending on his perception, becomes the major and preferred decisionmaking mode.

Mintzberg list of roles gives us an example of different roles that the CEO plays in an organisation and these are termed as interpersonal, informational, and decisional roles. As the head of the organisation the CEO has to perform numerous functions that are legal and social in nature. While performing these functions the CEO has to keep the strategies of his organisation in mind.

While staffing, training, motivating, irecting, and performing several other functions, he has to keep the strategic directions of the company in focus. The CEO has to essentially keep himself well-informed about the internal and the external environment and therefore has to create channels where from information will come to him. For this, he may have to travel, read periodicals, business magazines, conduct meetings within and outside the organisation, and also exchange information through writing letters, phone calls; faxes etc.

The CEO has to ensure processing and classification of information such that it may be useful as and when required. He also has to give the information in proper perspective of the strategic management to create the desired impact within the organisation. While performing his informational role, the CEO has to keep the strategic focus. Lets suppose you are acting like a CEO of some company, which role would you like to play and why? The decisional roles that the CEO has to perform are vital for the company.

The CEO perceives and interprets the information to draw conclusions based on which strategic directions are evolved. He has to take important decisions on resource allocation, like manpower and funds etc. and exercise control so that the resources are most optimally used for the growth of the organisation.

Role of a CEO

The CEO of a company has to play pivotal role in negotiating with unions, major suppliers, and customers etc. with strategic directions of growth in focus. He has to communicate with stakeholders, outside and within company. The formulation of strategies, plans, and their implementations are an important realm of CEOs. The planning staff in formulating the strategies often helps CEOs.

Even task groups are created that may visit various others companies and gather information, process it, and present it to CEOs that may help them to decide on the strategies. In the field of power equipment, BHEL has set up a team of managers who visited many companies vis, Escort, TVS, Siemens, etc. and suggested that future strategy should be to study business processes and reduce cycle times if it has to be competitive in the market, and accordingly various business units were given directive in this regards by the CEO. Which CEO in India you like the most and what kind of attributes you like in him?

Strategic management thrives in a congenial environment within the organisation. In case the CEO is autocratic in nature, the advantages of team work gets diminished. The CEO has to play a very positive role in ensuring participation and team orientation in his organisation for strategic management to prosper. The degree to the CEO plays his role in this regard determines the success of strategic management in the organisation.

Since the entire responsibility of the success of an organisation is dependent on CEOs, they play a dominant role in formulation of strategies and should display a strong will, a high level of company orientation, and a high sense of self-esteem. So, now is the need for you to ponder over, what makes a particular organisation successful or why certain organisations fail?

Strategic Management

The role of carefully formulated strategies is quite significant in all types of organisations-business or non-business, public sector or private sector, large or small, in developed countries or underdeveloped countries. Looking at the importance of strategies in organisational effectiveness, a new branch of management, known as strategic management has been developed which deals with strategy formulation and implementation.

The systems approach of management suggests interaction of an organisation with its environment on continuous basis. This interaction can better be maintained through formulation of suitable strategies. In fact, the function of formulation of strategies has become so important that it is equated with total top management function because it is the top management which is primarily responsible for organisational adaptation to the needs of environment.

Careful strategies play significant role in the success of an organisation. If we look at the Indian industrial scene over the last generation or so, we find that great names like Martin Bum, Jessops, Andrews have touched the rock bottom, while total unknowns few years ago like Reliance, Larsen and Toubro, etc., have touched gigantic heights.

Similarly, companies like Hindustan Lever, ITC Limited, TISCO, TELCO, have maintained their high profile. There are numerous such examples of good companies in the Indian scene as well as the world over which have been successful because they have adopted suitable strategies. This happens because strategies contribute in several ways in managing an organisation; the more important of them-are as follows:

Framework for Operational Planning

Strategies provide the framework for plans by channelling operating decisions and often pre-deciding them. If strategies are developed carefully and understood properly by managers, they provide more consistent framework for operational planning. If this consistency exists and applied, there would be deployment of organisational resources in those areas where they find better use.

Strategies define the business area both in terms of customers and geographical areas served. Better the definition of these areas, better will be the deployment of resources. For example, if an organisation has set that it will introduce new products in the market, it will allocate more resources to research and development activities, which is reflected in budget preparation.

Clarity in Direction of Activities

Strategies focus on direction of activities by specifying what activities are to be undertaken for achieving organisational objectives. They make the organisational objectives more clear and specific. For example, a business organisation may define its objective as profit earning or a non-business organisation may define its objective as social objective. But these definitions are too broad and even vague for putting them into operation.

They are better spelled by strategies, which focus on operational objectives and make them more practical. For example, strategies will provide how profit objective can be sharply defined in terms of how much profits is to be earned and what resources Of how much profit is to be earned and what resources will be required for that. When objectives are spelled out in these terms, they provide clear direction to persons in the organisation responsible for implementing various courses of action. Most people perform better if they know clearly what they are expected to do and where their organisation is going

Increase Organisational Effectiveness

Strategies ensure organisational effectiveness in several ways. The concept of effectiveness is that the organisation is able to achieve its objectives within the given resources. Thus, for effectiveness, it is not only necessary that resources are put to the best of their efficiency but also that they are put in a way which ensures their maximum contribution to organisational objectives.

In fact, taking strategic management, which states the objective of the organisation in the context of given resources, can do this. Therefore, each resource of the organisation has a specific use at a particular time. Thus, strategies ensure that resources are put in action in a way in which these have been specified. If this is done, organisation will achieve effectiveness

Personnel Satisfaction

Strategies contribute towards organisation effectiveness by providing satisfaction to the personnel of the organisation. In organisation where formal strategic management process is followed, people are more satisfied by definite prescription of their roles thereby reducing role conflict and role ambiguity. If the decisions are systematised in the organisation, everyone knows how to proceed, how to contribute towards organisational objectives, where the information may be available, who can make decisions, and so on. Such clarity will bring effectiveness at the individual level and consequently at organisational level.

Strategies provide all these things in the organisation through which everything is made crystal clear. Looking into the role of strategy, Ross and Kami have suggested "without a strategy the organisation is like a ship without a rudder, going around in circles. It is like a tramp; it has no place to go." They ascribe most business failures to lack of strategy, or the wrong strategy, or lack of implementation of a reasonably good strategy. They conclude from their study that without appropriate strategy effectively implemented, failure is a matter of time.

STRATEGY IN ACTION

Managing strategy requires the consideration of a wide range of factors to develop a coherent long-term direction for an organisation. In 1953, just four years after Ingvar Kamprad had produced his first mail order catalogue featuring locally produced furniture; he opened his first store in Almhult, Sweden. Since then, he and his successors have created a global network of stores in 28 countries. Initially stores were opened only in Scandinavia, but as greater levels of success were experienced, stores were build in countries further afield where the rewards, but also the risks of failure, were much higher.

In all these countries the retailing concept of Ingvar Kamprad remained the same: 'to offer a wide range of furnishing items of good design and function at prices so low that the majority of people can afford to buy them'. In the 1980s, Andres Moberg became the chief executive. However, the influence of Ingvar Kamprad could still be found. IKEA had always been frugal in its approach. In its early years it had relocated to Denmark to escape Swedish taxation.

Echoes of the same philosophy and style could be seen in Anders Moberg. He would arrive at the office in the company Nissan Primera, dressed in informal clothes, and clock in just as other employees did. When abroad he travelled on economy class air tickets and stayed in modest hotels. He expected his executives to do likewise. Such prudence was extended to the company whose shares where held in trust by a Dutch charitable foundation and not traded. Furthermore, IKEA's expansion plan envisaged only internal funding with 15 per cent of turnover being reinvested.

The 1980s saw rapid growth. IKEA benefited from changing customer attitudes, from status and designer labels to functionality, encouraged by an economic recession. It also developed a number of unique elements which came to make up IKEA's winning business formula: simple, high quality Scandinavian design, global sourcing of components, knockdown furniture kits that customers transported and assembled themselves, huge suburban stores with plenty of parking and amenities such as cafes, restaurants, wheelchairs and even supervised childcare facilities.

A key feature of IKEA's concept was universal customer appeal crossing national boundaries, with both the products and shopping experience designed to support this appeal. Customers came from different lifestyles: from new homeowners to business executives needing more office capacity. They all expected well-styled, high quality home furnishings, reasonably priced and readily available. IKEA met this expectation by encouraging customers to create value for themselves by taking on certain tasks traditionally done by the manufacturer and retailer, for example the assembly and delivery of products to their homes.

IKEA made sure that every aspect of its business system was designed to make it easy for customers to adapt to their new role. For example, information to assist customers make their purchase decisions was provided in a 200-page glossy catalogue; during their visit to the store customers were supplied with tape measures, pens and notepaper to reduce the number of sales staff required; furniture was displayed in 100 model rooms; and sales staff were expected to involve themselves with customers only when asked.

To deliver low-cost yet high-quality products consistently, IKEA also had 30 buying offices around the world whose prime purpose was to identify potential suppliers. Designers at headquarters then reviewed these to decide which would provide what for each of the products, their overall aim being to design for low cost and ease of manufacture. The most economical suppliers were always chosen over traditional suppliers, so a shirt manufacturer might be employed to produce seat covers.

Although the process through which acceptance to become an IKEA supplier was not easy, it was highly coveted, for, once part of the IKEA system, suppliers gained access to global markets, and received technical assistance, leased equipment, and advice on how to bring production up to world equality standards. By the mid 1990s IKEA was offering a range of 12,000 items, from 1,800 suppliers in 45 countries at prices 20-40 percent lower than for comparable goods.

However, by 1998 the means of achieving low cost was receiving some critical attention. It was reported that IKEA was sourcing its goods from suppliers in eastern Europe which paid its workers poverty level wages. Having to cope with widely dispersed sources of components and high-volume orders, made it imperative for IKEA to have an efficient system for ordering its suppliers, integrating them into products and delivering them to the stores.

This was achieved through a world network of fourteen warehouses. These provided storage but also acted as logistical control points, consolidation centres and transit hubs, and aided the integration of supply and demand, reducing the need to store production runs for long periods, holding down unit costs by minimizing the costs of inventory and helping stores to anticipate need and eliminate shortage.

By the end of the 1990s IKEA was turning its attention to new opportunities for growth. It had opened stores in Eastern Europe and the one-time Soviet republics, believing these represented great future potential. In 1997 it announced its plan to open twelve new stores a year internationally in cities such as Frankfurt, Shanghai, Chicago, and Roclab in Poland and to double manufacturing capacity by building up to twenty factories in eastern Europe by 2002.

There were also plan to develop new areas of business. In partnership with a building contractor, IKEA was market testing in Sweden 'flat packed' housing which could be assembled by two men and a crane in a week at prices about 30 per cent less than the going rate. It was also developing new sources of supply, entering into an agreement with a timber company to develop new wood material for furniture. However, the company was also facing problems. IKEA was experiencing growing competition on an international front.

It had decided to implement a programme of cost savings, rationalising its supply chain and product range in order to cut purchasing costs by an overall average of 10 per cent. The company had stated the intention of cutting what had become 2,400 suppliers by one-quarter and focusing on increased volumes with a smaller range of products and fewer suppliers. In 1996, Ingvar Kamprad announced that IKEA would be split into three, comprising the retailing operations, an organisation holding the franchise and trademarks, and a third arm involved mainly in finance and banking.

The first two would form the core of the group, controlled at arm's length by trust-like organisations; the latter's shares would be jointly owned by Kamprad's three sons. The structure was devised in an effort to ensure that the privately held organisation should not be broken up or sold off in a succession battle after Ingvar Kamprad retired. He also wanted to ensure that it would not be put under the sorts of external pressures for continual growth often faced by publicly quoted companies. Internally, IKEA's strategy was managed at different levels.

A committee of senior executive at headquarters in Denmark was responsible for overseeing investment in new market and stores; responsibility for product development and purchasing lay with IKEA of Sweden; and country managers tailored the presentation and marketing of products to home territories. In 1996, Ingvar Kamprad announced that IKEA would be split into three, comprising the retailing operations, an organisation holding the franchise and trademarks, and a third arm involved mainly in finance and banking.

The first two would form the core of the group, controlled at arm's length by trust-like organisations; the latter's shares would be jointly owned by Kamprad's three sons. The structure was devised in an effort to ensure that the privately held organisation should not be broken up or sold off in a succession battle after Ingvar Kamprad retired. He also wanted to ensure that it would not be put under the sorts of external pressures for continual growth often faced by publicly quoted companies.

Internally, IKEA's strategy was managed at different levels. A committee of senior executive at headquarters in Denmark was responsible for overseeing investment in new market and stores; responsibility for product development and purchasing lay with IKEA of Sweden; and country managers tailored the presentation and marketing of products to home territories.

STRATEGY APPROACHES

Example

Honda

Honda is now one of the leading manufacturers of motorbikes. The company is credit with identifying and targeting an untapped market for small 50cc bikes in the US, which, enabled it to expand, trounce European competition and severely damage indigenous US bike manufacturers. By 1965, Honda had 63% of the US market. But this occurred b accident.

On entering the US market, Honda's planned strategy was to compete with the larger European and US bikes of 250ccs and over. These bikes had a defined market, and we sold through dedicated motorbike dealerships. Disaster struck when Honda's larger machines developed faults—they had not been designed for the hard wear and tear imposed by US motorcyclists. Honda had to recall the larger machines. Honda had made little effort to sell its small 50 cc motorbikes—its staff rode them errands around Los Angeles.

Sports goods shops and ordinary bicycle and department stores had expressed an interest, but Honda did not want to confuse its image in its target' market of men who bought the larger bikes. The faults in Honda's larger machines meant that reluctantly, Honda had no alternative but to sell the small 50cc bikes just to raise money. They proved very popular with people who would never have bought motorbikes before. Eventually the company adopted this new market with enthusiasm with the slogan: You meet the nicest people on a Honda.' The strategy had emerged, agents managers' conscious intentions, but they eventually responded to the new situation.

5 Ps

Henry Mintzberg overview of the work of many writers on strategy suggests five ways in which the term strategy is used. A strategy can be a plan, ploy pattern, position or perspective. They are not mutually exclusive.

Activity 1 (10 Minutes)

Here are some issues of strategy. Which of Mintzberg's categories (plan, position, ploy, perspective, pattern) do you think they fit into?

a. The general manager of the Beardsley Hospital prepares a strategy. To minimize the time doctors spend walking from place to place she has rearranged the hospital so that services are clustered around patients. She has the resources so that this change will be phased in over three years, firstly Ophthalmology, secondly Oncology, thirdly Pediatrics, and so on.

b. Two market traders sell fruit and vegetables. One decides to specialise in exotic fruits, as he feels there are enough well-off and/or experimentally minded people in his area to make it worth his while.

Competences

The distinctive competence of an organisation is what it does well, uniquely, or better than its rivals. For example, for a relatively undifferentiated product like cement, the ability of a maker to run a truck fleet more effectively than its competitors will give it competitive strengths. Strategic opportunities must be related to the firm's resources.

A strategic approach involves identifying a firm's competences. Members of organisations develop judgments about what they think the company can do well—its core of competence. T4ese competences may come about in a variety of ways.

— Experience in making and marketing a product or service

— The talents and potential of individuals in the organisation

— The quality of co-ordination

Ad hoc choices

The planned strategy of selling large bikes had to give way to a strategy which had emerged' by accident, almost. Henry Mintzberg develops this theme further.

Definition

Emergent strategies do not arise out of conscious strategic planning, but from a number of ad hoc choices, perhaps made lower own the hierarchy. They may not initially be recognised as being of strategic importance. Emergent strategies develop out of patterns of behaviour in contrast to planned strategies or senior management decisions, which are imposed from above. An activity will make the point clearer.

Activity 2 (20 Minutes)

Aldebaran Ltd is a public relations agency founded by an entrepreneur, Estella Grande, who has employed various talented individuals from other agencies to set up in business. Estella Grande wants Aldebaran Ltd to become the largest public relations agency in North London. Management consultants, in a planning document, have suggested growth by acquisition. In other words, Aldebaran should buy up the other public relations agencies in the area.

These would be retained as semi-independent business units, as the Aldebaran Ltd group could benefit from the goodwill of the newly acquired agencies. When Estella presents these ideas to the Board there is general consensus with one significant exception. Livia Strange, the marketing director, is horrified. 'How am I going to sell this to my staff? Ever since we've been in business, we've won business by undercutting and slugging off the competition. My team has a whole culture based on it. I give them champagne if they pinch a high value client. Why acquire these new businesses—why not stick to pinching their clients instead?' What is the source of the conflict?

Explicit Strategies

Entrepreneurs often have a theory of the business, which they mayor may not document.

— Implicit strategies may exist only in the chief executive's head

— Explicit strategies are properly documented Some plans are more explicit than others. With these in mind, Mintsberg identified eight styles of strategic management.

Different Approaches to Strategic Decision

Before we proceed to undertake strategic management process, particularly strategy formulation, it is desirable to identify the various approaches, which are applied In strategic decision making. This is essential because different approaches put varying emphasis on various elements of strategic management. There are different approaches to strategic decision making because an organisation may differ from other organisations in terms of:

1. Degree of formalisation in decisionmaking process from highly formalised and structured to informal and unstructured process
2. Managerial power relationship from the dominant role of the strategist to compromise of different interest groups; and
3. Nature of environment from highly complex to simple and stable.

These differences determine the kind of approach individual organisations would adopt in their decisionmaking process, Including strategic decision making. However, authors have described various approaches that are available for adoption in strategic decision-making differently. For example, Mintsberg has classified various approaches into three forms (he has referred to these as modes). These are entrepreneurial, planning, and adaptive.

As against this classification, Steiner et al have a fivefold classification: formal structured, intuitive anticipatory, entrepreneurial opportunistic, incremental, and adaptive. The difference between these two sets of classification can be resolved to some extent. Formal structured approach resembles planning approach; incremental and adaptive approaches have common factors than differences and, therefore can be grouped together; entrepreneurial approach is basically based on intuition and anticipation as these elements require high level of vision in strategists to anticipate opportunities and threats posed by the relevant environment.

Therefore, for further analysis, three types of approaches will be taken. These are:

1. Entrepreneurial opportunistic approach
2. Formal structured approach, and
3. Adaptive approach.

Entrepreneurial Opportunistic Approach

Entrepreneurial opportunistic (or simply entrepreneurial) approach is adopted, generally, by heads of family managed organisations and is characterised by pushing an organisation ahead in the face of environmental odds. The basic features of strategy making under this approach are as follows:

1. The focus in this approach is on capitalising the opportunities rather than problem solving. There is constant search of opportunities in the environment either formally or otherwise.
2. Decision power is centralised in the entrepreneur who is capable of, making bold and unusual decisions.
3. The bold and unusual decisions made in the face of environmental uncertainty, lead the organisation to move forward by unusual leaps and thrive with corresponding gains.
4. The most important objective in this approach is growth and expansion, assets, turnover, and market share. Thus, decision-making becomes emergent process as against formal process.

Suitability and Limitations

Entrepreneurial approach is suitable in those organisations where key strategists have very high stake in the outcomes of a strategy. They are in a position to lead the organisation from front sidelining the views of other stakeholders. Usually, such strategists have very high level of aspirations, high level of vision about the future business scenarios, and have high risk bearing profile.

A basic advantage of this approach is that such decisions are made which may defy the basic principles of management textbooks. This is the reason that such organisations outperform their counterparts adopting formal structured approach. Exhibit presents examples of how organisations have grown faster by adopting this approach.

Application Of Entrepreneurial Approach

There are numerous examples throughout the world, which suggest that organisations have achieved phenomenal growth through this approach.

1. Akio Morita, Chairman of Sony Corporation, Japan, asked his research and design engineers to design a walkman (a minicassette player). Pat came the reaction that this would not succeed in the market. But he insisted on that and walkman made a roaring success.
2. Dhirubhai Ambani, Chairman of Reliance Industries, saw the business opportunity in highpriced premium fabrics in India, which was unheard at that time. This made roaring success in the market. Later on, he conceived many projects based on this approach. Today, Reliance has become number one in the private sector in India.
3. In early 1980s, when Hero group of Ludhiana considered addition of other products in its personal transport product, it chose to add fourstroke motorcycle which was not considered highly lucrative at that time as compared to scooter. In a personal chitchat, Brijmohan All Munjal, the present Chairman of Hero Honda Motors, commented on the choice of motorcycle in comparison to scooter, "future personal transport mode will be dominated by motorcycles and not by scooters. In the age of increasing fuel cost and speed oriented transport, motorcycles would have an edge over scooters." Though many did not agree with him, he proved himself right. Today, Hero Honda's motorcycle sales have crossed 10 lakh per annum with its Splendor being the World's number one brand in twowheelers.
4. Mansukhbhai Kothari of Kothari Products conceived the idea of introducing Paan Masala when he saw that paanchewers were facing problem during travelling because either paan (betel) was not available, or not available of right quality, or the process of preparing paan was a time-consuming activity. For such people,

he introduced an alternative to paan which was subsequently branded as Paan Parag. The product met with tremendous success.

The above discussion shows only the positive aspects of entrepreneurial approach This approach has one basic limitation that if the strategists do not have intuition and vision required for doing something new and extra ordinary, the strategies are likely to fail. There have been several such cases. For example, Sunrise Industries entered the toilet soap market with Yuva and Piyu brands in 1980s.

Both the products failed against the massive competition posed by then existing players particularly Hindustan Lever. Similarly, Suraj Automobiles introduced dieselbased motorcycles to provide saving in fuel cost but the product failed. There are numerous such cases of failures. Therefore, entrepreneurial approach is not suitable for all entrepreneurs.

Formal Structured Approach

Formal structured (or simply formal) approach involves strategic decision making in anticipation of the future state that the organisation wants to be in. Strategic decisions are based on socioeconomic purposes of the organisation, values of top management, external opportunities and threats, and organisation's strengths and weaknesses. The basic features of this approach are as follows:

1. Strategy making is based on analysis of various factors, which affect the strategy.
2. It involves systematic and structured approach to the solution of problems and also the task of assessing the cost and benefit of various alternatives.
3. It is a comprehensive process, which produces a set of integrated decisions and strategies.

In India, most of the multinationals follow this approach in which they have formalised and structured their strategic decisionmaking process.

Suitability and Limitations

Suitability and limitations of formal approach depend on type of organisation, management styles, complexity of environment, complexity of production processes, nature of problems and purpose of planning system.

A basic advantage of this approach is that it generates enough information, which enables decision makers to make decisions in complex situations. However, when decision system becomes too formalised and highly structured, decision making process becomes slow because of emergence of professional bureaucracy, which relies on standardisation of skills. Decisionmaking is decentralised and takes place where the expertise exists. With the result, unusual decisions are hard to come by.

Adaptive Approach

Adaptive approach of strategic decision-making is basically reactive and tries to assimilate the change in decisionmaking contextvarious factors, particularly environmental ones, affecting strategic decisions. Various features of strategic decision-making under adaptive approach are as follows:

1. Decision-making is basically meant for problem solving, rather than going for new opportunities. Adaptation process is adopted to meet the threats by changed environment as against the decision making to meet the anticipated changes in environment which entrepreneurial approach suggests.
2. Decisions are made in sequential, incremental steps, one thing at a time necessitated by environmental changes. The basic orientation is to maintain flexibility to adapt the decisions to more pressing needs.
3. Various interest groups and stakeholders put considerable pressure on decision-making process so as to protect their own interests. Thus, the ultimate decision Is a compromised one which may be, sometimes, at the cost of optimising organisational effectiveness.
4. Since decision-making is incremental and fragmented, there is lack of integrative decision-making. With the result, systems approach of decision-making is missing.

In India, most of the public sector organisations follow adaptive approach in their decision making because of the power distribution between organisations' management and controlling ministries of Government. Those organisations in the private sector, which cannot anticipate likely future scenarios, either based on vision and intuition or through formal and structured approach of environmental analysis, follow this approach in their strategic decisionmaking process.

Suitability and Limitations

Adaptive approach of strategic decision-making is suitable for those organisations, which tend to play the role of followers rather the role of leaders in the industry sector concerned. This approach saves them from high risk since the strategic decisions are based' on the actual environmental factors. If these factors are less dynamic, this approach produces satisfactory results. However, this approach suffers from one basic limitation.

Environmental adaptation as a continuous process works well so long as there is continuity in environmental changes, which can be assimilated quickly by the organisations adopting this approach. When the environmental factors change fast, this approach does not work because by the time, the organisations adopt one change, which has some lead-time, environment changes further making previous adaptation unworkable. In the present context of global competition, perhaps, this approach is not very suitable to achieve meaningful competitive advantage.

Combining Different Approaches

We have seen above that various approaches of strategic decision making have their positive and negative aspects and each of these is suitable for particular type of organisations and the nature of environment. Since there are many variables, which affect strategic decision-making, many organisations follow a combination of different approaches. The experts on strategic management also hold this view, For example, Sumantra. Ghoshal, Professor of Strategic Leadership, comments that "it may be useful for Reliance to think whether it should follow a bit of Hindustan Lever's structured processes, just as much as it may be productive for Hindustan Lever to consider ways of broadening its systems and culture to the entrepreneurial approach.

In fact, Hindustan Lever has restaged the need for infusing entrepreneurial approach in developing business level strategies. According to its former Chairman, Keki Dadiseth, "Hindustan Lever has grown in size. While it has its own obvious benefits, it also brings some drawbacks. What we need to master is the art of creating and preserving the entrepreneurial ability and connectedness of a small company within a large company. There may be different ways in which various approaches may be combined together. More common ways are as follows:

1. Adaptive entrepreneurial
2. Structured adaptive
3. Entrepreneurial structured
4. Adoption of different approaches for different businesses, and
5. Adoption of different approaches at different stages of organisational life.

While combining two or more approaches together the individual organisations can do better if they evaluate their culture, human resources, and leadership styles and the nature of environment in which an organisation or its different businesses operations

Strategic Management Process

Strategy formulation

1. Formulation of organisational mission and objectives
   - Formulating mission and mission statement
   - Business definition in terms of customer, product, and technology
   - Formulating long-term broad objectives
2. Environmental analysis
   - Analysis of general environment
   - Industry and competition analysis

- — Preparation of environmental threat and opportunity profile

3. Organisational analysis
   - — Analysis of strengths and weaknesses in different areas
   - — Preparing organisational capability profile
   - — SWOT analysis
   - — Defining core competence and distinctive competence
   - — Developing competitive advantage through
   - — Generic competitive strategies
   - — Strategic intent
   - — Benchmarking
   - — Synergistic approach
   - — Critical success factors approach
   - — Preparing competitive advantage profile
4. Strategic alternatives
   - — Stability strategy
   - — Retrenchment strategy
   - — Turnaround strategy
   - — Divestment strategy
   - — Liquidation strategy

Growth strategy

- — Concentric expansion strategy
- — Vertical integration strategy
- — Diversification strategy
- — Merger and acquisition strategy

Joint venture strategy

- — Strategic alliance
- — Combination strategy
- — Business restructuring strategy

5. Choice of strategy
   - — Focusing on strategic alternatives
   - — Evaluating strategic alternatives

— Considering decision factors
— Strategy choice

Strategy Implementation

1. Activating strategy
   — Institutionalisation of strategy
   — Resource mobilisation and allocation
   — Translating general objectives into specific objectives
2. Procedural implementation
3. Structural implementation
   — Designing organisation structure
   — Prescribing organisational systems
4. Functional Implementation Prescribing policies and strategies in
   — Production/ operations
   — Marketing
   — Finance
   — Human resources
5. Behavioural implementation
   — Leadership implementation
   — Managing organisational culture
   — Creating values and ethics
   — Corporate governance
   — Managing organisational politics
6. Organisational change and innovation
   — Initiating and implementing organisational change
   — Managing organisational innovation
   — Creating learning organisation

Strategy evaluation and control

1. Designing evaluation and control system
   — Setting criteria for evaluation and control

— Setting standard in respect of these criteria

2. Exercising control
   — Strategic control
   — Financial performance control
   — Social performance control

References

Barney, J., "Firm Resources and Sustainable Competitive Advantage", *Journal of Management*, vol 17, no 1, 1991.

Chaffee, E., "Three models of strategy", *Academy of Management Review*, vol 10, no. 1, 1985.

David, F., *Strategic Management*, Columbus:Merrill Publishing Company, 1989.

Drucker, Peter., *The Practice of Management*, Harper and Row, New York, 1954.

3

Evolution of Successful Business Management

Contemporary societies and the business world are inseparable. But so are all human beings and the planet. From a systems perspective, all human institutions, individuals and the environments in which they live and operate are inextricably interconnected in a complex and elegant web of mutually influential relationships.

And yet, this understanding is hardly reflected in the functioning of the business world. Business life, as a legitimate money making practice, it is not the "universal human activity it is sometimes thought to be. It is, instead a remarkably modern and culturally peculiar phenomenon" whose infancy was triggered by the industrial revolution during the 18th century and supported by individualism and the Calvinist Protestant ethic.

From an evolutionary perspective, it is not inconceivable to consider the transformation of the ends and means of business. "For thousands of years, business existed only at the fringes of society. Society thought little of people in business, and people in business expected little of society. Profit was their only reward because power, social status, and even social acceptability were closed to them. In this context,... the idea that making a profit was the only goal of business might have some sense". But in a time when the values of the business world largely influence the values of society as a whole and the possibilities of future generations, the purposes and goals of business need to be questioned and expanded.

Merchant makes a useful distinction between different ethical approaches. She explains the paradigmatic assumptions of three kinds of ethics-egocentric, homocentric, and ecocentric ethics. Her framework helps to identify the dominant ethical stance of modern business: the egocentric ethic. In this approach, the wellbeing and happiness of the individual is sought. It encourages the individual to act in ways that brings about the personal good, assuming that a society constituted of fulfilled individuals equals the collective good.

However, there are some pitfalls to this ethical position. "Because egocentric ethics is based on the assumption that the individual good is the highest good, the collective behaviour of human groups or business corporations is not a legitimate subject of investigation". Also, "it includes the assumption that humans are 'by nature' competitive and capitalism is the 'natural' form of economics" and as a result "ecological effects are external to human economics and cannot be adjudicated". The point is that the trickle down economic theory does not work in reality.

Rich people become richer while poor people become poorer. That is, the egocentric ethic does not bring about social good. Another possibility is the homocentric ethic, which goes beyond individualistic self-interest in order to promote the collective good. However, it assumes that humans have a special place in the universe and this entitles them to exploit the rest of the world for their own purposes. So the homocentric ethic is good but not good enough as a new business ethic.

The ecocentric ethical approach is the one that can bring a balance between human progress and preservation of the natural world. The ecocentric ethic embraces a systems view of the world—in contrast to the ego and homocentric ethics which are rooted in a reductionistic and mechanistic paradigm. Koestenbaum points out that "an evolutionary transformation of who we are, how we behave, how we think, and what we value" is necessary to resolve the paradox between business as usual and the contemporary global challenges that call for social and environmental responsibility. He connects this evolutionary transformation to the basic human quest for meaning, purpose, and fulfilment which have been left behind in the hectic life style of industrial societies.

Unless such issues of purpose and meaning are addressed, humans cannot make intelligent decisions come Monday morning—

much less develop a long term strategy toward sustainability. Human depth makes business sense, he argues, and it is precisely the depth required to move from the egocentric business ethic to a broader perspective that advances the wellbeing of individuals, societies, ecosystems and future generations. "The more you understand the human condition, the more effective you are as a business person".

And the more we understand the interconnected nature of the universe, the more competent we are as shapers of sustainable and evolutionary organisations. To focus beyond the bottom line does not implies forgetting about the "profit motive" but transcending it toward a mode of wealth creation that pursues personal, social and ecological gains in addition to financial results. "The gift of working for sustainability is its meaningfulness".

Role of Images and Metaphors

The business world is heavily influenced by images and metaphors that shape the strategies, structures and processes of organisations. Solomon analyses common metaphors that he considers ways not to think about business. "How a person thinks about business—as a ruthless competition for profits or as a cooperative enterprise whose aim is the prosperity of the community—preshapes much of his or her behaviour and attitudes toward fellow employees or executives, competitors, customers, and the surrounding community".

"It's a jungle out there" is one of the most pervasive metaphors that brings into business the classical Darwinian view of the survival of the fittest where the rule is kill or be killed. But this metaphor is grounded on fundamentally wrong scientific premises. Evolutionary systems theory shows that cooperation is an essential strategy in nature, and the jungle metaphor completely ignores this fact.

Closely related to the jungle metaphor is the conception of business as war and the marketplace as the battlefield. "Military metaphors are intrinsically nationalistic, alarmist, pessimistic, conservative, and authoritarian. This has grim implications for the mental health of a productive organisation. Paranoia is not usually conducive to creativity or competitiveness". Less violent but as dehumanising as the jungle and war metaphors is the idea of business as a money-making machine. Mechanistic thinking is reflected in many management methodologies and approaches, and the machine metaphor "transforms everything human into something cold and mechanical. Emotions, affections, and relationships disappear, to be replaced by mere causes and effects".

The ideals of efficiency and control, two of the most appealing concepts for managers and planners, are derived directly from Newtonian physics while more holistic and organic concepts are revolutionising contemporary physics and engineering themselves. The machine metaphor has not been replaced but rather "improved" through information technologies.

The information processing capacity of computers has overexcited managers and made them forget that what we need is not more information but more wisdom which requires human experience and ethical sensitivity. What is common to these metaphors are the assumptions that match what Eisler has called the dominator model of social organisation—a win-loose paradigm that involves ranking, power over others, hierarchies of control, competition and the institutionalisation of violence.

Unless we transcend the dominator paradigm, which seems to permeate the thinking and actions of people in Western civilisations, it will be difficult to come up with alternative metaphors and new visions to guide the evolution of the business world and the emergence of evolutionary corporations. The new sciences, also known as the sciences of complexity, offer new insights that support the idea of an interconnected, collaborative, participatory, and creative universe. New metaphors and powerful images are being born as this new scientific understanding spreads.

For instance, Moore introduces the powerful idea of business ecosystems as a metaphor for the new type of cooperative and competitive relationships that take place in today's business world. He argues that the traditional understanding of competition—from a dominator model point of view—is no longer adequate to the new realities, and that an ecosystemic understanding of business interactions has profound implications for corporate strategy. "We have only just begun the process of discovering and inventing the new organisational forms that will inhabit the 21st Century. We need the courage to let go of the old world, to relinquish most of what we have cherished, to abandon our interpretations about what does and doesn't work".

Leadership and Innovation for Sustainability

The challenge for the evolution of the business world is clearly articulated by Nattrass and Altomare who explain that "it is no longer sufficient to be a smart organisation, one that can scan the commercial environment, detect variations, and react accordingly. If we restrict ourselves to reacting to signals when it comes to human impact... we may well end up focusing the organisational resources just on minimizing the pain of irreversible damage.

The business organisations need to become conscious of the evolutionary role business plays in the future of the planet and to take responsibility for that role." Following the image of a business ecosystem embedded and entangled in a socio-cultural and bio-physical context, we can appreciate the need to move from reactive and even proactive organisational strategies to an interactive mode involving coevolution. The economy is one of the most relevant aspects of the socio-cultural context in which business operates.

From a systems perspective, the economy cannot be detached from society and the natural environment. Such an integrated view of economy, society, and nature is encompassed in the notion of a sustainable economy which, according to Milbrath, is one that preserves and enhances a well-functioning ecosystem; provides humans with the products and services necessary for a good and dignified life; provides opportunities for fulfilling work and self-realisation; achieves and maintains economic justice; and utilises resources at a sustainable rate that does not deplete future generations. Some organisations are taking the lead by creating business opportunities through the creation of a sustainable economy.

An extraordinary example is the well-known case of Interface, Inc. They have introduced innovations such as the lease of carpet tiles that allows them to be in charge of the whole life cycle of their products, eliminate waste, reduce costs, inspire personnel, and protect the environment. Interface is living up to its goal of becoming one of the first names in industrial ecology. Their vision, as articulated by their Founder, Chairman and CEO, Ray C. Anderson, says it all:

> Interface will be environmentally sustainable. But our mission is larger. We will also be financially sustainable, for the simple reason that our corporation must survive and that we must assure the livelihood of our associates and the investment of all our stakeholders. We will be socially sustainable, respecting the communities in which we work, positively influencing all those whose lives we touch, and taking care not to deplete the human spirit on which we depend... Our sustainability goals—financial, social, and environmental—are inextricably bound together, which is why we make such a point out of doing well by doing good.

When reviewing the case of Interface with my executive MBA students,. They see the detailed and comprehensive changes implemented by Interface to fulfil its vision as an exception to the business world. However, there is enough evidence of the move toward sustainability that if a corporation or institution does not pay attention to the revolution of "natural capitalism" it will lose competitive advantage. "The move toward radical resource productivity and natural capitalism is beginning to feel inevitable rather than merely possible".

Paul Ray, in his sociological studies, has identified a fast growing segment of the US population—currently 50 million people—that embrace a social and ecological consciousness. He calls them the "cultural creatives." These are the individuals who are willing to live and act in ways that bring about a sustainable culture. There are businesses that understand the implications of the emergence of this segment and in the last decades new products and services have been developed to satisfy the needs and support the values of the cultural creatives.

A clear case is the relatively new family of funds aimed at individuals who want to make money while making a difference. Socially responsible investing (SRI) does not seek moral perfection but tries to affect positive change and promote best practices. The growth and performance of SRI supports the argument put forward by Hawken, Lovins, and Lovins in terms of the inevitability of the move toward sustainability because it makes business sense.

Many pension-fund managers believe that they cannot take an ethical stand because of their fiduciary duty to their clients. However, socially and environmentally responsible stock indexes are outperforming their ethically neutral counterparts. Environmental and social issues can have profound impact on a company bottom line. "Virtue... can bring more than its own reward".

Some of the rewards received by companies engaged in sustainable practices include:

— Increase in eco-efficiency that impacts the bottom line;
— Attraction of talented people as well as generation of employee commitment and motivation;
— Innovation of new products and services that meet environmental criteria as well as of production processes that close the loop;
— Development of the knowledge base and core competencies for the market of the future;
— Improvement of relations with local residents concerned with the wellbeing of their communities;
— Promotion of industry-wide self-regulation and impact on legislation;
— Achievement of quality standards under ISO and the International Chamber of Commerce environmental criteria;
— Inclusion in socially and environmentally responsible mutual funds and investment portfolios;
— Attention to media and activist pressures that affect consumer's perceptions; and o, the reward that comes from knowing that it is the right thing to do.

There are many business opportunities still unexplored in the challenge of sustainability. Those companies that are willing to engage in processes of learning, innovation and management of complexity—the processes of adjusting the sails to the uncontrollable winds of change—are the ones with the greatest possibilities of profiting from the sustainability trend.

Business Knowledge and Complexity

Knowledge has always been relevant for the good performance of business. However, the kind of relevant knowledge to develop and maintain competitive advantage has changed over time (figure 1).

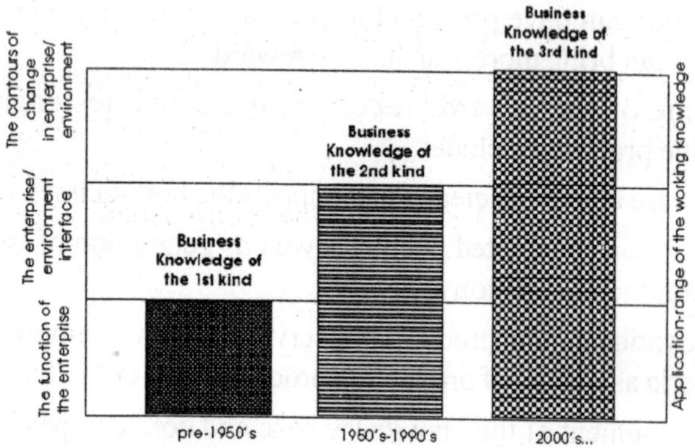

Figure 1. Business knowledge for evolutionary management.

During the first half of the 20th century, successful companies focused on improving their internal processes—production and managerial operations needed to be efficient. Scientific management, as developed by Frederick W. Taylor, is an example of business knowledge of the first kind. But increase in competition and expansion of the economy made it necessary to focus beyond the enterprise itself in order to learn more about the market, the industry, the consumers. Business knowledge of the second kind, therefore, is contextual.

The work of Michael Porter on competitive advantage is a quintessential example of this kind of knowledge with great impact in the 80's. These two stages of business knowledge reflect a reductionistic and mechanistic scientific paradigm that is portrayed in the outdated-but-still-in-use business metaphors of the jungle, war, and machine. The companies of the 21st century, the emerging evolutionary corporations, transcend that.

Business knowledge of the third kind comprises an understanding of the socio-cultural and bio-physical dynamics of the organisational environment and draws insight from the sciences of complexity to infuse strategy and tactics for innovative value creation. The centrality of knowledge in contemporary management brought into being the thriving field of knowledge management (KM). Mark McElroy has described two generations of knowledge management. First generation KM focuses on knowledge sharing—how to distribute existing organisational knowledge, usually through technology—while second generation KM focuses on knowledge creation—how to satisfy organisational needs for new knowledge, usually through processes of learning and innovation. Learning has become one of the main sources of sustainable competitive advantage. But it is not simply learning processes the ones that create value in the business world.

It is learning through collaboration—that is, organisational learning. Knowledge and innovation are the result—the byproducts—of ongoing collaborative processes that create the conditions for creativity and synergy. This is the vision of a learning organisation, which, in words of Peter Senge, is a place where

> people continually expand their capacity to create the results they truly desire, where new and expansive patterns of thinking are nurtured, where collective aspiration is set free, and where people are continually learning how to learn together.

The machine metaphor applied to an organisation removes its human character and makes it a static and sterile system. The fact is that organisations are human activity systems that reflect the purposes, values, expectations and emotions of the people that comprise them. A more appropriate metaphor for the organisation is a living organism - an image that makes explicit the dynamic complexity of organisational life. Complex systems are evolving systems. A living organism is capable of self maintenance, self-renewal, and self-transcendence.

Evolution is a process of self-organisation into higher levels of functional and structural complexity. These features of complex evolving systems offer new insights for the design of organisational strategies, structures, and processes. "The company that acts like a living organism will naturally be a learning organisation absorbing and reacting to information in an evolutionary manner. Companies that are conceived of as machines, rather than living organisms, are unlikely to be aware of external shifts in public opinion or be sensitive enough to their key relationships, because they will not be sensitive to the unexpected".

Bib Pictre Redefined

The vision of a sustainable future is compelling, inspiring, meaningful. It is also critical -the wellbeing of future generations depends on the ability to live in partnership with Earth. But there is even more depth to the sustainability challenge. It is evolutionary. The evolutionary perspective can be adequately thought of as the "big picture"—but it is not a static and permanent image of the larger context of the human existence, but rather an understanding of the dynamic processes of change of which we are a part.

In this sense, evolution is the big moving picture and we humans are key actors. How long is long-term in the business world? Five, ten, twenty years... Regardless of the exact variation, in evolutionary terms, it is very short. Long-term for the Iroquois Indians is seven generations. This is closer to the long term required for evolutionary change agency in which humans, individually and collectively, need to engage. The planet was formed 4.6 billion years ago. Humans have lived on Earth for about 2.5 million years. Civilisations developed about 10,000 years ago and written histories only cover 5,000 years approximately. In the last 200 years (0.00000044% of Earth time), humans have brought more change on the planet than in the past billion years. An analogy may help gain perspective on these time spans:

> Imagine a movie that runs a full year representing all the time since the origin of the earth. Each frame in the motion picture is the equivalent of one year of real time. The normal movie speed of twenty-four frames a second has to be increased about six times to 146 frames (years) per second to fit this movie into a single year. That means that 8.752 years of real time would flash by during each minute of the movie.... A day of the movie would represent 12,602.240 years. Imagine that the movie begins on January 1, coinciding with the origin of the earth, and ends with the present time at New Years' Eve the following year. As the movie runs for weeks, no sign of life is seen. The first glimmers of one-celled microbial life do not develop until March....
>
> In the year long movie, more complex life forms... do not develop until August and September. Larger and still more complex multicellular organism do not appear until November. Dinosaurs appear about December 13th and become extinct after about thirteen days. Mammals appear about December fifteen. The genus Homo does not develop until five hours before midnight on December 31. Homo sapiens sapiens (modern humans) developed only 100,000 years ago; eleven minutes before midnight. Civilisation does not appear until one minute before midnight. A lifetime of a modern human would be only one-half of a second.

> The industrial era has lasted about two seconds. During that era, humans have used up and scattered a large proportion of the resources in the earth's crust, altered and exploited ecosystems to serve strictly human needs, held all other species at their mercy, and driven many species to extinction. They are now well on the way to poisoning the biosphere and changing the earth's climate. In comparison to the dinosaurs who survived on the planet thirteen days, can Homo sapiens last even one day? Microbes that long precede us will still be here long after we are gone.

Banathy provides a historical view of societal evolution. Each stage of societal evolution builds on another. Technological innovation can be seen as one of the motors of change, moving from technologies that allow us to survive and satisfy the basic human needs to technologies that expand the physical and cognitive capacities. The acceleration in the rate of change, the trend toward global integration, and the emergence of the systems paradigm.

Each one of these stages represent periods of relative stability. However, the transitions from one stage to another are periods of utter confusion and chaos in which the status quo cannot be maintained given the changes in the environment. During these transitions —or bifurcation points -the next stage of societal evolution cannot be predicted. Chaos theory, one of the pillars of the sciences of complexity, describes a phenomenon called the butterfly effect: in bifurcation points, the turbulent conditions in a complex dynamic system make possible the overall transformation of the system through small changes.

Individuals and organisations may ask themselves "what difference will I make if I behave ethically in society?" and the thought of a single initiative of social and environmental responsibility against all the unsustainable practices of society at large seems to discourage ethical and innovative initiatives. The popular quote from Margaret Mead, "never doubt that a small group of thoughtful, committed individuals can change the world; indeed, it's the only thing that ever has," gains new meaning through the lens of the sciences of complexity. Prigogine, in his work Order out of Chaos expresses this idea in the following way:

The threat lies in the realisation that in the universe the security of stable, permanent rules are gone forever. We are living in a dangerous and uncertain world that inspires no blind confidence. The hope arises from the knowledge that even small fluctuations may grow and change the overall structure. As a result, individual activity is not doomed to insignificance". Contemporary global societies are currently experiencing another bifurcation. A new stage in societal evolution is about to be born. The key difference from the previous transitions from one stage to the other is that this is the first time in human history that we are able to explain what is happening while it is happening. This gives us an unprecedented opportunity. With the new understanding of evolutionary dynamics and systemic approaches to the participatory design of strategies, structures and processes, the species can stop drifting upon the currents of change and begin to adjust its sails in view of sustainable evolutionary futures.

There are many indications that the new evolutionary stage could be labelled "sustainable society"—but in evolution there are no guaranties, and devolution or extinction are always possibilities. "We can take responsibility, individually and collectively, for the conscious evolution of our human systems. We can hold others—individuals, corporations, and governments—accountable as well. It no longer matters "who is to blame"; what matters is that we all take responsibility for the direction and impact of our society. In this generation, in our era, humans have become integral agents of evolution. More than that, we are evolution becoming conscious of itself".

Business Education

The creation of the evolutionary corporations that will bring about a sustainable society is a task that begins today. Organisations can begin doing things in new ways, to design new strategies, to implement new processes and structures. But these actions require capable people that understand the challenges, that embrace the new scientific paradigm, that can think long term, that are committed to the creation of meaning. "An actual change to a more sustainable way of life... require(s) a degree of change in understanding and attitudes. Education is one of the ways in which moral values and positions are developed in society. A transition to sustainability may therefore require some change in current educational programmes".

Bowers considers that educators are not yet aware of the cultural myths and assumptions that underlie their practice. Most educational innovators are still "caught in the myth of an anthropocentric universe.... The avalanche of information on the human impact on the environment is now so great that it is almost inconceivable that it is still being ignored by people who represent themselves as the leaders in education. But unfortunately this is the case". Unless business education, dedicated to the development of the talent for the business world, reflects the emergent evolutionary paradigm both in processes and contents, companies will continue to respond to new realities with old approaches. An essential task in business education "would be to develop a wider concept of social and environmental responsibility".

Contemporary business education fails to help business students achieve sufficient educational breadth, particularly with regard to their role and responsibility in an increasingly interconnected planet. "By developing curricular projects linked to community needs, [business] faculty can further their students' technical skills when helping them simultaneously develop greater interpersonal, inter-cultural, and ethical sensitivity".

Evolutionary corporations have strong and explicit core values that embrace sustainability; recognise the business benefits of sustainability; are committed to organisational learning and to the human development of their people; understand the evolutionary systems perspective; have an expanded sense of responsibility & accountability; seek financial robustness; and accept their role as agents of socio-cultural evolution.

Business education needs to facilitate the development of the knowledge, skills, values and attitudes that will cover the spectrum of evolutionary management, bringing a more balanced perspective to the overlay emphasised financial bottom line. Banathy differentiates between maintenance and evolutionary learning. The first is adaptive. It involves the acquisition of fixed viewpoints, methods, and rules of dealing with known and recurring events. It maintains the status quo, and it is appropriate during periods of socio-cultural stability. In contrast, evolutionary learning is innovative.

It enables the learner to cope with uncertainty and change, renew perspectives and creatively design co-evolutionary human systems. It is a more appropriate learning approach during bifurcation points.

Educational systems in general have been focused primarily on maintenance learning and the creation of knowers that know a lot about existing business knowledge and approaches. But new realities and global challenges call for evolutionary learning and the empowerment of learners capable of generating new knowledge and processes to respond to the changing socio-cultural and bio-physical environment.

Milbrath suggests that educational institutions need to reorient their efforts toward helping students learn systems thinking, futures design, probabilistic decision making, integrative analysis, creativity, values inquiry, and ethical reasoning. Following a similar perspective, the business education programmes of EGADEseek to elicit creative problem solvers, transformative agents, ethical visionaries, self-directed learners, managers of complexity, cross-cultural leaders, and technology shapers.

This vision informs the contents and processes of the courses we offer in order to facilitate the development of competencies such as nonlinear systemic thinking, systems design, selfmotivation, openness to change and uncertainty, empathy and innovation. In the courses, we are introducing collaborative and self-directed learning methodologies and we encourage the adaptation and application of the knowledge covered in the active organisational contexts of the students.

Business education need to include evolutionary systemic approaches and the vision of a sustainable economy. Ethical innovation cannot happen through a top-down mandate, but rather occurs as the result of self-organising, collaborative and creative processes within an organisation that has made explicit the values and the commitment to move toward sustainability.

References

Bowers, C. A., *Education, Cultural Myths, and the Ecological Crisis: Toward deep changes,* New York: SUNY, 1993.

Capra, Fritjof, *The Web of Life: A new scientific understanding of living systems*, New York: Anchor books, 1996.

Hawken, Paul; Lovins, Amory and Lovins, L., Hunter. *Natural Capitalism: Creating the next industrial revolution,* New York: Little, Brown, and Company.

4

Mission and Vision of Business Organisations

Organisational mission encompasses the broad aims of the organisation; it defines what for the organisation strives. Therefore, the process of defining mission for any organisation can be best understood by thinking about it at its inception. Truly speaking, an organisation's mission lies in the basic philosophy of those who create and manage the organisation as shown in figure Philosophy. Philosophy, in the context of management of an organisation, consists of an integrated set of assumptions and beliefs about the way the things are, the purpose of the activities, and the way these should be.

These assumptions and beliefs of those who create an organisation (owners) and those who manage it (managers, specially the decision makers) become base for defining vision of the organisation. These assumptions and beliefs are sometimes explicit, and occasionally implicit, in the minds of the decision makers. The philosophy of a person has its origin in two premises-fact premises and value premises. Fact premises represent the descriptive view of how the world behaves. They are drawn from research findings and the experiences. Value premises represent the view of the desirability of certain goals and activities.

Vision of an organisation has a long-term orientation and is derived from organisational philosophy. Vision represents a challenging portrait of what the organisation and its members can be in the future. Therefore, the organisation should create projections about where it should go and what major changes lie ahead. Once the vision is established, persistent and enthusiastic communication of it throughout the organisation is required so that various subsystems embrace it with commitment.

Key decision makers' philosophy and visionary long-term concept of the organisation taken together define organisation's mission in the form of desires, beliefs and assumptions in the following form:

1. The product and service offered by the organisation can provide benefits at least equal to its price.
2. The product or service can satisfy the needs of the customers not adequately served by others presently.
3. Technology used in producing product or service will be cost and quality competitive.
4. The organisation can grow and be profitable than just survive in the long run with the support of various constituents.
5. The organisation will create favourable public image which will result in contributions from environment.
6. Entrepreneur's self-concept of the business can be communicated and adopted by employees and stakeholders.
7. The organisation will be able to satisfy the entrepreneur's needs and aspirations which he seeks to satisfy through the organisation.

At the initial stage, the above elements go into mission formulation. As the organisation grows or is forced by competitive forces to alter its product, market, and technology, there may be need for redefinition of the mission. However, the revised mission will reflect the same set of elements as the original-like type of product to be offered, type of customer to be served, type of technology to be employed, growth of organisation, favourable public image, self-concept of entrepreneur, and needs and aspirations of entrepreneur, though in modified form.

Characteristics of Mission

Every organisation has mission either defined explicitly or may be deduced from the actions of its top management. For a large organisation, where its members do not have face-to-face contact, explicit mission statement is desirable as it serves the purpose of communicating to the members about the corporate philosophy, identity, character, and image, which govern their behaviour in the organisation.

Further, section of the society dealing with the organisation knows well in advance as how to, interact with the organisation. Therefore, while framing the mission statement, following points should be taken into consideration so that it serves the purpose for which it is prepared:

Features of a Good Mission

1. Mission should be clear, both in terms of intentions and words used;
2. It should be feasible, neither too high to be unachievable, nor too low to demotivate the people for work.
3. It should be precise but self-explanatory, neither too narrow so as to restrict the organisation's activities, nor too broad to make itself meaningless.
4. It should be distinctive, both in terms of the organisation's contributions to the society and how these contributions can be made.

Exhibit presents the mission statement of ITC Limited which is characterised by the following concerns:

Mission of ITC Limited

1. Concern for the ultimate customers-millions of customers.
2. Concern for the intermediate customers-the trade.
3. Concern for the suppliers-the sources of raw materials and ancillaries.
4. Concern for the employees-the most valued asset.
5. Concern for the competitors- wishing them well as healthy competition ultimately benefits the customers.
6. Concern for the shareholders-the investing public.
7. Concern for the national aspiration-India's future.

Objectives of Mission Statement

Objectives are more precise as compared to mission and used to specify the end results which an organisation wants to achieve. However, there are two problems in giving the precise definition of objectives.

— First, goals and objectives are used interchangeably, though there are some differences between the two.

— Second, the end results, expressed as objectives, may be time-specific or without this specification.

Therefore, objectives are defined in different ways. For example, McFarland has defined objectives in quite broad term which is as follows:

> "Objectives are oils, aims, or purposes that organisations wish over varying periods of time."
>
> Terry and Franklin have also used the term goal in defining an objective. They view that:
>
> "A managerial objective is the intended goal that prescribes definite scope and suggests direction to the planning efforts of a manager.

Features of Objectives

1. Each organisation, or group of individuals, has some objectives. In fact, organisations or groups are created basically for certain objectives. Members in the organisation or group try to achieve these objectives.
2. Objectives may be broad or they may be specifically mentioned. They may pertain to a wide or narrow part of the organisation. They may be set either for the long term or for the short term. For example, the basic objective of a business organisation may be to earn profit. This may be quite a broad objective. In order to achieve this broad objective, some specific objective may be set, for example, how much profit and in which period. Thus, general objectives may be translated into operative objectives to provide definite action.
3. Objectives may be clearly defined or these may not be clear and have to be interpreted by the behaviour of organisational

members, particularly those at top level. However, clearly defined objectives provide clear direction for managerial action.

4. Objectives have hierarchy. At the top level, it may be broad organisational purpose which can be broken into specific objectives at the departmental level. From departmental objectives, units of the department may derive their own objectives. This is possible because combining people into sections, departments, divisions, etc create organisation. All of them try to achieve organisational objectives and, at each level a unit may contribute to the fulfilment of tasks assigned to it. Thus, a hierarchy of objectives is created.
5. Organisational objectives have social sanction, that is, they are created within the social norms. Since organisations are social units, their objectives must conform to the general needs of the society. Various restrictions on organisational objectives are put through social norms, rules and customs.
6. An organisation may have multiple objectives. For example, Hindustan Lever Limited, under the chairmanship of T. Thomas formulated the following objectives:
   i. To expand and diversify in the area of chemicals;
   ii. To continue to control costs and improve productivity very rigorously;
   iii. To build up management skills for future growth;
   iv. To utilise R & D more effectively in creating new-business opportunities;
   v. To build a strong Board balancing the advantages of decentralising profit responsibility against the advantages of centralised controls on personnel, finance, and technology;
   vi. To communicate more openly and purposefully, internally as well as externally; and
   vii. To develop succession to the Board and to Chairmanship.

It can be emphasized that many of these objectives are functional objectives; many of these objectives are intertwined and interrelated. Sometimes, many of the objectives may be even incompatible. This happens because over a period of time, many interest groups exert their pressure on organisational objectives. For example, economic and social objectives of an organisation may be incompatible; the achievement of one may be at the cost of the other at one point of time, while at other time, both can be integrated.

7. Organisational objectives can be changed; new ones may replace old objectives. It is possible because organisations are free to set their objectives within the overall social norms. Since objectives are formulated keeping in view the environmental factors and internal conditions, any change in these may result into change in objectives. For example, in response to various changes in the social environment, the objectives of YMCA have been transformed from religion and spirituality to recreation and physical exercise.

Similarly, the Red Cross which was originally formed to hold itself in readiness in the war or any calamity to help the people found itself underemployed after Word War I and lost members' contributions, and public esteem. The Reg. Cross subsequently added another objective-that of preserving and improving public health.

Objectives and Goals

Objectives and goals are the end results which an organisation strives for. Since there may be different ways in expressing end results like market leadership (a qualitative measurement), or a certain percentage of increase in sales in a particular year (a quantitative measurement), the question is: for which result the term objectives should be used and for which result the term goal should be used. This problem arises because these two terms are used in variety of ways; many of them are conflicting.

- First, these terms are used interchangeably meaning one and the same thing. Therefore, there is no difference between the two. To make distinction between long-term and short-term orientations, these prefixes are used either with objectives or goals.
- Second, some authors use goals as the long-term results, which an organisation seeks to achieve, and objectives as the short-term results.
- Third, some writers reverse the usage referring to objectives as the desired long-term results and goals as the desired short-term results.

From this point of view, Ackoff has defined both the terms as follows:

> "Desired states or outcomes are objectives. Goals are objectives that are scheduled for attainment during planned period.,"

Thus, objectives and goals defined in this way convey two different concepts. The distinction between these two concepts is important because management needs both.

The Difference between Objectives and Goals may Be Drawn in Terms of the Following Four Dimensions.

1. Time Frame Objectives are timeless, enduring, and unending; goals are temporal, time-phased, and intended to be superceded by subsequent goals. Because objectives relate to the ongoing activities of an organisation, their achievement tends to be open-ended in the sense of not being bounded by time. For example, the survival objective of a business organisation is never completely attained since failure is always a future possibility.
2. Specificity Objectives are stated in broad, general terms, dealing with matters of image, style and self-perception. These are aspirations to be worked in the future. Goals are much more specific, stated in terms of a particular result that will be accomplished by a specific date. In the above example, survival as an objective is not very specific because it leads to different interpretation of the state of survival. On the other hand, goals can be expressed in terms of say achievement of 10 per cent growth in the net sales in the next year. This is more specific and time bound.
3. Focus Objectives are usually stated in terms of some relevant environment which is external to the organisation; goals are more internally focused and carry important implications about how resources of the organisation are utilised or will be utilised in future. Therefore, objectives are more generalised statements like maintaining market leadership, striving continuously for technological superiority. etc. A goal may imply a resource commitment requiring the organisation to use those resources in order to achieve the desired outcomes.
4. Measurement Both objectives and goals can be stated in terms, which are quantitatively measured, but the character of measurement is different. Generally quantitative objectives are

set in relative terms. For example, Reliance Industries has put its objectives like this: to acquire top position among the Indian companies. This objective may not be achieved in anyone year, but it is timeless and externally focused, providing a continuing challenge for the company. Quantitative goals are expressed in absolute terms. For example, a company has stated its goal to achieve 10 per cent growth in its sales in the next year. The achievement of this goal can be measured irrespective of environmental conditions and competitors' actions.

Hierarchy of Objectives

Organisational objectives form a hierarchy ranging from the broad aim to specific individual objectives.

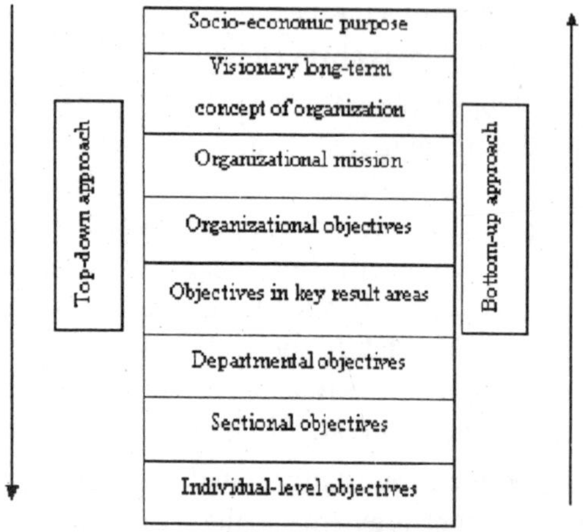

Hierarchy of organizational objectives

The process of assigning a part of a mission to a particular department and then further subdividing the assignment among sections and individuals creates a hierarchy of objectives. The objectives of each subunit contribute to the objectives of the larger unit of which it is a part.

In fact, the organisation itself can be thought of as a social unit and, as such, its objectives are the extension of the objectives of the society. This can be explained in terms of end-means chain which suggests that what is a means for one unit may be an end for another unit. For example, if accomplishment of the overall objectives is the responsibility of top management in the organisation, acquisition of the requisite means may be an end for the next lower level. In order to achieve this sub-objective, sub-means are necessary.

Obtaining these sub-means then becomes the responsibility and consequently the objective of still lower level. This process goes on till a decision can be drawn on the existing product or programme available in the organisation's environment. This is presented in figure

Top-down and bottom-up approach

Hierarchy of objectives can be explained in two approaches: topdown approach and bottom-up approach. Understanding of this phenomenon is essential because a question arises whether objectives should be set at the top and communicated lower down the line or it is in reverse direction. In the top-down approach, at the extreme top of the hierarchy is the purpose, which has two dimensions.

— First, there is the purpose of the society, such as requiring the organisation to contribute to the welfare of the people by providing goods and services at the reasonable cost.

— Second, there is the purpose of the business which may be the ultimate objectives of the business such as what an organisation would like to be. For example, mission might be described as the basic philosophy of the organisation.

However, the distinction between purpose and mission is not\ very obvious and are often used synonymously. At the next level of the hierarchy, overall organisational objectives as specified by various strategies and policies are defined. These lead to specify overall objectives in forms of quantitative standards. These objectives are further carried into divisional, departmental, and individual objectives.

At individual level, two types of objectives exist: performance of individuals which contributes to the achievement of organisational objectives and personal objectives of individuals which they want to satisfy while working in the organisation. At each level of objectives, managers of different levels are involved. For example, overall objectives are formulated by top management. It also sets objectives for all key-result areas where performance is necessary to achieve organisational objectives.

Middle-level managers are involved in the setting of key-result area objectives, divisional objectives, as well as departmental objectives. The primary concern of lower-level managers is the setting of objectives on the departmental and unit level as well as the objectives of their subordinates.

Although in the hierarchy of objectives, individual performance and objectives have been shown at the bottom level, managers at the higher levels also should set objectives for their performance and development. Thus, in top-down approach, upper-level managers determine the objectives for their subordinates, while in bottom-up approach, subordinates initiate the setting of objectives for their position and present them to their superiors.

There is a controversy whether an organisation should use the top-down approach for setting the objectives or it should use bottom-up approach. Proponents of top-down approach suggest that the total organisation needs direction through organisational objectives provided by the top management, which may include owners of the organisation. Proponents of the bottom-up approach, on the other hand, argue that top management needs to have information from lower levels in the form of objectives.

Subordinates are more likely to be motivated and committed by the objectives, which they initiate. While both approaches have certain positive and negative aspects, in order to take the advantages of both, a combination of the two is followed. To what extent both will be combined depends on situations such as size of the organisation, organisational culture, leadership styles of managers, etc.

Role of Objectives

Every organisation has some objectives, either specified or unspecified. Clearly defined objectives govern behaviour of organisation members, and as such, every organisation should specify its objectives clearly. However, contingency approach recognises that in some situations, either it may not be possible to set specific objectives or it is not desirable to set objectives.

Such situations require directional objective setting which identifies preferred style of action for the organisation or individual and an arena for activities. The emphasis switches from carefully formulating what objective is to be accomplished to consideration of a manager's thrust. This approach is more flexible than traditional objective-setting approach and suggests that under three conditions, it is not desirable or possible to set objectives:

i. In the formative period of an organisation's development when it is too early to set objectives;

ii. When the environment in which the organisation operates is unstable or uncertain owing to fast social, economic, technological, legal, or other changes; and

iii. When members cannot build enough trust or agreement to decide upon a common objective.

No doubt, in these situations, it may not be very desirable or possible to set objectives, but not all situations are like this. Specific objectives are appropriate in cases marked by the following conditions:

1. Managers want to narrow the focus and efforts of organisational members;
2. The environment is relatively stable and certain;
3. There are severe time and resource limitations; and
4. Organisational members require more specific conditions as a result of low tolerance for ambiguity and uncertainty.

Objectives should be specified because they perform a number of functions. For Example, Drucker maintains that objectives are essential in all key areas where performance and results directly contribute to the growth and survival of business for enabling managers to

i. Organise and explain the whole range of business phenomena by such objectives

ii. Verify the objective in actual business operation

iii. Predict employee behaviour

iv. Vouchsafe the soundness of decisions

v. Improve their performance.

Major Functions and Contributions

Defining an organisation

Every organisation works in an environment consisting of several forces. These forces provide both opportunities and threats. In order to take the best possible from the environment, it must define itself that is, what kind of company it is, or what kind of business it is in. This relates the organisation with its environment. For example, the following descriptions provide the kind of company each is or the business it is in.

— *Modern 'Food Industries Limited*: manufacturing and marketing of nutritional foods to the public.

— *India Photographic Company Limited*: a quality-oriented photographic system appealing to the consumer who desires instant photography.

— *Mirc Electronics Limited*: the provision of high quality product in the area of electronic entertainment.

Such a definition of the company in relation to its environment provides a clear thinking for the type of efforts the company should make so that it achieves its objectives. The failure to define the nature of the company based on its objectives and environment leads to confusion about the way in which the company wants to move.

Directions for decision-making

Objectives provide the directions for decision- making in various areas of the organisation's operation. The objectives set the limits and prescribe the areas in which the managers can make decision. Since there is no ambiguity about the ends to be achieved, managers are quite clear about the expectations, which the organisation has from its functions. From this point of view, clearly specified objectives serve a number of purposes.

— Clear definition of objectives encourages unified planning. Objectives embody the basic idea and fundamental theories as to what the organisation is trying to achieve. This is necessary to give the meaning and direction to the work of the people associated with the organisation. Such objectives are the focus for different individuals, and unifying effect arises when various plans prepared by several people are adjusted to a common objective.

— Objectives work as a motivating force by providing direction to organisational members. Individuals have framework to fit their personal needs with organisational objectives. All individuals desire a sense of accomplishment of meeting objectives. Thus, fulfilling of objectives itself is a source of motivation for the people in the organisation

— Voluntary coordination, an essential feature of the organisational objectives, is achieved easily if the objectives are clearly specified and mutually agreed upon. People tend to work within their own areas of discretion and adjust according to the needs of, others if they know their own and others' objectives.

Performance standards

Objectives provide standards against which performance of the organisation, its units, sub-units and individuals can be measured. Without performance standards, which are derived from the objectives, there cannot be any meaningful control activities in the organisation. Such control measures not only ensure the achievement of organisational objectives by taking corrective actions, if needed, but also put a psychological pressure on those who are responsible for achieving the organisational objectives.

Basis for decentralisation

Decentralisation includes assigning decision-making authority to lower-level people, thereby a subordinate is given considerable leeway in deciding to perform his work. Decentralisation is necessary for large-size organisations. However, independent decision-making authority to subordinates may lead to disintegration of the organisation unless there is a clear indication of the contributions of each unit towards the realisation of common objectives. Objectives indicate the contributions to be made by each unit for tying them effectively and allowing the managers concerned to exercise their individual skills and initiative.

Integrating

Organisation, Group and Individual. Clearly specified objectives may provide integration of organisation and its various groups and individuals. An organisation cannot exist apart from its individuals, and various groups associated with it, such as creditors, customers, etc. If the objectives are clear, these will communicate the relationship between the organisation and various groups and individuals. Therefore, the individuals and groups can better be integrated because they have clear basis for dealing with the organisation.

Objective Setting

Virtually all organisations have a formal, explicitly recognised, legally specified organ for setting the initial objectives or their amendments. Generally top management determines the overall objectives, which the members of the organisation unite to achieve. In some organisations, the objectives may be set by the vote of the shareholders; in others, by a vote of the members, by a small number of trustees or by a few individuals who own and run the organisations.

In large corporate entities, such bodies as board of directors, governing board, executive committee may set the objectives. These bodies may formulate or change the objectives according to the needs. In practice, the objectives are set in a complicated power play involving various individuals and groups within and without the organisation, and by reference to the values, which govern behaviour in general, and the specific behaviour of the relevant individuals and groups in a particular society.

There are many factors which enter into the struggle to determine the organisational objectives. From management point of view, these factors may be: value system of managers, particularly at the top level, organisational strengths and weaknesses, and external environment. As such, while setting the organisational objectives, managers should take into account all these factors. On the basis of this interaction, management should set the general objectives.

The general objectives are quite broad in nature and show the direction in which the organisation will like to proceed. For example, the general objectives of the business organisations may be survival, growth, contribution to the need of the society, profit earning, etc. These objectives may not be mutually exclusive; rather these can be achieved simultaneously. It is the question of giving relative importance to these.

General objectives are too broad and sometimes intangible to be transformed into action. As such, within the framework of general objectives, managers determine the specific objectives, which they and their units of the organisation will seek to attain. Most of these objectives tend to be of shorter range in character and have definite time limits within which the organisation has to achieve them.

The specific objectives may prescribe the manner in which the general objectives may be achieved as there is always ends-means chain. These objectives may be in the form of diversification of the firm, liquidation of unprofitable divisions, reorganisation of the company, etc. For example, a company has defined its specific objectives as expansion of present range of product, higher sale targets, import substitution, reducing cost without affecting the quality of the product, and expanding range of markets. These specific objectives may fulfil two criteria.

First, translation of general objectives into specific objectives should be tangible and meaningful. As far as possible, these objectives should be easily measurable as organisational performance is measured against these objectives. Second, short-term objectives should contribute to the long-term objectives. In fact, the time-bound objectives are set to make the achievement of long-term objectives more feasible. For example, long-term objectives involving plans for the distant future may fail to make individual objective tangible and meaningful standards for control. This can be overcome by setting short-term objectives as different steps or stages of long-term objectives.

Guidelines

1. Objectives must be clearly specified.
2. Objectives must be set taking into account the various factors affecting their achievement.
3. Objectives should be consistent with organisational mission.

4. Objectives should be rational and realistic rather than idealistic.
5. Objectives should be achievable but must provide challenge to those responsible for achievement.
6. Objectives should yield specific results when achieved.
7. Objectives should be desirable for those who are responsible for the achievement.
8. Objectives should start with the word 'to' and be followed by an action verb.
9. Objectives should be consistent over the period of time.
10. Objectives should be periodically reviewed.

Areas of objective setting

Organisational objectives are of multiple character. Even major objectives are multiple in nature. Thus, an organisation has to set objectives in many areas. However, what objectives should be selected must meet three criteria:

(i) They must be consistent with the values of the management in the organisation.

(ii) They must pinpoint the organisational strengths and weaknesses.

(iii) They must satisfy the external environmental forces.

From these points of view, the organisation will set its objectives in several areas. For example, Peter Drucker has emphasised the areas, which an organisation must emphasize as its objectives. These are: "Market standing, innovation, productivity, physical and financial resources, profitability, manager performance and development, worker performance and attitude, and public responsibility."

Some research studies also indicate that companies set objectives in different areas. A research study on setting objectives in 65 companies shows that organisations set objectives in terms of corporate growth, maximisation of profit or return's, supply of quality products, employee satisfaction, and other objectives strengthening of manufacturing base, maintaining market leadership, change in product mix, technological leadership, growing returns to shareholders, social obligations, interest of consumers and labour, maintaining organisational assets as national assets, export development, and funds management.

In another study of 28 companies, it has been found that the companies emphasize objectives in five broad areas in varying proportion-profit, marketing, growth, employee, and social In a study of 72 companies, conducted later, it has been found that the companies have emphasized their objectives in the areas of growth through expansion in the same line of business, diversification in related product lines, manufacturing products requiring high technology., development of product base, and cooperative existence with rival companies.

It can be emphasized here that objectives are intertwined and interrelated. For example, growth of the company may result into profitability, consequently shareholder's higher returns either in terms of higher dividend or in terms of bonus and consequently higher dividend. However, the emphasis on the strategic management may differ in these two cases.

Various, objectives identified above are more in the form of common denominators rather than a true reflection of the objectives that the companies actually set for themselves. In the case of individual companies,- there may be wide variations in the objectives that they set. The examples of two companies-Bharat Heavy Electricals Limited (BHEL) and Associated Cement Companies (ACC) Limited illustrate what objectives have been set by these companies.

Translating General Objectives

Organisational objectives, discussed so far, are of general and broad nature. They provide direction for action on continuous basis. However, these objectives are too general and, sometimes, intangible to be transformed into action. In order to make these operative, managers determine specific objectives within the framework of general objectives, which the organisation and its various units will seek to achieve within a specific period. For example, growth is one of the vital objectives of every organisation.

This provides direction for undertaking various activities through which growth can be achieved. However, this is very general and does not provide clue about how much growth in what period of time. In order to overcome this problem, organisations set specific objectives to be achieved in specified time. For example, Tata Group has set growth objective in terms of doubling group turnover in four years and doubling net profit in three years. Such a specific objective provides sharp focus on the activities that may be undertaken to achieve this volume of growth..

Most of the specific objectives tend to be of short range in character and have definite time limits within which the organisation has to achieve these. Translation of general objectives into specific and operative objectives must fulfil two criteria.

1. Translation of general objectives into specific objectives should be tangible and meaningful. As far as possible, these objectives should be easily measurable as organisational performance is measured against these objectives.
2. Specific objectives should contribute to the achievement of general objectives. In fact, time-bound objectives are set to make the achievement of general objectives more feasible. For example, long-term objectives involving plans for the distant future may fail to make individual objectives tangible and meaningful standards for control. This can be overcome by setting specific objectives at different stages of general long-term objectives.

Change in Objectives

Organisational objectives are not static but dynamic and these are modified over the period of time to have better alignment of the organisation with its environment. This process is known as objective or goal succession. This may happen in three specific conditions:

1. If existing objectives have been achieved and the organisation has no alternative, it must adopt new objectives for its continuous existence.
2. If it is not desirable to pursue the existing objectives because of change in environment and/ or internal conditions, the organisation has to evolve new objectives.
3. If the existing objectives are such that they cannot be achieved, the organisation has to modify or alter them.

The change in objectives may take the character of objective multiplication expansion, or substitution of objectives depending on the situations. Many organisations have expanded their objectives over the period of time. For example, Reliance has expanded its objectives to include petrochemical business along with its textile business and the contribution of petrochemicals to its revenues is significantly more than textiles.

Similarly,. ITC Limited has added hotel, paper- and packaging business in its fold along with tobacco business. Many organisations have transformed themselves from a mere marketing organisation to manufacturing organisations like Hindustan Lever, Voltas, etc. Similarly, many organisations have substituted their original objectives with new objectives. For example, Re-Cross Society was established primarily for helping those who suffered from war or any other casualty.

After the World Wars, this objective became meaningless and the Red Cross has now adopted the objective of preserving and improving public health. YMCA transformed itself from religious and spiritual exercises to recreational and physical exercises because of changed social environment. From management point of view, following factors are important to effect changes in organisational objectives.

Change in organisational objectives

Change in aspiration level of top management and other key strategists of the organisation requires a change in organisational objectives. In one way, the organisation becomes a means for satisfying personal needs and ambitions of promoters. and/ or top-level managers who perform the role of key decision makers. These personal needs and ambitions are reflected in organisational objectives.

Whenever there is any change in -aspiration level, it affects the organisational objectives; there will be a change in the objectives or a change in priority ordering of objectives. For example, Dhirubhai Ambani, the chairman of Reliance Industries Limited, once commented that he had the ambition of being number one industrialist of the country. The result is: he set highly ambitious objectives for Reliance and it grew at very fast rate. Change in organisational objectives caused by a change in aspiration level of management is more often found when a new team of executives or new chief executive from outside the organisation having no commitment to the past strategies and objectives takes over the reins of management.

Change by coalition groups

Coalition refers to combination of two or more individuals, groups, or organisations for common objectives. Thus, coalition is goal-oriented alliance among individuals, groups, or organisations with different interests and is formed to mobilise joint efforts. Coalition concept is very common in political parties where two or more political parties combine themselves to fight against the third. Business organisations have similar coalition.

A business organisation is viewed as consisting of a number of groups such as owners, managers, suppliers, employees, government agencies, etc. In this coalition, each group has a bargaining power and the result of complex bargaining process determines, to a great extent, the objectives of the organisation. Emergence of a certain interest group as more dominant and powerful, necessitates modification of organisational objectives. For example, change in ownership of a company, owner being a dominant group in the coalition, may necessitate change in the company's objectives.

Change in environment

An organisation, being a subsystem of the broader societal system, has to work within the framework provided by the society and its various constituents, commonly referred to as external environment or just environment of the organisation. The organisation sets its objectives and strategies taking environmental variables into account.

The environment is dynamic and changes over time. Any change in the environment may disturb the present working of the organisation, necessitating change in the organisation's operations including change in objectives. For example, after the liberalisation of Indian economy in 1990s, many foreign companies entered in India making the business environment quite competitive.

In such a situation, existing Indian organisations had to change their strategies and objectives. For example, in pre-liberalisation era, automobile companies, particularly in two-wheeler and car segment, did not emphasize on product innovation because they were operating in sellers' market. In the post-liberalised era, product innovation became one of their objectives to face competition effectively. Similar phenomenon has happened in other segments too.

Life-cycle of organisation

Organisations have life cycles similar to human beings and pass generally through different stages in their life cycle from infancy to adulthood, maturity and then possibly decay as in old age. At each stage of life cycle, there may be specific thrust on an objective or set of objective presents relationship between life cycle, organisational objectives and strategic focus of the organisation.

Objectives and strategic focus

How much time will be taken by an organisation to reach to a particular stage of its life cycle from its previous stage cannot be determined. Some organisations complete the life cycle quickly while others lake lot of time. For example, Toes, established in 1907, is still going great and its hunger for expansion is yet to be satiated. As against this, many leasing and hire purchase companies establish in 1980s have completed their life-cycle and have exited. Similar was the case with Soya extraction companies. The major determinants of life cycle are quality of promoters, their management philosophy, and nature of industry.

COMPARATIVE ANALYSIS

Objectives of Madras Fertilizers Ltd.

1. To produce and market fertilizers and bio-fertilizers and market agro-chemicals, efficiently and economically, in an environmentally sound manner;
2. To take up and implement schemes for saving energy;
3. To continuously upgrade the quality of human resources promote organisational and management development.
4. To continually improve plant and operational safety;
5. To take up R&D schemes.

National Thermal Power Corporation Ltd.

In line with the Corporation's mission, the Corporation's objectives are as under:

1. To add generating capacity by installing thermal power plants including gas based power plants as per the prescribed time schedules, cost and reliability levels.
2. To establish transmission systems adequate fro the evacuation of power from the generating units set up by the Corporation within the prescribed time schedules, costs and reliability levels.
3. To operate and maintain the existing generating units and the transmission systems in an efficient manner so as to unsure higher availability and reliability levels.
4. To manage and financial operation of the Corporation in accordance with sound commercial practices to enable generation of adequate internal resources in order to be able to contribute in the National Power Development Programme.
5. To take up environmental and rehabilitation measures in coordination with the programme of the State governments and other agencies concerned and to initiate requisite studies in this behalf.
6. To develop and implement a well-knit Human Resources Development Policy, result oriented personnel development Programme and an organisational culture, which motivates employees to contribute their best towards achievement of organisational objectives.
7. To develop and utilise specialised technical expertise as well as general managerial skills in enabling employees to achieve professional excellence and organisational goals.
8. To strengthen in house technical and managerial capabilities not only to be self reliant to cater to the needs for setting up of its projects/transmission system and their operation but also for providing consultancy services to the organisations within the country and abroad.

The objectives and goals in National Thermal Power Corporation Ltd. have been put together for comparison purposes and to ascertain the difference between these two terms.

Concept of Mission of Business

The basic concept of mission of business is expressed in terms of products, markets, and geographical scope along with a statement of uniqueness. At business levels the mission statement becomes sharper and gets focused on specifics. It is detailing out of the vision statement that reflects the strategic posture of a company. The mission statement is an expression of business purpose as well as needed excellence to achieve a position of competitive leadership.

Statement by Lalita D. Gupta Joint Managing Director & Chief Operating Officer, ICICI In 45th Annual Report 1999-2000

> "We have taken the leadership role in bringing the new economy paradigm to the India Financial Sector. We have used the power of technology to forge relationships with several key multinationals and to establish virtual partnerships with our corporate clients. We will continue to ride the technology paradigm and retain the cutting edge."

The primary information contained in a mission statement should be the required degree of excellence for assuming a position of competitive leadership, a clear definition of the present position, and future expected scope in business. So, again you will take the example of your own university and write down the mission statement and put down the purpose of the mission statement. Usually Short- term goals are achievable in reasonably short span of a time frame of three to five years. Business scope is explicit in stating what is to be included and excluded. Purpose of defining business scope is to clearly enumerate specification of current and future product, market and geographic coverage of business.

Many firms suffer from marketing myopia and the contrast between the current and future scope is an effective diagnostic tool to caution against the myopic position of company. Information contained in mission statement should provide a way of selecting a method to pursue a position of either leadership or a definite competitive advantageous position. Lets take up few examples:

a. HCL: The environment for computer companies became quite competitive by 1991. A need was felt to provide a feeling of oneness in the organisation. So management felt to assess the internal strength and design a customer -centric mission statement for team-building, mutual trust and empowerment.

b. Similarly RANBAXY realised that competition in pharmaceuticals industry was becoming tough and it could not survive just by selling generic drugs. Later, measures were taken to communicate it extensively throughout the company down to the level of workers.

Last but not the least in UTI too an extensive corporate planning exercise was undertaken in 1992. That is the time when they formulated their Mission statement.

MOTIVATING PEOPLE, THE PEPSI WAY

Pepsi fosters belongingness and ownership in employees from whom it also demands a lot.

— It awards onetime scholarship to children of employees to study abroad

— It has set up multiskilled capability centre in Delhi which offers training tools to employees growing from supervisory to manager cadre

— It has introduced awards for best performing sales people in a country

— It celebrates Pepsiday which is a day long carnival with families

— It supplies free beverages at employees weddings

— It sends flowers to employees on birthdays

— It encourages people to preferably use blue cars as blue is Pepsi's corporate colour.

Vision of a firm is in fact its corporate philosophy.

BHEL Vision 2001

Vision

A worldclass, innovative, and profitable engineering enterprise providing total business solutions mission. To be the leading Indian engineering enterprise providing quality products, systems and services in the fields of energy, transportation, industry infrastructure and other potential areas.

Values

— Meeting commitments made to external and internal customers
— Faster learning, creativity and speed of response
— Respect for dignity and potential of individuals
— Loyalty and pride in the company
— Team playing
— Zeal to excess
— Integrity and fairness in all matters

The major components of a vision statement must consist the following.

i. Mission of the firm in terms of product, market, and geographical scope and a way to attain a desired competitive position.
ii. Clear identification of business units and their interrelationship in terms of shared resources and concerns.
iii. Statement of corporate philosophy, corporate policy and values

Objectives of BHEL

The objectives of BHEL are formulated in terms of growth, profitability, image, and continuity, which are as follows:

— *Growth*: To ensures a steady growth in business so as to fulfil national aspirations from BHEL and expand international operations.
— *Profitability*: To provide a reasonable and adequate return on capital employed primarily through improvements in operational efficiency, capacity utilisation and productivity, and generate adequate internal resources to finance the company's growth.
— *Image*: To build up a high degree of customer confidence by sustaining international standard of excellence in product quality, performance and service, particularly in regard to supply of spares and after-sales service; to fulfil the expectations which stakeholders like Government as owner, employees, customers and the country at large have from BHEL.

— *Continuity*: To invest in human resources development, sustained research and development, strive for excellence in management and other long-term objectives to ensure a leadership status for BHEL..

Objectives of ace limited

1. To strive continuously to maintain the leadership of the cement industry by modernisation, expansion and the establishment of wide and efficient marketing network.
2. To achieve a fair and reasonable return on the capital employed by promoting productivity throughout the company.
3. To ensure a steady growth of business by strengthening the Company's position in the cement sector and also by diversifying into other areas consistent with the overall corporate objectives.
4. To maintain the high quality of the Company's products and services, and to ensure supply of these products and services at fair prices.
5. To promote and maintain fair and harmonious industrial relations, and an environment for the effective involvement, welfare and development of staff at all levels.
6. To promote research and development efforts in the areas of product development, energy and fuel conservation, to innovate and optimize productivity.
7. To discharge its obligations to society specifically in the areas of integrated rural development schemes and safeguarding of environment and natural ecological balance.

UNDERSTANDING OBJECTIVE, MISSION AND VISION

Vision

Aspirations, expressed as strategic intent, should lead to an end; otherwise they would just be castles in the air. That end is the vision of an organisation or an individual. It is what the firm or a person would ultimately like to become. For instance, some of you, say in 10 years, or may be even earlier, would like to become general managers managing an SBU in a large, diversified multinational corporation.

Or some others among you would like to believe that you will be an entrepreneur in 1015 years owning your own company dealing with IT services and employing cuttingedge technology to serve a global clientele. A firm thinks like that too. Witness what Tata Steel says about its vision:

"Tata Steel enters the new millennium with the confidence of a learning, knowledge based and happy organisation. We will establish ourselves as a supplier of choice by delighting our customers with our service and our products. In the coming decade, we will become the most cost competitive steel plant and so serve the community and the nation."

A vision, therefore, articulates the position that a firm would like to attain in the distant future. Seen from this perspective, the vision enencapsulates the basic strategic intent.

Understanding Vision

A vision is more dreamt of than it is articulated. This is the reason why it is difficult to say what vision an organisation has. Sometimes it is not even evident to the entrepreneur who usually thinks of the vision. By its nature, it could be as hazy and vague as a dream that one experienced the previous night and is not able to recall perfectly in broad daylight. Yet it is a powerful motivator to action. And it is from the actions that a vision could often be derived. Henry Ford wished to democratise the automobile when he visualised that an affordable vehicle could be available for the masses. Walt Disney probably wanted to make people happy.

Vision has been defined in several different ways. Kotter defines it as a "description of something (an organisation, corporate culture, a business, a technology, an activity) in the future". ElNamaki considers it as a "mental perception of the kind of environment an individual, or an organisation, aspires to create within a broad time horizon and the underlying conditions for the actualisation of this perception".

Miller and Dess view it simply as the "category of intentions that are broad, all-inclusive, and forward thinking". The common strand of thought evident in these definitions and several others available in strategic management literature relates to 'vision' being future aspirations that lead to an inspiration to be the best in one's field of activity

Benefits of Having a Vision

Parikh and Neubauer point out the several benefits accruing to an, organisation having a vision. Here is what they say:

— Good visions are inspiring and exhilarating
— Visions represent a discontinuity, a step function and a jump ahead so that the company knows what it is to be
— Good visions help in the creation of a common identity and a shared sense of purpose
— Good visions are competitive, original and unique. They make sense in the market place, as they are practical
— Good visions foster risktaking and experimentation
— Good visions foster longterm thinking.
— Good visions represent integrity; they are truly genuine and can be used for the benefit of people.

Process of Envisioning

The process of envisioning is a difficult one as we see from what Collins and Porras have to say about it. According to them, a well conceived vision consists of two major components: core ideology and envisioned future. The core ideology defines the enduring character of an organisation that remains unchangeable as it passes through the vicissitudes of vectors, such as, technology, competition, or management fads.

The core ideology rests on the core values (the essential and enduring tenets of an organisation) and core purposes (an organisation's reason for being)." The envisioned future too consists of two components: a 1030 years of audacious goal and a vivid description of what it will be like to achieve that goal. The process envisioning is indeed fascinating as can be seen from which presents a vivid description by a young and dynamic inheritor of the Birla group"

Mission

While the essence of vision is a forward looking view of what an organisation wishes to become, mission is what an organisation is and why it exists. Several years ago Peter F Drucker raised important philosophical questions related to business: What is the business? What will it be? And what should it be? These three questions, though simply worded, are in reality the most fundamental questions that any organisation can put to itself. The answers are based on the analysis of the underlying needs of the society that any organisation serves to fulfil. The satisfaction of that need is, then, the business of the organisation.

Organisations relate their existence to satisfying a particular need of the society. They do this in terms of their mission. Mission is a statement, which defines the role that an organisation plays in a society. It refers to the particular needs of that society, for instance, its information needs. A book publisher and a magazine editor are both engaged in satisfying the information needs of society but they do it through different means. A book publisher may aim at producing excellent reading material while a magazine editor may strive to present news analysis in balanced and unbiased manner. Both have different objectives but an identical mission.

A mission was earlier considered as the scope of the business activities a firm pursues. The definition of mission has gradually expanded to represent a concept that embodies the purpose behind the existence of an organisation. Thompson defines mission as the "essential purpose of the organisation, concerning particularly why it is in existence, the nature of the businesses it is in, and the customers it seeks to serve and satisfy" Hunger and Wheelen say that mission is the "purpose or reason for the organisation's existence".

Now there is not much difference of opinion about the definition of mission. Yet, you finds instances of organisations confusing mission with vision or objectives. In strategic management literature, mission occupies a definite place as a part of strategic intent.

Most organisations derive their mission statements from a particular set of tasks they are called upon to perform in the capsulates the basic strategic intent light of their individual, national or global priorities Several public sector organisations, set up in India during the

1950s and 60s owe their existence to the vision of Jawaharlal Nehru, the first prime minister, who enunciated and tirelessly worked for the national aim of building a strong and self reliant India by laying the foundations of many of the basic infrastructure industries. Mission statements, whether derived from set priorities or not, could be formulated either formally or informally.

Usually, entrepreneurs lay down the corporate philosophy, which an organisation follows, in its strategic and operational activities. Such a philosophy may not be consciously and formally stated but may gradually evolve due to the entrepreneur's actions. Generally an entrepreneur has a perception of the type of organisation that he, wants his company to be. Mission statements could be formulated on the basis of e-vision that an entrepreneur decides on in the initial stages of an organisation's, growth.

As an entrepreneur of an organisation formulates a mission statement for the organisation you want to work for? Major strategists could also contribute to the development of a mission statement. They do this informally by lending a hand in the creation of a particular corporate identity or formally through discussions and the writing down of a mission statement.

Chief executives plan a major role in formulating a mission statement both formally and informally. They may set up executive committees to formally discuss and decide on a mission statement or enunciate a corporate philosophy to be followed for strategic management. Consultants may also be called upon to make an in depth: analysis of the organisation to suggest an appropriate mission statement.

B N Sinha, (managing director of the Scientific Instrument Company Ltd) who took the help of, a management consultant in deciding his company's mission and purpose, describes the process of formulating a mission: as a starting point, we spent quite a bit of time on identifying the 'mission' of business. After a lot of discussion, he identified the mission as follows: to be a vibrant organisation set on contributing to the scientific and technical progress of the country; keeping its customers and employees satisfied in terms of service and work reward; giving adequate return on investment to the shareholder.

Characteristics of a Mission Statement

Organisations legitimize themselves by performing some function that is valued by society. A mission statement defines the basic reason for the existence of that organisation. Such a statement reflects the corporate philosophy, identity, character, and image of an organisation. It may be defined explicitly or could be deduced from the management's actions, decisions, or the chief executive's press statements. When explicitly defined it provides enlightenment to the insiders and outsiders on what the organisation stand for. In order to be effective, a mission statement should possess the following seven characteristics communicated

1. *It should be feasible:* A mission should always aim high but it should not be an impossible statement. It should be realistic and achievable its followers must find it to be credible. But feasibility depends on the resources available to work towards a mission. In the sixties, the US National Aeronautics and Space Administration (NASA) had a mission to land on the moon. It was a feasible mission that was ultimately realised.
2. *It should be precise:* A mission statement should not be so narrow as to restrict the organisation's activities nor should it be too broad to make itself meaningless. For instance, 'Manufacturing bicycles' is a narrow mission statement since it severely limits the organisation's activities, while mobility business' is too broad a term, as it does not define the reasonable contour within which the organisation could operate.
3. *It should be clear:* A mission should be clear enough to lead to action. It should not be a high sounding set of platitudes meant for publicity purposes. Many organisations do adopt such statements but probably they do so for emphasizing their identity and character. For example, Asian Paints stresses 'leadership through excellence', while India Today see itself as 'the complete news magazine'. The Administrative Staff College of India considers itself as 'the college for practising managers' and Bajaj Auto believes in 'Providing, value for money, for years'. To be useful, a mission statement should be clear enough to lead to action. The ITC's stated corporate philosophy of aligning its organisational

activities with national priorities helps it in choosing areas for diversification like the hotel, paper and agroindustry.

4. *It should be motivating:* A mission statement should be motivating for members of the organisation and of society, and they should feel it worthwhile working for such an organisation or being its customers. A bank, which lays great emphasis on customer service, is likely to motivate its employees to serve its customers well and to attract clients. Customer service, therefore is an important purpose for a banking institution.
5. *It should be distinctive:* A mission statement, which is indiscriminate, is likely to have little impact. If all scooter manufacturers defined their mission in a similar fashion, there would not be much of a difference among them. But if one defines it as providing scooters that would provide 'value for money, for years' it will create an important distinction in the public mind.
6. *It should indicate major components of strategy:* A mission statement along with the organisational purpose should indicate the major components of the strategy to be adopted. The chief executive of Indal expressed his intentions by saying that his company "begins its fifth decade of committed entrepreneurship with the promise of a highly diversified company retaining aluminium as its mainline business, but with an active presence in the chemical, electronics and industrial equipment business". This statement indicates that the company is likely to follow a combination of stability, growth and diversification strategies in the future.
7. *It should indicate how objectives are to be accomplished:* Besides indicating the broad strategies to be adopted a mission statement should also provide clues regarding the manner in which the objectives are to be accomplished. The Centre for Development of Telematics (CDOT) had set its first three yearsmission (198487) as developing, designing, and engineering a large digital exchange suitable for Indian conditions and its second mission (198790) as developing the technological prerequisites for an integrated systems digital network of the future. 14 These mission statements specially deal with the objectives to be achieved within a given time period. So,

check your mission statement, which you framed for your business school, fulfills all the seven purposes.

Goals

The next step for the company, after formulating the mission statement, is the establishment of major goals. The goals designate specific results the businesses want to achieve. In this context, the purpose of goals is to specify, as accurately as possible, as to what is to be done, if the company is to attain its mission. Goals are more specific than the mission but less specific than objectives. Objectives define and refine the goals further. Strategic goals help managers to establish end results of activities in general without getting bogged down in issues of measurement and timing.

Goals, in general, can be longterm or short-term. Short-term goals generally cover a period of about one year. Longterm goals cover a time period beyond one year. Sometimes, there is a category of intermediate goals, which cover a time period of between one and five years. Longterm goals are usually related to such issues as customer satisfaction, improvements in product quality, worker efficiency and productivity, innovation and so on. These longterm goals require management to do strategic planning in terms of longterm profitability and in terms of longterm investments in equipment, people, research and development and so on.

Goal characteristics

According to M.D. Richards, meaningful goals should have four characteristics.

— First, goals should be sufficiently specific so that they are precise and measurable. It would assist management in monitoring the progress towards achievement of these goals at each specific point in time.

— The second characteristic is concerned with the issues that a goal addresses. A goal should only address important issues. Short-term goals and objectives should be left to the lower management to plan and achieve. Such important issues as reducing costs or improving quality should be included in goals, which are to be achieved by top or middle management. For example, Boeing's goal of being a market leader in aircraft business by maintaining a minimum of 60 percent market share is an important issue that a goal addresses.

— A third characteristic of well constructed goals is that they should be realistic and challenging. Challenging goals motivate managers to be innovative and ambitious about improving the operations. However, the goals have to be realistic and compatible with the resources available. An unrealistic goal would cause resentment among employees. For example, Boeing Company decided to achieve a 30 percent unit cost reduction by improving efficiency of operations. However, the time period they projected in achieving this goal was 6 years. This goal was considered challenging and realistic. The goal would have been unrealistic and unachievable if they had projected the time period for such cost reduction much less than 6 years'.

— The fourth characteristic of realistic goals is the specification of time period in which a given goal is to be achieved. For example, when Boeing decided to cut the per unit cost by 30 percent, they put the time frame to be 6 years. Deadlines, if realistic, can inject a sense of urgency into goal attainment and can motivate employees to work hard and with dedication. The dedication becomes even higher when appropriate rewards are related with the timely goal attainment.

Some of the strategic goals established by Elpaso Electric Company in various areas of concern are taken from their annual report and are briefly stated below:

1. Customer Service
   - Provide a quality of service to customers at least equal to the highest standards in the industry.
   - Maintain reliability of service to customers at a level above 99 percent.
   - Insure that customers are educated on the safety aspect of focusing electricity.
2. Community Service: Promote economic growth and increased development of the company's total service area. Provide job

opportunities and an investment in the service area, which promotes a higher standard of living for all citizens a Cooperate with and serve the educational institutions located in the service area in a manner consistent with other leaders in the industry.

3. Shareholder Relations
   - Assure that all expenditures are made in such a way as to protect and enhance the shareholder's investment.
   - Provide a rate of return to the shareholders, which is competitive with other investments.
   - Base all company involvement in new programmes or projects on solid economic principles.
4. Employee Management Obligations
   - Monitor and strive to improve the quality of management and supervision. Attract, develop and retain able and loyal employees.
   - Provide equal employment opportunities and a high degree of training along with modem, professional tools.
5. Corporate Communications
   - Make an assertive effort to provide informative communications on relevant company issues.
   - Keep senior management apprised and educated on current topics of interest. Enhance the community image of the company by being receptive to the needs of customers and the community.

References

Barney, J., "Firm Resources and Sustainable Competitive Advantage", *Journal of Management*, vol 17, no 1, 1991.

Chaffee, E., "Three models of strategy", *Academy of Management Review*, vol 10, no. 1, 1985.

David, F., *Strategic Management*, Columbus:Merrill Publishing Company, 1989.

Drucker, Peter., *The Practice of Management*, Harper and Row, New York, 1954.

Hamel, G. & Prahalad, C.K., "Strategic Intent", *Harvard Business Review*, May-June 1989.

Hammer, M. and Champy, J., *Reengineering the Corporation*, Harper Business, New York, 1993.

Lamb, Robert, *Boyden Competitive strategic management*, Englewood Cliffs, NJ: Prentice-Hall, 1984.

Levinson, J.C., *Guerrilla Marketing, Secrets for making big profits from your small business*, Houghton Muffin Co. New York, 1984.

5

The Power of Business Strategy

Game of Business

Business competition is very similar to sports. In business, teams of individuals face each other in competition for employees, customers, product innovations, and profits-among other goals. The major difference between sports and business is the relevant time frame. As in sports, business organisations that win consistently excel at preparation, planning, and execution. They know their situation, know where they want to go, and determine how best to go there.

Maybe more importantly, these organisations have their finger on the pulse of the markets, customers, technologies, and other innovations that may change the rules of the game and the factors that lead to success. And these dominant companies are willing to adjust their game plans accordingly. Strategy is the business word for game plan. All businesses have strategies, either planned or unplanned.

Power of Business

The essence of business can be depicted in a simple diagram (Figure 1). This diagram suggests that a business is a flow model, a going concern. First, there's the business idea that motivates us to begin a business. Let's say we decide to use the grandmother's recipes to open a restaurant. We figure that since we all loved Grandma's cooking, others would too. In order to realise and deliver the promise of the business idea, we must use a package of assets: people, property, and relationships.

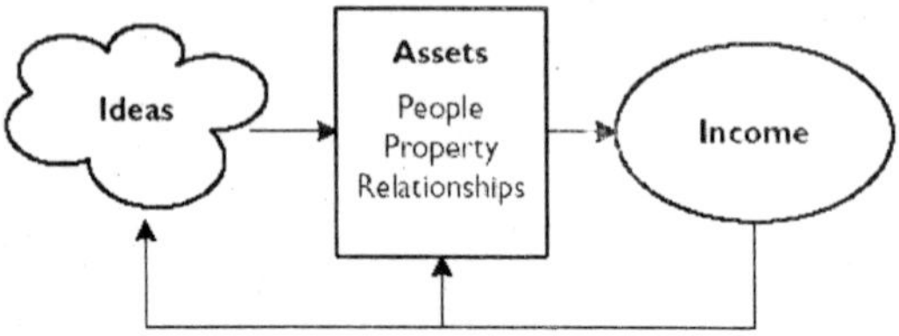

Figure 1. A simple model of business

We'll need a location, tables, chairs, china, silverware, and a lot of restaurant equipment and supplies. We'll need cooks, waiters and waitresses, dishwashers, and other employees. We'll need a liquor license, public health certificates, and accounts with food suppliers of meat, produce, and so forth. These assets must then generate income, which is used to refuel the assets and invest in new ideas to keep the business going. Let's examine each component of the model. It all begins with a business idea. Now, a business idea is more than just an idea.

A business idea has two defining characteristics. First, a good business idea meets an unmet need in the market. The product or service that we offer must satisfy a customer's unmet need. This may mean a brand-new product or service or it may mean finding a way to provide a product or a service at a lower price than is currently available. In the case of the restaurant, the unmet need may be as simple as providing a good place for authentic Italian food. Certainly, there are other restaurants, and other Italian restaurants, but the idea is to package the food, wine list, and ambiance in a way that will be attractive to patrons.

Second, a good business idea drives transactions. Whatever product we offer to customers, they must be willing to exchange their money for the product or service. The test of a good business idea is whether people will give up their cash to get the products or services in enough numbers to keep operations going.

Our Italian restaurant idea, when communicated to the public (by advertising and/or word of mouth), must create a demand for hungry people to select the establishment for lunch or dinner. The ultimate test is whether the business idea will meet the unmet needs of the market in a way that customers will return, again and again-and satisfy the business need to generate income.

Once we have a business idea, we must assemble the assets to construct the business. Usually we need money, financial capital. Also we need employees, human capital. Finally, we need relationships: with suppliers, the government, customers, distributors, and others to make the business work. Linking the business idea with the right asset mix is what creates the power of a business and it's that link that's the business strategy.

So, while we start with Grandma's recipes, in putting together the plan, we must make many decisions and undertake many activities. That is, we must construct the strategy. The location, the market we target (families, upscale diners, college students, and so forth), the decor we select, the pricing of the entrees, the wine list, the training and performance of the wait staff, the quality of the foodstuffs, and the preparation of the food-all will play a role in the success.

These strategic decisions we make in building the organisation and business model are endless. The link between the business idea and the assets we select is the business strategy. It doesn't matter whether we are operating a small restaurant or a giant telecom, automobile, or chemical company; this coordination between the business idea and the asset mix we select is the power of the business.

The result of the idea-asset connection is the income the business generates. The lifeblood of a business is the cash flow, which is used to replenish the assets and develop new ideas to keep the business going. If an asset does not contribute to generating income, we should get rid of it! If, for example, we generally have unused tables in the dining room and yet the cocktail lounge is crowded, we should consider reconfiguring the assets: fewer dining tables, more space in the bar! Later on we will discuss how we can develop strategies based on the efficient and optimal use of the assets.

The cash flow that the business generates is the source of keeping the business going, investing in new ideas and new assets, and reaching the financial goals. We can consider revenue and income and profit: all of these terms reflect the activity of the business. But, at the end of the day, the most important consideration to the business owner is cash flow.

BASICS OF STRATEGY

So, business strategy is the selection of ideas and assets to meet the long-term goals. Of course, we must begin with goals-What do we want to accomplish by operating this business? There are many reasons for going into business. For now, let's just think about what "strategy" means. We can break down strategy into three components:

— Create the strategy-What should we do?

— Implement the strategy-How do we do it?

— Evaluate the strategy-How well are we doing in meeting the long-term goals?

Formulating a business strategy is a complex task even for the smallest of organisations. Furthermore, whether you're the manager of a small group in an organisation or the CEO of a large company, you'll be working with strategic issues. Creating the business strategy begins with the business idea. In the case of the Italian restaurant, the business idea is authentic Italian cooking, based upon Grandma's recipes. But as we know, the idea is not enough.

We cannot raise capital simply by presenting samples of Grandma's cooking to the loan committee down at the bank. Rather, we must present a comprehensive plan to the lenders that details the complete picture of the restaurant, so that the bank may judge whether we'll be able to acquire the assets we need and generate enough income to completely repay the debt.

We also won't be able to hire good cooks without fully explaining how the ideas for the business will provide a good place to work now and into the future. If these people cannot see a viable business in the idea, they're not likely to commit to working to prepare the foods that will turn the recipes into revenues. Also, without a good idea of what we want the restaurant to be, we won't be able to inspire the waiters and waitresses to provide the service that will make the restaurant a special experience that will delight the customers and keep attracting business.

So formulating a strategy requires us to develop a complete picture of the business in operation, even before we implement the plan. The development of this vision of the business requires that we address a series of questions that will lead to a successful strategy.

STRATEGY DEVELOPMENT

Since strategy is the bundle of decisions and activities that we choose to reach the long-term objectives and since we must picture the entire business before we actually start turning the ideas into business strategies, we have a lot of thinking to do. Can we structure this strategic thinking process? Yes, as a start we should address the following questions. As we do, we will begin to see the strategy emerge.

What Is the Business Idea? This question forces us to decide what business we are in. This is very obvious for a new business, but it can be tricky for existing businesses. Organisations act and react and sometimes find that their business idea becomes diluted or too ambiguous to describe. As a result, managers and employees lose the focus on the founding principles that made the business successful.

Wal-Mart is an example of a company that does not lose focus and is true to its business idea. For Wal-Mart the business idea is low prices, "Always!" for a galaxy of products that most people need or want. Every aspect of the Wal- Mart operation is dedicated do delivering low prices to its customers. Wal-Mart extracts cost savings in the products it stocks by being tough on suppliers and executing a sophisticated, high-technology supply chain.

Corporate overhead is kept very low. Sam's Clubs provide another low-price option through bulk purchasing and selling. Customers may not have all the brand choices, but the selection of goods is offered at lower prices than for comparable goods sold elsewhere. Sears, on the other hand, is a retailer that has not enjoyed the growth or financial success of Wal-Mart. If we explore the history of Sears, the company has bounced around with its own brands and with national brands. It once tried to move up-market, seeking higher-income customers, and confused its clientele with higherprice point goods.

Sears has at different times been a catalogue merchant and discontinued its use of the catalogue. For a while, Sears emphasized "The Softer Side of Sears," seeking to promote its clothing and housewares lines and de-emphasizing the successful hardware and appliance lines. In 2002, Sears acquired Lands' End, a mail-order retailer of traditional clothing, placing some Lands' End goods in

Sears stores and selling the goods through direct mail catalogues and the Internet.

The casual observer of Sears might ask, "What is the business idea of the company?" There doesn't seem to be a clear answer. If we compare the results of Sears and Wal-Mart, we find a striking comparison. Founded in 1906, Sears had revenues of $41.1 billion in 2001. Wal-Mart, started in 1969, had 2001 revenues of $193.3 billion, almost five times the Sears sales results.

Answering that basic question-What business are we in?-also leads us to consider what businesses and markets we should not be in. Sometimes it is important to say "no" to a business idea, if it does not fit the plan. We should select the best business ideas and then focus on the decisions and activities that support those ideas.

Business Purpose

Philosophers often address the question, why do we exist? Answers usually lead to religious or secular big picture notions. Businesses need practical answers to the question, why do we exist? The answer is the long-term objectives. Clearly, every business has financial objectives, because every business is based upon a capital investment, which should produce an expected rate of return to the owners. Yet, businesses typically aspire to be more than just an engine for returns to shareholders.

Customer satisfaction, contributions to the community, and a good place to work for employees are frequently important components of long-term objectives. Some firms provide a broader notion of their business purpose as a guide to their strategy development. Here's how Ben & Jerry's Ice Cream, for example, expresses its purpose: "Ben & Jerry's is founded on and dedicated to a sustainable corporate concept of linked prosperity. The mission consists of three interrelated parts." It then defines its product mission, economic mission, and social mission.

Its product mission is "To make, distribute & sell the finest quality all natural ice cream & euphoric concoctions with a continued commitment to incorporating wholesome, natural ingredients and promoting business practices that respect the Earth and the Environment." Its economic mission is "To operate the Company on a sustainable financial basis of profitable growth, increasing value for the stakeholders & expanding opportunities for development and career growth for the employees." Finally, its social mission is "To operate the company in a way that actively recognises the central role that business plays in society by initiating innovative ways to improve the quality of life locally, nationally & internationally."

Other companies have a broad, but simple business purpose. Merck, the large pharmaceutical company, lists among its company values "Our business is preserving and improving human life." The American Red Cross states that it "will provide relief to victims of disasters and help people prevent, prepare for, and respond to emergencies." For the BMW Group, "The BMW brand means ground-breaking innovations and fascinating design."

The business purpose should guide the decisions and activities of the organisation to create a consistent, successful, and meaningful reality. In order to achieve successful results, businesses must communicate why it's important that they exist and what it is that they stand for.

Advantage

Most businesses must compete with others in trying to meet unmet consumer needs. In order to be successful at attracting customers and keeping them, the business must have an advantage over the others. In the case of the new Italian restaurant, we believe that Grandma's recipes for authentic Italian food will be the advantage we have over other, more generic Italian restaurants in the area.

If the advantage is meaningful for consumers, it should differentiate us from the others and lead to a successful business. Differentiation of the product, service, or business model highlights the competitive advantage. 7 UP, the soft drink, for years differentiated itself from the soft drink leaders through its campaign, "The Un-Cola." Since 1960, Avis Rent A Car System has been proclaiming, "We try harder" to provide superior customer service, because it was Number 2.

In the same industry, Enterprise Rent-A-Car has succeeded by targeting car rentals away from airports with its line, "Pick Enterprise.

We'll pick you up." Your advantage must target unmet needs of customers. These examples suggest that companies can look to areas in which other companies fail to completely satisfy an important customer need and then create a business idea to satisfy that need and make it their advantage.

Of course, if such an approach is successful, competitors will respond and copy the advantage, leading to a new cycle of innovation in the product or service that is being offered. This is what makes a market economy great. Through the competition of firms, consumers benefit by getting better and better products and services. Innovation is rewarded. Progress is ensured.

Role of Customers

If we attempt to satisfy an unmet need, we must know who has that need, since all customers are not the same. Gillette and Norelco compete for men who shave. Gillette meets the needs of those who use cream and a razor; Norelco targets those who prefer an electric shaver. Neither company focuses on men with beards. This simple case describes the need that all businesses have for market segmentation.

Few businesses try to serve the entire market for their product or service. And even if they do, they usually find ways to structure the organisation to serve each market segment. In the automobile industry, General Motors tries to cover the entire market, but its division into Chevrolet, Pontiac, Oldsmobile, Buick, Cadillac, and Saturn attempts to match operating units with different market segments.

As we develop the plan for strategy, we must consider for which market segments the business idea is viable, so the idea will drive transactions. Pricing considerations are a dominant factor in market segment analysis. Going back to the Italian restaurant idea, if Grandma's recipes require that we charge $24 for a plate of spaghetti to break even, regardless of how good it might taste, few patrons would be willing to pay that much for spaghetti and the business idea would fail to drive the necessary transactions to sustain the business.

With the wide availability of travel services on the Internet, travel agents have had to adjust from serving a broad segment to a narrow one. As travel agents had their commissions cut to zero by the airlines, they now charge clients a service fee ($15-$30 per ticket) for reserving and issuing airline tickets. Since customers can go online and get tickets from the airlines directly or from providers like Travelocity or Orbitz, without paying a service fee, travel agents must segment the market and sell to those who are not willing or able to use the computer to secure airline tickets.

As a result of these significant changes, the market for travel agent services has shrunk considerably. The contemporary travel agent must identify only those clients who are willing to pay extra for their services, rather than those who are willing and able to go online and serve themselves. Market segmentation is a key component in building a successful strategy. In order to do segmentation, significant market and customer understanding and analysis are necessary.

Product

Our product is the benefits that we deliver to the customers. In the classic and popular TV show Cheers, the location was a tavern, but this bar delivered more than just drinks and pub food. As the theme song said, "Sometimes you want to go where everybody knows your name, and they're always glad you came." In a way, Starbucks has borrowed the Cheers model in building its business.

Starbucks is in the coffee business, but its stores deliver the same benefits as the Cheers bar: a comfortable place to get good coffee and share it with the same people regularly, read the paper, or just chat with friends. The product is a bundle of benefits surrounding a relatively expensive cup of coffee. Starbucks sells the experience as much as the coffee. And the experience rationalises the higher price.

When customers buy a product or a service, they go through six phases:

— purchase
— delivery
— use
— supplements
— maintenance
— disposal

Purchase involves recognition of needs, searching for alternatives, deciding, and buying. If the product is not consumed immediately at purchase (like a pint of beer) or carried away (like groceries), the customer must consider delivery options. Some products are easy to use; for others training or experience is necessary. Many products require supplements to make them work. As products are used, sometimes maintenance and repair can be a concern. Finally, if anything remains of a product after use, the question of disposal may arise.

In the process of developing the product strategy, we must not only consider the benefits delivered to the users to meet their unmet needs. We might also consider which of the six areas of the product use cycle we are also going to serve. Here are some examples. While most furniture stores either provide delivery or subcontract it to a third party, Ikea, the Swedish furniture giant, does not.

Ikea sells knockdown furniture that is disassembled into smaller packages that the buyer can take directly and then assemble at home. Home Depot, as another example, rents pickup trucks on-site for customers to take large items or quantities of supplies to their location. Volkswagen initiated the bundling of service with the car and included all routine maintenance with the sale of a new car.

Other manufacturers have since followed this practice. Indeed, the parts and service departments at all automobile dealerships are there to supply supplements and maintenance. In many case, these departments bring in more money than car sales. Car dealers also provide disposal of cars, through taking them in as trades on the purchase of new cars. Many computer vendors offer and sell training classes, so customers can use hardware and software efficiently.

Camera stores sell instruction on photography and film development (and now digital enhancement) so that customers can use cameras better and realise more benefits from them and from the vendors. Deciding on the product is more complex than first meets the eye. On the other hand, this product complexity can lead innovative companies to new and successful strategies.

Product Distribution

The heart of any business idea is in completing the transaction. That's when the customer receives your product or service in exchange for money. The environment in which that transaction occurs is called the distribution channel. One significant strategic decision we must make is the choice of distribution channel. Channels vary in their operation, cost, and effectiveness to reach particular market segments.

For retail products and services, business-to-consumer (B2C), channels include the following:

— company-owned retail stores

— franchised retail stores

— department stores

— direct mail

— the Internet

In business-to-business (B2B) circumstances, channels include the following:

— manufacturer representatives

— direct sales

— the Internet

Let's look at these various channels for computer sales. Before Hewlett-Packard and Compaq merged in 2002, the companies competed in outlets like Best Buy, CompUSA, and Circuit City. For HP and Compaq, the channel of choice was department stores. Neither company owned any stores. The retail stores would order computers, stock them in inventory, and then deliver them to customers. That was the environment for transactions.

Michael Dell founded Dell Computer in 1984 with a different distribution model. Dell decided that there was significant advantage in building the computers to order, eliminating the retail stores altogether, and relying on a direct-to-consumer sales approach, using telephone and Internet channels. Customers would call Dell, design the features that they needed and wanted in a computer, pay, and then receive delivery at their doorstep a few days later.

The Dell model has shown to have many strengths and has made Dell the 800-pound gorilla of the computer business. By going directly to the customer, Dell eliminated the costs of the retailer. More importantly, by building the computers to order, Dell kept its inventory of parts low; since computer component prices usually fall over time, a better cost structure was created. But Dell also received the customers' money in advance of delivering the machine, so the cash cycle for the company was positive. The customers also explicitly paid for delivery through a third party, such as UPS.

Finally, because of low inventories, Dell got the newest technologies to the market before HP and Compaq, which had older-technology computers sitting in inventory. In summary, Dell created a new business model for computer sales by switching from the traditional distribution channel. Dell offered customers a custom computer with the latest technology at a very competitive price. It also created a lower cost structure and a better cash flow. As a result, Dell achieved the dominant position in the industry. Then, of course, Gateway copied the Dell model, but it added distribution through its own stores. Both Compaq and HP began direct sales channels, in addition to the big box stores.

Finally, IBM withdrew from the retail store channel and now relies on direct sales. The point of all this is that strategically Dell figured out how to add more value for customers, not just by lowering prices, but also by using technology to go the customer directly and eliminating costs from the old way of doing business. Another significant example of channel management has occurred in the travel business. As little as five years ago, travel agents sold virtually all of the airline tickets in the market.

Travel agents-independent manufacturers' representatives-would shop all of the airlines' reservation systems and meet the customers' requirements for schedule, price, and/or class of service. The airlines paid the agents a commission based upon the price of the ticket, usually 10%. The travellers never saw the fee paid to the agent as a cost to them. Things changed as the airlines grew their frequent flyer programmes.

More and more customers wanted a specific airline, rather than other features, so that they would earn points toward free travel. As the airline brands, through their frequent flyer programmes, grew stronger; the airlines realised that they could sell directly, without travel agents. Over time, the airlines capped commissions, then cut them to 5%, and ultimately eliminated them entirely. These changes forced travel agents to charge an explicit fee for their services.

Additionally, Internet options, like Orbitz, permit customers to replicate what travel agents can do, but without paying the fee. Rather, the customer pays by spending the time making the reservation and by bearing the risk of errors. As with computer sales, the travel example demonstrates major changes in the way in which business is done, solely by changing the channel of distribution. Clearly, the Internet creates new distribution opportunities in many markets.

And new strategies will continue to emerge as technologies evolve and offer new possibilities for selling channels. The current trend is toward using multiple distribution channels rather than just one. Multiple channels complicate operations, but may provide better results.

Trends in Business

Have you ever noticed how many manufactured products that you use are marked "made in China"? Did you know that over 80% of college students do all their financial transactions on the Internet or through ATMs? What percentage of cars on the road are SUVs? Are you aware that 45% of the U.S. adult population is invested in the stock market directly or through 401(k) and similar plans? Did you know that the difference between 9% and 6% for a 30-year mortgage for $150,000 is over $300 per month? Are you aware that experts predict a serious shortage of nurses in the U.S. over the next five years?

The world, markets, population, tastes, technology, and economic factors are changing-as they always have. And to sustain a successful business, we must know what the changes will be and how they may affect the business and then adjust the strategy. Sometimes changing events or factors really do not affect the business. So it's important to know and understand the things that drive success in the markets.

Wayne Gretzky, the greatest hockey player of all time, was famous for saying, "Some people skate to the puck. I skate to where the puck is going to be." Likewise, in developing the business strategy we must consider where the various changing trends- economic, legal, demographic, competitive, and social-will lead and anticipate both the trends and the business policies we must adopt.

Business Operation

In this context, "how" is used in two ways.

First, how do we do business from a business operation point of view? Are we cost- and efficiency-oriented? Are we sales- and growth-oriented? Are we customer-focused? Are we financially driven? Are the employees the most important asset? It's a matter of priorities. Call it the philosophy of doing business or call it the operational strategy. Two companies in the same industry can have the same objectives, but try to get there in two very different ways.

For a small business example, take two insurance agencies. One is managed very tightly; the owner is very frugal, drives a Toyota, and brown bags his lunch every day. The other agency is run by an owner who is very extravagant, drives a Lexus, and eats at the club every lunch. They compete in the same markets, but operate in very different ways. It's a matter of priorities. By operating in these different ways, the owners are defining a part of their strategy. For example, if a buyer is looking for a discounted price, which happens in all markets, the frugal operator has bigger margins and may be willing to give up profit for growth, while the extravagant owner has much less room to move and may be unable to lower the price and must, therefore, forego the sale. If the trend in the industry required more discounting in the future, the extravagant owner would be at a big disadvantage.

The second way to view the question "How shall we do business?" is the style of doing business. Are we aggressive competitors? Or are we willing to ally with the competitors? What image do we want to project? In this case, it's a matter of values. Businesses have morals, personalities, habits, and images, just like the humans who operate them. In fact, businesses usually acquire the traits of the leaders who started them or who lead them to be successful.

General Electric bears the distinct markings of Jack Welch, but still seeks the inventiveness of its founder, Thomas Edison. Microsoft reflects the hard-driving characteristics of Bill Gates. Enron took on the values of its leadership. Every business can choose how it will do its business. For example, an organisation can establish a zero-tolerance rule for integrity.

With the recent spate of ethical problems with companies like Enron, Tyco, WorldCom, Merrill Lynch, and Aldelphia, a more careful eye is being cast toward the values that a company espouses and lives. The regulators of publicly traded companies (SEC and the stock exchanges) are adopting new rules for protecting investors and the integrity of the capital markets. Even within these guidelines, however, each firm can choose its own set of values as a matter of strategy.

Strategy Implementation and Evaluation

Developing a strategy is one thing, putting it in action is quite another. Studies have shown pretty consistently that the three biggest barriers to strategic success are these:

— A failure to communicate the strategy clearly throughout the organisation

— Inconsistency between management talk and management action

— A lack of top management support for strategic initiatives

Something your dad probably told you years ago sums it up: "Say what you mean and mean what you say." Easier said than done, though! Implementing a strategy requires leadership and attention to detail as strategic ideas flow through the entire organisation and become real. Wal-Mart's strategy of being the low-cost retailer touches every aspect of the company, including executive pay, office locations, and other components of overhead.

Evaluating the strategy is a matter of management and measurement systems. In order to judge whether we're reaching the long-term objectives, we must measure the results. If we want high customer satisfaction, we must honestly measure customer attitudes toward the products and/or processes. If we want to be number one or two in every product market, we must accurately measure the market share and that of the competitors.

References

Barney, J., "Firm Resources and Sustainable Competitive Advantage", *Journal of Management*, vol 17, no 1, 1991.

Chaffee, E., "Three models of strategy", *Academy of Management Review*, vol 10, no. 1, 1985.

David, F., *Strategic Management*, Columbus:Merrill Publishing Company, 1989.

Drucker, Peter., *The Practice of Management*, Harper and Row, New York, 1954.

Hamel, G. & Prahalad, C.K., "Strategic Intent", *Harvard Business Review*, May-June 1989.

Hammer, M. and Champy, J., *Reengineering the Corporation*, Harper Business, New York, 1993.

Lamb, Robert, *Boyden Competitive strategic management*, Englewood Cliffs, NJ: Prentice-Hall, 1984.

Levinson, J.C., *Guerrilla Marketing, Secrets for making big profits from your small business*, Houghton Muffin Co. New York, 1984.

6

Strategy Formulation

Formulation, the second phase in the strategic management process, produces a clear set of recommendations, with supporting justification, that revise as necessary the mission and objectives of the organisation, and supply the strategies for accomplishing them. In formulation, we are trying to modify the current objectives and strategies in ways to make the organisation more successful. This includes trying to create "sustainable" competitive advantages—although most competitive advantages are eroded steadily by the efforts of competitors.

A good recommendation should be: effective in solving the stated problem(s), practical, feasible within a reasonable time frame, cost-effective, not overlay disruptive, and acceptable to key "stakeholders" in the organisation. It is important to consider "fits" between resources plus competencies with opportunities, and also fits between risks and expectations.

There are four primary steps in this phase:

— Reviewing the current key objectives and strategies of the organisation, which usually would have been identified and evaluated as part of the diagnosis

— Identifying a rich range of strategic alternatives to address the three levels of strategy formulation outlined below, including but not limited to dealing with the critical issues

— Doing a balanced evaluation of advantages and disadvantages of the alternatives relative to their feasibility plus expected effects on the issues and contributions to the success of the organisation

— Deciding on the alternatives that should be implemented or recommended.

In organisations, and in the practice of strategic management, strategies must be implemented to achieve the intended results. The most wonderful strategy in the history of the world is useless if not implemented successfully. This third and final stage in the strategic management process involves developing an implementation plan and then doing whatever it takes to make the new strategy operational and effective in achieving the organisation's objectives.

THREE LEVELS OF STRATEGY FORMULATION

The following three aspects or levels of strategy formulation, each with a different focus, need to be dealt with in the formulation phase of strategic management. The three sets of recommendations must be internally consistent and fit together in a mutually supportive manner that forms an integrated hierarchy of strategy, in the order given.

— *Corporate Level Strategy:* In this aspect of strategy, we are concerned with broad decisions about the total organisation's scope and direction. Basically, we consider what changes should be made in the growth objective and strategy for achieving it, the lines of business we are in, and how these lines of business fit together. It is useful to think of three components of corporate level strategy:

(a) growth or directional strategy,

(b) portfolio strategy, and

(c) parenting strategy.

— *Competitive Strategy:* This involves deciding how the company will compete within each line of business (LOB) or strategic business unit (SBU).

— *Functional Strategy:* These more localised and shorter-horizon strategies deal with how each functional area and unit will carry out its functional activities to be effective and maximize resource productivity.

Corporate Level Strategy

This comprises the overall strategy elements for the corporation as a whole, the grand strategy, if you please. Corporate strategy involves four kinds of initiatives:

— Making the necessary moves to establish positions in different businesses and achieve an appropriate amount and kind of diversification. A key part of corporate strategy is making decisions on how many, what types, and which specific lines of business the company should be in. This may involve deciding to increase or decrease the amount and breadth of diversification. It may involve closing out some LOB's (lines of business), adding others, and/or changing emphasis among LOB's.

— Initiating actions to boost the combined performance of the businesses the company has diversified into: This may involve vigorously pursuing rapid-growth strategies in the most promising LOB's, keeping the other core businesses healthy, initiating turnaround efforts in weak-performing LOB's with promise, and dropping LOB's that are no longer attractive or don't fit into the corporation's overall plans. It also may involve supplying financial, managerial, and other resources, or acquiring and/or merging other companies with an existing LOB.

— Pursuing ways to capture valuable cross-business strategic fits and turn them into competitive advantages -- especially transferring and sharing related technology, procurement leverage, operating facilities, distribution channels, and/or customers.

— Establishing investment priorities and moving more corporate resources into the most attractive LOB's.

It is useful to organise the corporate level strategy considerations and initiatives into a framework with the following three main strategy components: growth, portfolio, and parenting.

Growth objective and strategies

Growth objectives can range from drastic retrenchment through aggressive growth. Organisational leaders need to revisit and make decisions about the growth objectives and the fundamental strategies the organisation will use to achieve them. There are forces that tend to push top decision-makers toward a growth stance even when a company is in trouble and should not be trying to grow, for example bonuses, stock options, fame, ego.

Leaders need to resist such temptations and select a growth strategy stance that is appropriate for the organisation and its situation. Stability and retrenchment strategies are underutilised. Some of the major strategic alternatives for each of the primary growth stances (retrenchment, stability, and growth) are summarised in the following three subsections.

Growth strategies

All growth strategies can be classified into one of two fundamental categories: concentration within existing industries or diversification into other lines of business or industries. When a company's current industries are attractive, have good growth potential, and do not face serious threats, concentrating resources in the existing industries makes good sense.

Diversification tends to have greater risks, but is an appropriate option when a company's current industries have little growth potential or are unattractive in other ways. When an industry consolidates and becomes mature, unless there are other markets to seek, a company may have no choice for growth but diversification.

There are two basic concentration strategies, vertical integration and horizontal growth. Diversification strategies can be divided into related (or concentric) and unrelated (conglomerate) diversification. Each of the resulting four core categories of strategy alternatives can be achieved internally through investment and development, or externally through mergers, acquisitions, and/or strategic alliances -- thus producing eight major growth strategy categories. Comments about each of the four core categories are outlined below, followed by some key points about mergers, acquisitions, and strategic alliances.

Vertical Integration: This type of strategy can be a good one if the company has a strong competitive position in a growing, attractive industry. A company can grow by taking over functions earlier in the value chain that were previously provided by suppliers or other organisations ("backward integration"). This strategy can have advantages, e.g., in cost, stability and quality of components, and making operations more difficult for competitors. However, it also reduces flexibility, raises exit barriers for the company to leave that industry, and prevents the company from seeking the best and latest components from suppliers competing for their business.

A company also can grow by taking over functions forward in the value chain previously provided by final manufacturers, distributors, or retailers ("forward integration"). This strategy provides more control over such things as final products/services and distribution, but may involve new critical success factors that the parent company may not be able to master and deliver. For example, being a world-class manufacturer does not make a company an effective retailer.

Some writers claim that backward integration is usually more profitable than forward integration, although this does not have general support. In any case, many companies have moved toward less vertical integration during the last decade or so, replacing significant amounts of previous vertical integration with outsourcing and various forms of strategic alliances.

Horizontal Growth: This strategy alternative category involves expanding the company's existing products into other locations and/or market segments, or increasing the range of products/services offered to current markets, or a combination of both. It amounts to expanding sideways at the point(s) in the value chain that the company is currently engaged in. One of the primary advantages of this alternative is being able to choose from a fairly continuous range of choices, from modest extensions of present products/markets to major expansions -- each with corresponding amounts of cost and risk.

Related Diversification (aka Concentric Diversification): In this alternative, a company expands into a related industry, one having synergy with the company's existing lines of business, creating a situation in which the existing and new lines of business share and gain special advantages from commonalities such as technology, customers, distribution, location, product or manufacturing similarities, and government access. This is often an appropriate corporate strategy when a company has a strong competitive position and distinctive competencies, but its existing industry is not very attractive.

Unrelated Diversification (aka Conglomerate Diversification): This fourth major category of corporate strategy alternatives for growth involves diversifying into a line of business unrelated to the current ones. The reasons to consider this alternative are primarily seeking more attractive opportunities for growth in which to invest available funds, risk reduction, and/or preparing to exit an existing line of business. Further, this may be an appropriate strategy when, not only the present industry is unattractive, but the company lacks outstanding competencies that it could transfer to related products or industries. However, because it is difficult to manage and excel in unrelated business units, it can be difficult to realise the hoped-for value added.

Mergers, Acquisitions, and Strategic Alliances: Each of the four growth strategy categories just discussed can be carried out internally or externally, through mergers, acquisitions, and/or strategic alliances. Of course, there also can be a mixture of internal and external actions. Various forms of strategic alliances, mergers, and acquisitions have emerged and are used extensively in many industries today.

They are used particularly to bridge resource and technology gaps, and to obtain expertise and market positions more quickly than could be done through internal development. They are particularly necessary and potentially useful when a company wishes to enter a new industry, new markets, and/or new parts of the world. Despite their extensive use, a large share of alliances, mergers, and acquisitions fall far short of expected benefits or are outright failures. For example, one study published in Business Week in 1999 found that 61 percent of alliances were either outright failures or "limping along."

Research on mergers and acquisitions includes a Mercer Management Consulting study of all mergers from 1990 to 1996 which found that nearly half "destroyed" shareholder value; an A. T. Kearney study of 115 multibillion-dollar, global mergers between 1993 and 1996 where 58 percent failed to create "substantial returns for shareholders" in the form of dividends and stock price appreciation; and a Price-Waterhouse-Coopers study of 97 acquisitions over $500 million from 1994 to 1997 in which two-thirds of the buyer's stocks dropped on announcement of the transaction and a third of these were still lagging a year later.

Many reasons for the problematic record have been cited, including paying too much, unrealistic expectations, inadequate due diligence, and conflicting corporate cultures; however, the most powerful contributor to success or failure is inadequate attention to the merger integration process. Although the lawyers and investment bankers may consider a deal done when the papers are signed and they receive their fees, this should be merely an incident in a multi-year process of integration that began before the signing and continues far beyond.

Stability strategies

There are a number of circumstances in which the most appropriate growth stance for a company is stability, rather than growth. Often, this may be used for a relatively short period, after which further growth is planned. Such circumstances usually involve a reasonable successful company, combined with circumstances that either permit a period of comfortable coasting or suggest a pause or caution. Three alternatives are outlined below, in which the actual strategy actions are similar, but differing primarily in the circumstances motivating the choice of a stability strategy and in the intentions for future strategic actions.

1. *Pause and Then Proceed*: This stability strategy alternative (essentially a timeout) may be appropriate in either of two situations:
   (a) the need for an opportunity to rest, digest, and consolidate after growth or some turbulent events—before continuing a growth strategy, or
   (b) an uncertain or hostile environment in which it is prudent to stay in a "holding pattern" until there is change in or more clarity about the future in the environment.
2. *No Change*: This alternative could be a cop-out, representing indecision or timidity in making a choice for change. Alternatively, it may be a comfortable, even long-term strategy in a mature, rather stable environment, e.g., a small business in a small town with few competitors.
3. *Grab Profits While You Can*: This is a non-recommended strategy to try to mask a deteriorating situation by artificially supporting profits or their appearance, or otherwise trying to act as though the problems will go away. It is an unstable, temporary strategy in a

worsening situation, usually chosen either to try to delay letting stakeholders know how bad things are or to extract personal gain before things collapse. Recent terrible examples in the USA are Enron and WorldCom.

Retrenchment strategies

— *Turnaround*: This strategy, dealing with a company in serious trouble, attempts to resuscitate or revive the company through a combination of contraction (general, major cutbacks in size and costs) and consolidation (creating and stabilising a smaller, leaner company). Although difficult, when done very effectively it can succeed in both retaining enough key employees and revitalising the company.

— *Captive Company Strategy*: This strategy involves giving up independence in exchange for some security by becoming another company's sole supplier, distributor, or a dependent subsidiary.

— *Sell Out*: If a company in a weak position is unable or unlikely to succeed with a turnaround or captive company strategy, it has few choices other than to try to find a buyer and sell itself.

— *Liquidation*: When a company has been unsuccessful in or has none of the previous three strategic alternatives available, the only remaining alternative is liquidation, often involving a bankruptcy. There is a modest advantage of a voluntary liquidation over bankruptcy in that the board and top management make the decisions rather than turning them over to a court, which often ignores stockholders' interests.

Portfolio strategy

This second component of corporate level strategy is concerned with making decisions about the portfolio of lines of business (LOB's) or strategic business units (SBU's), not the company's portfolio of individual products. Portfolio matrix models can be useful in re-examining a company's present portfolio. The purpose of all portfolio matrix models is to help a company understand and consider changes in its portfolio of businesses, and also to think about allocation of the resources among the different business elements.

Business Screen: These models consider and display on a two-dimensional graph each major SBU in terms of some measure of its industry attractiveness and its relative competitive strength. The BCG Growth-Share Matrix model considers two relatively simple variables: two primary models are the BCG Growth-Share Matrix and the GE growth rate of the industry as an indication of industry attractiveness, and relative market share as an indication of its relative competitive strength. The GE Business Screen, also associated with McKinsey, considers two composite variables, which can be customised by the user, for

(a) industry attractiveness and

(b) competitive strength

The best test of the business portfolio's overall attractiveness is whether the combined growth and profitability of the businesses in the portfolio will allow the company to attain its performance objectives. Related to this overall criterion are such questions as:

— Does the portfolio contain enough businesses in attractive industries?
— Does it contain too many marginal businesses or question marks?
— Is the proportion of mature/declining businesses so great that growth will be sluggish?
— Are there some businesses that are not really needed or should be divested?
— Does the company have its share of industry leaders, or is it burdened with too many businesses in modest competitive positions?
— Is the portfolio of SBU's and its relative risk/growth potential consistent with the strategic goals?
— Do the core businesses generate dependable profits and/or cash flow?
— Are there enough cash-producing businesses to finance those needing cash
— Is the portfolio overlay vulnerable to seasonal or recessionary influences?

— Does the portfolio put the corporation in good position for the future?

It is important to consider diversification vs. concentration while working on portfolio strategy, i.e., how broad or narrow should be the scope of the company. It is not always desirable to have a broad scope. Single-business strategies can be very successful.

Some of the advantages of a narrow scope of business are:

(a) less ambiguity about who we are and what we do;

(b) concentrates the efforts of the total organisation, rather than stretching them across many lines of business;

(c) through extensive hands-on experience, the company is more likely to develop distinctive competence; and

(d) focuses on long-term profits.

However, having a single business puts "all the eggs in one basket," which is dangerous when the industry and/or technology may change. Diversification becomes more important when market growth rate slows. Building stable shareholder value is the ultimate justification for diversifying -- or any strategy.

Parenting strategy

This third component of corporate level strategy, relevant for a multi-business company, is concerned with how to allocate resources and manage capabilities and activities across the portfolio of businesses. It includes evaluating and making decisions on the following:

— Priorities in allocating resources

— What are critical success factors in each business unit, and how can the company do well on them

— Coordination of activities and transfer of capabilities among business units

— How much integration of business units is desirable.

COMPETITIVE STRATEGY

In this second aspect of a company's strategy, the focus is on how to compete successfully in each of the lines of business the company has chosen to engage in. The central thrust is how to build and improve the company's competitive position for each of its lines of business. A company has competitive advantage whenever it can attract customers and defend against competitive forces better than its rivals.

Companies want to develop competitive advantages that have some sustainability. Successful competitive strategies usually involve building uniquely strong or distinctive competencies in one or several areas crucial to success and using them to maintain a competitive edge over rivals. Some examples of distinctive competencies are superior technology and/or product features, better manufacturing technology and skills, superior sales and distribution capabilities, and better customer service and convenience.

> Competitive strategy is about being different. It means deliberately choosing to perform activities differently or to perform different activities than rivals to deliver a unique mix of value.

> The essence of strategy lies in creating tomorrow's competitive advantages faster than competitors mimic the ones you possess today.

We will consider competitive strategy by using Porter's four generic strategies as the fundamental choices, and then adding various competitive tactics.

Porter's Four Competitive Strategies

He argues that a business needs to make two fundamental decisions in establishing its competitive advantage:

(a) whether to compete primarily on price or to compete through providing some distinctive points of differentiation that justify higher prices, and

(b) how broad a market target it will aim at (its competitive scope).

These two choices define the following four generic competitive strategies. Which he argues cover the fundamental range of choices. A fifth strategy alternative (best-cost provider) is added by some sources, although not by Porter, and is included below:

— *Overall Price (Cost) Leadership*: appealing to a broad cross-section of the market by providing products or services at the lowest price. This requires being the overall low-cost provider of the products or services. Implementing this strategy successfully requires continual, exceptional efforts to reduce costs -- without excluding product features and services that buyers consider essential. It also requires achieving cost advantages in ways that are hard for competitors to copy or match. Some conditions that tend to make this strategy an attractive choice are:

- The industry's product is much the same from seller to seller
- The marketplace is dominated by price competition, with highly price-sensitive buyers
- There are few ways to achieve product differentiation that have much value to buyers
- Most buyers use product in same ways -- common user requirements
- Switching costs for buyers are low
- Buyers are large and have significant bargaining power

2. *Differentiation*: appealing to a broad cross-section of the market through offering differentiating features that make customers willing to pay premium prices, e.g., superior technology, quality, prestige, special features, service, convenience. Success with this type of strategy requires differentiation features that are hard or expensive for competitors to duplicate. Sustainable differentiation usually comes from advantages in core competencies, unique company resources or capabilities, and superior management of value chain activities. Some conditions that tend to favour differentiation strategies are:
   - There are multiple ways to differentiate the product/service that buyers think have substantial value
   - Buyers have different needs or uses of the product/service
   - Product innovations and technological change are rapid and competition emphasizes the latest product features
   - Not many rivals are following a similar differentiation strategy
3. *Price (Cost) Focus*: a market niche strategy, concentrating on a narrow customer segment and competing with lowest prices,

which, again, requires having lower cost structure than competitors. Some conditions that tend to favour focus are:

— The business is new and/or has modest resources

— The company lacks the capability to go after a wider part of the total market

— Buyers' needs or uses of the item are diverse; there are many different niches and segments in the industry

— Buyer segments differ widely in size, growth rate, profitability, and intensity in the five competitive forces, making some segments more attractive than others

— Industry leaders don't see the niche as crucial to their own success

— Few or no other rivals are attempting to specialise in the same target segment

4. *Differentiation Focus*: a second market niche strategy, concentrating on a narrow customer segment and competing through differentiating features.

Best-Cost Provider Strategy. This is a strategy of trying to give customers the best cost/value combination, by incorporating key good-or-better product characteristics at a lower cost than competitors. This strategy is a mixture or hybrid of low-price and differentiation, and targets a segment of value-conscious buyers that is usually larger than a market niche, but smaller than a broad market. Successful implementation of this strategy requires the company to have the resources, skills, capabilities to incorporate up-scale features at lower cost than competitors.

This strategy could be attractive in markets that have both variety in buyer needs that make differentiation common and where large numbers of buyers are sensitive to both price and value. Porter might argue that this strategy is often temporary, and that a business should choose and achieve one of the four generic competitive strategies above.

Otherwise, the business is stuck in the middle of the competitive marketplace and will be out-performed by competitors who choose and excel in one of the fundamental strategies. His argument is analogous to the threats to a tennis player who is standing at the service line, rather than near the baseline or getting to the net. However, others present examples of companies who seem to be able to pursue successfully a best-cost provider strategy, with stability.

Competitive Tactics

Two categories of competitive tactics are those dealing with timing and market location.

Timing Tactics: When to make a strategic move is often as important as what move to make. We often speak of first-movers, second-movers or rapid followers, and late movers. Each tactic can have advantages and disadvantages. Being a first-mover can have major strategic advantages when:

(a) doing so builds an important image and reputation with buyers;

(b) early adoption of new technologies, different components, exclusive distribution channels, etc. can produce cost and/or other advantages over rivals;

(c) first-time customers remain strongly loyal in making repeat purchases; and

(d) moving first makes entry and imitation by competitors hard or unlikely.

However, being a second- or late-mover isn't necessarily a disadvantage. There are cases in which the first-mover's skills, technology, and strategies are easily copied or even surpassed by later-movers, allowing them to catch or pass the first-mover in a relatively short period, while having the advantage of minimising risks by waiting until a new market is established. Sometimes, there are advantages to being a skilful follower rather than a first-mover, e.g., when:

(a) being a first-mover is more costly than imitating and only modest experience curve benefits accrue to the leader;

(b) the products of an innovator are somewhat primitive and do not live up to buyer expectations, thus allowing a clever follower to win buyers away from the leader with better performing products;

(c) technology is advancing rapidly, giving fast followers the opening to leapfrog a first-mover's products with more attractive and full-featured second- and third-generation products; and

(d) the first-mover ignores market segments that can be picked up easily.

Market Location Tactics: These fall conveniently into offensive and defensive tactics. Offensive tactics are designed to take market share from a competitor, while defensive tactics attempt to keep a competitor from taking away some of the present market share, under the onslaught of offensive tactics by the competitor. Some offensive tactics are:

— *Frontal Assault*: going head-to-head with the competitor, matching each other in every way. To be successful, the attacker must have superior resources and be willing to continue longer than the company attacked.

— *Flanking Maneuver*: attacking a part of the market where the competitor is weak. To be successful, the attacker must be patient and willing to carefully expand out of the relatively undefended market niche or else face retaliation by an established competitor.

— *Encirclement*: usually evolving from the previous two, encirclement involves encircling and pushing over the competitor's position in terms of greater product variety and/or serving more markets. This requires a wide variety of abilities and resources necessary to attack multiple market segments.

— *Bypass Attack*: attempting to cut the market out from under the established defender by offering a new, superior type of produce that makes the competitor's product unnecessary or undesirable.

— *Guerrilla Warfare*: using a "hit and run" attack on a competitor, with small, intermittent assaults on different market segments. This offers the possibility for even a small firm to make some gains without seriously threatening a large, established competitor and evoking some form of retaliation.

Some Defensive Tactics are:

— Raise Structural Barriers: block avenues challengers can take in mounting an offensive

— Increase Expected Retaliation: signal challengers that there is threat of strong retaliation if they attack

— Reduce Inducement for Attacks: e.g., lower profits to make things less attractive. Keeping prices very low gives a new entrant little profit incentive to enter.

The general experience is that any competitive advantage currently held will eventually be eroded by the actions of competent, resourceful competitors. Therefore, to sustain its initial advantage, a firm must use both defensive and offensive strategies, in elaborating on its basic competitive strategy.

Cooperative Strategies

Another group of "competitive" tactics involve cooperation among companies. These could be grouped under the heading of various types of strategic alliances, which have been discussed to some extent under Corporate Level growth strategies. These involve an agreement or alliance between two or more businesses formed to achieve strategically significant objectives that are mutually beneficial. Some are very short-term; others are longer-term and may be the first stage of an eventual merger between the companies.

Some of the reasons for strategic alliances are to: obtain/share technology, share manufacturing capabilities and facilities, share access to specific markets, reduce financial/political/market risks, and achieve other competitive advantages not otherwise available. There could be considered a continuum of types of strategic alliances, ranging from:

(a) mutual service consortiums,

(b) licensing arrangements,

(c) joint ventures,

(d) value-chain partnerships.

Functional Strategies

Functional strategies are relatively short-term activities that each functional area within a company will carry out to implement the broader, longer-term corporate level and business level strategies. Each functional area has a number of strategy choices, that interact with and must be consistent with the overall company strategies.

Three basic characteristics distinguish functional strategies from corporate level and business level strategies: shorter time horizon, greater specificity, and primary involvement of operating managers. A few examples follow of functional strategy topics for the major functional areas of marketing, finance, production/operations, research and development, and human resources management. Each area needs to deal with sourcing strategy, i.e., what should be done in-house and what should be outsourced?

Marketing strategy deals with product/service choices and features, pricing strategy, markets to be targeted, distribution, and promotion considerations. Financial strategies include decisions about capital acquisition, capital allocation, dividend policy, and investment and working capital management. The production or operations functional strategies address choices about how and where the products or services will be manufactured or delivered, technology to be used, management of resources, plus purchasing and relationships with suppliers.

For firms in high-tech.. industries, R&D strategy may be so central that many of the decisions will be made at the business or even corporate level, for example the role of technology in the company's competitive strategy, including choices between being a technology leader or follower. However, there will remain more specific decisions that are part of R&D functional strategy, such as the relative emphasis between product and process R&D, how new technology will be obtained, and degree of centralisation for R&D activities.

Human resources functional strategy includes many topics, typically recommended by the human resources department, but many requiring top management approval. Examples are job categories and descriptions; pay and benefits; recruiting, selection, and orientation; career development and training; evaluation and incentive systems; policies and discipline; and management/executive selection processes.

Concept of Interdisciplinary Thinking

The concept of interdisciplinary with respect to the thinking/ intellectual process is in its infancy stage within the literature; more specifically, applied to the strategy formulation process in management. The presented thoughts are intended to serve as suggestions for improving the effectiveness of strategy formulation process.

However, the term interdisciplinary in itself means combining fields and/or interests of study that are mutually exclusive. The basic premise behind IT is simple: solicit thoughts from a diverse selection of associates specialising in different academic backgrounds, such as ones representing the broad arts and sciences. It is often understood that many corporations encounter the limitation of staffing professionals representing diverse academic backgrounds.

Knowledge can certainly be perceived as an intangible, by where implementation may potentially yield tangible outcomes for any organisation. Moreover, the field of management crosses the wide boundaries of the arts and sciences, warranting the notion of viewing business solutions and challenges three-dimensionally. It is no longer sufficient to consider business problems one-dimensionally.

Needless to state, the assessment of business core strategies requires change and innovation if corporations are to meet the demands of environmental changes, such as globalisation and interpreting confronts from different vantage points. Organisations must continuously change according to derivatives in the respective environment in which they function in order to remain competitive.

Divisional Stakeholders

The foundation for business strategy development lies in the opportunity to effectively implement strategic management tools. The process usually involves stakeholders within (internal) and outside (external) of the corporation. There is no question the single most important asset of any corporation is its people. One characteristic of a modern organisation is all stakeholders involved in the analysis and actions of strategic planning. The internal stakeholders are normally involved in the daily operational functions of the business; therefore, they possess at different ranges, knowledge of potential benefit to the corporation.

Internal associates, include, but not limited to, company associates/employees and management. External associates, such as the greater community/customers and stockholders, etc, each may potentially contribute towards the strategy formulation process, also. While soliciting such individuals may be of a challenge, the outcomes may be worthwhile for business considerations. A suggestion for inclusion of knowledge input is by way of a survey, soliciting for feedback/input, in general terms. The analysis of feedback from customers, suppliers, etc. is critical in formulating strategy directly associated with competition from respective corporations.

Interdisciplinary Organisations

While the concept of IT may be new in terms of jargon; however, some organisations implement the process to some degree. The range of implementation is based on such factors as organisational motivation and knowledge management, among others. In spite of, in order for its effectiveness to truly be assessed, full implementation is necessary.

Furthering the discussions, it is necessary to incorporate human resources, which are responsible for attracting and hiring qualified candidates for positions, among other duties to the development aspects of IT within an organisation. Moreover, the basic notion is to hire highly competent individuals representing diverse academic training backgrounds and working history. Human resources must be involved in the strategic planning process of any organisation; this provides them with an understanding of what is taking place and how to best recruit future associates.

Conventional hiring practices within corporations normally mirror the specific description of that position and the academic/professional preparatory background to fit that description. A movement towards hiring professionally diverse employees is emerging within many companies. An interdisciplinary approach to this would feature a description fitting the job; however, perhaps also interviewing candidates that may qualify by professional experience and not directly an academic background.

Perhaps the academic degree for a respective position may necessitate business, but a particular candidate may possess an engineering degree with relevant job experience. The respective human resource department in a company should consider asking themselves the following questions in an attempt to analyse their staff and strive for building an interdisciplinary team:

1. What are the departmental associates' current academic and professional backgrounds? This would enable HR to focus on

specific skills/individuals necessary for departmentalised services.

2. How ethnically diverse is the company? With diversity brings problem solving skills representing different sociological backgrounds, which potentially may result in business problems viewed from a different lens.
3. How can we (HR) solicit department management and identify diverse professional needs beneficial for the entire organisation? By HR being apart of the departmental meetings would provide insight into hiring needs. Furthermore, this process would benefit each department by HR sharing knowledge distributions by way of other respective departments.
4. Where and how can we recruit a diverse professional workforce? Conduct a needs assessment to see how many associates with what particular background(s) are needed. Next, consider advertising and/or contacting universities if positions are entry to middle-management levels. Please note that majors outside of business may be critical in strategy development process given candidate qualifications and interests. Simply restricting within the boundaries of business majors may result in not viewing a particular valid vantage point representing society, best captured by a sociologist, for example. Utilising headhunters can assist with a more skilled caliber of talent.
5. What type of training/in-service programme do we need to design and deliver for new hires, especially if they are new to the industry? If recruitment efforts are from interdisciplinary collegiate programmes will require additional training on corporate business, etc. However, recruited associates having little to no conceptualisation of interdisciplinary thinking, etc. will require a series of in-services detailing the concept of interdisciplinary thinking and how it is/will be implemented.

Key questions HR should consider are endless; however, the questions are critical in formulating an interdisciplinary team. Furthermore, recruiting from universities offering interdisciplinary majors is a key advantage. Such programmes offer potential candidates that possess specific training and exposure to diverse fields of study, which supports broad problem solving skills as a result of the programme of study.

However, HR should study the university programmes to see which programme(s) better match company needs. An important step to building interdisciplinary organisations is to provide leadership. The type of leadership required to successfully incorporate the concept of Interdisciplinary Thinking somewhat differs from traditional support from leadership. Leadership associates should develop query skills, with a focus on soliciting all members of the organisation for knowledge. This juncture does not complete the process as it is then required to expose and synthesise the thoughts gathered.

This process enables all the stakeholders responsible for strategy formulation to some degree to see the yielding results and provides a reflection opportunity. It is as this time where the executive team can prioritise from the list of strategies solicited and develop meaningful corporate strategies. These strategies should be few in number and specifically focused on some general aspect of the corporation's mission/vision statement(s).

Strategy Questioning Phase

A critical component to any strategy development process is the questioning phase, where a list of questions should be considered focusing on key strategic considerations for the respective corporation. More importantly, the strategic management tools implemented should begin the questioning phase. The presented questions should take into consideration the weaknesses of the company and follow with a detailed plan of action to remedy the challenge. Alternatively, the questions can be viewed from a standpoint of company growth or diversification, etc.

Regardless of the direction, questioning strategies within the formulation process are critical in allowing for contributors to reflect and exchange thoughts from one another. Organisations should consider themselves as life-long learning organisations, where continuous developmental efforts are implemented to increase intellectual contributions from one of the most important assets of any organisation-its associates.

Enhancing associates' levels of understanding concerning their respective roles and the overall business will potentially increase the quality of input. One such method of transferring associate knowledge to organisational strategies is by way of innovating the questioning phase. The strategy formulation process requires an organisation to prioritise its objectives by way of intellectual contributions of knowledge (thinking), in order to best determine how to achieve the desired results.

More specifically, this process requires thoughts about any possible issues affecting the business, such as marketing, accounting, production, etc. The design process requires first, the implementation of strategic management tools, such as the SWOT analysis to be conducted. At that point, a look at the external/internal environment (SWOT) is the starting point for a corporation to begin the strategy formulation process. When a department or group of associates has finalised the SWOT analysis, the following such questions should be considered next:

1. What is/are the weaknesses as a corporation?
2. What is the most optimal recovery/growth opportunity?
3. How can this be accomplished?
4. Who will be involved and to what extent, exactly?
5. How will the strategies be subsidised?
6. How will implementation of strategies be assessed?

The key above questions are required to better conceptualise the strategic functions ahead. They are derived at the conclusion of a SWOT analysis. This process does not limit the input from internal associates, but also the external community, too. The formulation stage requests the inclusion of interdisciplinary teams throughout the process. While the formulation process is traditional in nature, the intellectual input from stakeholders, internally and externally, is a suggestion to further strengthen the process.

More important, organisations soliciting knowledge from associates provides a better understanding of what is taking place from a different lens, environmentally, both on an external context and internal context from within the organisation. This process can support the notion that managers have and may continue not to be exact in their decision-making. The inclusion of stakeholders' contributions benefits both the corporation and the associates.

It provides "buy-in" with respect to selected strategies and ensures stakeholders are continuously updated and professionally developed as to the organisation's strategic progress.

Interdisciplinary Formula

The concept of bringing associates from within and outside of the corporation to disclose thoughts, feelings, and general knowledge about the organisation will require a building of trust. Once trust is established, ideas will begin to surface, organisationally, allowing the minds to come together. A socially-balanced organisation is supportive of trust building where associates can feel safe expressing their ideologies without being criticised.

As an example. Company "X" is looking to conduct an internal/ external audit to measure their stance within the industry and to pinpoint what options for advancement may be viable for the company. The process begins with the gathering of data from respective departments, by a multitude of options, such as departmentalised meetings, survey, etc. When conducting this process (SWOT), it will require departments, such as accounting, marketing, engineering, research & development, etc. to input strategies directly relating to the company.

What one department may consider a company strength may be considered a weakness by another respective department. It is for this reason that a process must be created to ensure trust and responsibility, company-wide. Associates' intuitive thinking is a critical strategy often overlooked in the strategy formulation processes.

A recommended method is to gather input and have a meeting with department managers to list the data where others (from other departments) can see and contribute input. Interdisciplinary thinking can be challenged if respect and acceptance/openness is not provided to participating interdisciplinary team members.

A list of meaningful SWOT results can then be compiled by way of departmentalised input. This process can then be furthered to include what the executive cabinet has considered either by way of lists and/or their SWOT analysis. Ultimately, it is the recommendation of the executive team/CEO that selects strategies; however, it would be of interest to compare commonalities and/or insights generated as a result of soliciting associates.

Thinking process

Leadership and management roles have become ever so complex in business on a global scale. While the discussions thus far have alluded to increased leadership and involvement of stakeholders in strategy formulation, many challenges require immediate attention for a seamless transition into innovative practices. A major task of leaders is to synthesise thoughts representing an entire corporation and vertically integrate it as one and to ensure that thinkers (associates) are effectively and efficiently thinking (like managers). Thinking is indeed an intricate process and can be defined differently by many.

Is thinking an art or a science? Arguably, if you consider the actual process that occurs in one's brain, it can be considered a science; however, if you view what thoughts are triggered through the thinking process in the brain, it can be considered an art. Complex enough, the art and science of thinking is an integral component of strategy formulation and requires a thorough conceptualisation and support from leadership.

A classical example from the technical world is "GIGO: garbage in garbage out." To this end, certainly warrants lean thinking strategies to be modelled by administration. It should be made a routine of by associates within the corporation. A brief, yet concise discussion on interpersonal relationships within departments is necessary. More specifically, managing intellect representative of different personality/ characteristic styles within a department can be challenging and potentially skewing momentum towards common goals and objectives to be integrated in the data gathering process (SWOT).

There may be multiple fashions to addressing this interdepartmental challenge, but a recommendation is to incorporate a "agree to disagree" statement; however, considering and rationalising each solicited statement representing each individual associate by leadership/management. The underlying point is that stakeholder participation leads to increased effectiveness within the organisation.

While the hope is that common thinking as a result of the organisational mission/ vision takes place, one can certainly expect to encounter differences of opinion. It is critical for leaders to manage this and treat as it sensitive as it can destroy any trust building that may be in existence. Once trust is inhibited, social disengagement may occur coupled with lack of intellectual contributions.

Supporting Organisational Assets

The discussions thus far have surfaced a valuable organisational asset that can certainly be considered as a prime characteristic of effective and efficient organisations. The critical asset to the success of any corporation is its stakeholders and their state of commitment to the corporation coupled with their emotional/social well-being. After all, it is the intellectual contributions stemming from such stakeholders that contributes to the strategy formulation process and potentially yields desired organisational outcomes.

The environment in which we live and work in today has changed; family values, job commitments, career goals, etc. all play a critical role in the daily situations an average worker encounters. To this end, such issues can tend to sometimes cause stress and anxiety in the lives of people, which certainly has a direct impact on performance at work and at home. This is one phenomenon that executives must learn to foster. Furthermore, a lower level of tolerance for any organisation may be the lack of commitment offered by the stakeholder(s). This can be true and relational to management and even executives within an organisation, too.

According to Ghoshal, the lack of energy and focus is one cause limiting the performance of managers, where only "10%" of manages possess both high levels of energy and focus by effectively leading their company. This may certainly reflect onto associates and executives of an organisation as well. In order for corporations to strive for higher performance and success in their respective industry will require strategies aimed at assisting stakeholders manage their personal and professional lives.

A sample of organisational strategies to assist associates has ranged from providing breakfast in the morning to day care for children. Since life and managing the different roles individuals confront has become increasingly challenging, perhaps a recommendation to house a psychologies (confidential) many prove to be effective in assisting individuals with their personal and professional challenges. All too often mangers have been assumed to serve as support structures for associates; however, the service may be limited as they serve as direct supervisors, where many associates may not wish to disclose personal happenings with them.

A company psychologist serves as a neutral party within the organisation. Is there any one way an organisation can manage commitment from its stakeholders? How can this process be accomplished without associates feeling cornered and micromanaged, whereby disenfranchising them from the company? This is a sensitive topic where one simple rationale to this may not exist, other than continuous support structures, creating an organisation that solicits and encourages feedback, and respects each individual alike.

A family-like ambiance needs to be created where each individual is welcomed, collaborates socially and professional with others, and is encouraged/ recognized for doing so. Moreover, associates need to trust one another and feel autonomous, too (Gratton, 2003). A simple success factor is when employees feel wanted, empowered to contribute thoughts, and recognised for their intellectual efforts as a result of contributing to an organisation's strategy formulation process.

References

Harrison, E. Frank, *The Managerial Decision-Making Process* (5th ed.), Boston: Houghton Mifflin, 1999.

McCall, Morgan W., Jr., & Kaplan, Robert K., *Whatever it takes: The realities of managerial decision making* (2nd ed.), Englewood Cliffs, NJ: Prentice-Hall, 1990.

Porter, Michael E., *Competitive Strategy: Techniques for analyzing industries and competitors*, New York: Free Press, 1980.

Williams, Steve W., *Making better business decisions: Understanding and improving critical thinking and problem solving skills*, Thousand Oaks, CA: Sage Publications, 2002.

7

Basics of Strategic Planning

Effective Strategic Planning was created for staff and board members of community development organisations. It describes the process for developing an organisational strategic plan, from preparation to development and implementation. Worksheets are provided to assist with planning tasks. The manual includes information on:

— When to undertake strategic planning

— Who should be involved

— The five elements of a strategic plan

— A case study of strategic planning

— How to organise the plan for presentation

Nonprofit community development organisations face an array of challenges and opportunities carrying out their missions. Failing to identify these challenges or opportunities -and plan accordingly—can lead to organisational paralysis, decline and eventual collapse. Strategic planning is an essential process in every organisation's success.

Through a productive strategic planning process, your organisation's leadership will clarify and affirm the mission and values of the organisation and define its role in the community. The process can also identify external and internal challenges and opportunities that you may encounter and help you design well thought-out strategies to address them. Properly used, strategic planning is a powerful tool to keep your organisation energised, focused and effective.

STRATEGIC PLANNING PROCESS

The sequence of the basic steps involved in the strategic planning process is shown below.

The Basic Steps of Strategic Planning

— Prepare To Plan

— Define and Review Organisational Vision, Mission, Activities and Values

— Do an Environmental Scan or SWOT (strengths, weaknesses, opportunities and threats) Analysis.

— Identify Strategic Issues

— Develop Strategic Goals and Objectives

— Create Implementation Plans To Achieve Goals and Carry Out Objectives

— Monitor and Evaluate Periodically and Adjust if Necessary

Strategic planning should not be confused with other planning processes such as business planning, programme planning or community planning, also referred to as neighbourhood planning. Although closely related, strategic planning focuses on establishing your organisational direction, setting priorities and identifying obstacles and opportunities that may limit or enable you to carry out your mission.

Business plans and programme work plans are often by products of the strategic planning process. After organisational priorities are set and strategic goals and objectives are articulated, these plans a re used to describe the implementation details of various strategies such as budget, staffing, funding sources and evaluation activities. A community planning process can assist the organisation in identifying strategic issues based on an analysis of existing conditions in the community. These issues are often used in the strategic planning process. A community plan might also identify potential roles for an organisation to fill in the community.

Preparing To Plan

Before undertaking a strategic planning process, your organisation will need to decide when it is the appropriate time to embark on such a journey. The final decision to engage in a strategic planning process should be made by the leadership or governing board. Once the decision is made, your organisation will need to allocate financial, board, staff and time resources to the strategic planning process, and design a process that fits your situation.

If your organisation is in the early stages of formation, a strategic planning session can assist leadership in selecting an area on which to initially focus organisational resources and attention. It will also help your nonprofit establish programme goals and guidelines. For more seasoned organisations, a strategic planning process is most necessary when leadership is considering a major shift in programmes or services, or if major changes in the environment or community (governmental, demographics, funding, etc.) cause a shift in focus or a redirection of resources.

The process is also important if the organisation has experienced rapid growth. A strategic planning process should not be done when your organisation is in the middle of a crisis or in the process of changing key board members or staff. If your leadership is focused on resolving a short-term crisis, they will not direct adequate attention and resources toward the strategic planning process. Complete acceptance or buy-in is essential for the successful implementation of the plan. This also holds true if the organisational leadership is in the middle of a transition. New leadership may not embrace a plan reflecting the philosophies and priorities of the previous leadership.

Organisational Leadership

Before proceeding with a strategic plan, the board of directors of the organisation must support the decision to undertake the process and commit to seeing it through to completion. Planning for the future success of the organisation is the responsibility of the board of directors.

Failing to obtain the support and commitment of the board of the directors can result in limited input and participation from leadership. It may also lead to a strategic plan that is not fully embraced by the leadership. This sense of ownership is crucial because the board of directors will be responsible for overseeing the implementation of the plan.

Designing the Planning Process

Time is probably the most important element to consider in designing the planning process. Allow approximately three to nine months to conduct all of the tasks related to the process and additional time for review and approval by the full leadership. As mentioned earlier, if your organisation is in the middle of a crisis and cannot allocate adequate time and attention to the process, leadership may wish to consider postponing the process. In designing the planning process, the leadership needs to consider the objectives it seeks to achieve.

In addition to producing the elements of the plan (such as clarification of your organisation's mission and vision or identification of strategic goals and objectives), the planning process can be designed to achieve other objectives.

These include increasing the sense of ownership by the board of directors in current organisational activities, strengthening partnerships with other organisations or institutions, building greater public support and understanding of the organisation, and increasing the interaction between board and staff. In the early stages, it may be helpful to survey the leadership regarding any other "nonplanning" objectives to be achieved. Other factors to consider include time availability, internal capacity and access to external resources.

Planning Roles

Depending on its "non-planning" objectives, your organisation may decide to design a process with different levels of board, staff, consultant and external participation. However, keep in mind that the board of directors is ultimately responsible for approving and allocating the resources to implement the plan. At a minimum, the full board of directors needs to be kept informed throughout the process.

After selecting a planning approach, you will need to identify your organisation's capacity and resources to carry out the planning tasks.

You should also fill the following roles:

— *Leader:* To keep the process moving and make sure that the people who need to be involved are. Often the board chair, strategic planning committee chair or executive director fills this role.

— *Facilitator:* To help with difficult discussions and heated debates, and to enable everyone to participate and focus on the task at hand. Keep in mind that the facilitator's ability to make decisions is limited, so key board or staff may not be the best option for filling this role.

— *Researchers, interviewers, writers:* To research, conduct interviews, perform calculations and projections, and document the process and produce the written plan. If available, this is a role that staff and volunteers often fill.

In addition to finding internal or external sources to fill the above roles, identify the following resources:

— *Financial resources:* Funding for consultant and facilitator expenses, rental of adequate space for the planning sessions, and materials and supplies needed for the planning process.

— *Skills, knowledge, expertise:* It may be helpful to have individuals with knowledge and expertise in fields related to the programmes or activities conducted by your organisation. Those professionals may include attorneys, bankers, real estate developers, human service professionals, etc. If your organisation does not have the expertise in-house, check with local colleges and universities, professional groups and clubs, and the local chamber of commerce.

After all the above elements in the plan are identified, the full design should be approved by the organisational leadership and shared with the participants in the planning process.

ELEMENTS OF A STRATEGIC PLAN

Five elements comprise a strategic plan:

— Define mission, vision, activities and values

— Scan the environment using a SWOT analysis

— Identify and prioritise strategic issues

— Define strategic goals and objectives

— Establish an implementation plan and schedule

Foundation of the strategic plan

The foundation of the strategic plan is the vision, mission, activities and values of the organisation. When articulated in formal statements, they provide the framework for identifying strategic goals. The statements provide a vision or target goal for the organisation to achieve and define what the organisation does and why. They should be created or reviewed as the first step in formulating the organisation's strategic plan. Building and Managing a Better Board, one of the manuals in the Community Development Library's Governanceseries, has more information and exercises on writing vision, mission, activities and values statements.

A vision statement tells everyone the type of community or world the organisation envisions for its constituency as a result of the work of the organisation. A mission statement describes what the organisation will do, who it will do it for and how it will achieve the vision. The mission statement is often the only statement many people will read about an organisation.

An activities statement describes the business or general activities you will use to achieve the organisation's mission. A values statement describes the principles and beliefs that guide the operations of the organisation. These statements provide a filter through which important decisions for the organisation and the standards for evaluating the effectiveness of your programmes and activities can be screened.

As the "owners" or representatives of the membership of the organisation, the board of directors is responsible for creating or modifying the mission, vision, activities and values statements. Staff members can also be involved since they are responsible for day-to-day activities and may provide a valuable perspective on the work. Before you create or review your vision, mission, activities and values, take time to review the history of your organisation. This will help refresh the memories of long-tenured board members and provide a better foundation for newer members.

Schedule a retreat where board members and staff describe (chronologically) major events leading to the creation of the organisation, individuals who played significant roles, victories and programme accomplishments, funding sources and other supporters, and your organisation's focus at various points in time. Reviewing the history will give board members a collective sense of what role the organisation has filled in the past and can assist them in deciding what it can be in the future.

Vision

Even if your organisation has a vision, mission and activities statement, it is helpful to go through several exercises that may either affirm the exiting statements or provide a basis to modify them. To create the vision, board members should provide answers to the following questions:

— As a result of the work of the organisation, how will the community or the lives of the organisation's constituents be changed?
— What will the community look like? How will its members interact?
— How will the organisation be perceived in the community? What will be its image?

When people describe the organisation, what terms will they use? Your vision will serve as the overall goal for which strategies will be developed to achieve.

Mission

The mission describes the approach the organisation will take to achieve the vision. To articulate your mission, board members should answer the following questions:

— What will the organisation do to accomplish the vision?
— What types of services or products will the organisation provide?
— Who will be the primary beneficiaries of these activities?

Values

Values are your core beliefs and principles. They define why you carry out your mission the way you do and help develop strategic objectives and work plans. To define your organisation's values, board members should answer the following questions:

— Why is it important for this organisation to carry out its activities?
— In all of the organisation's activities, what should be the underlying principles that cannot be compromised?

Environment Using a SWOT Analysis

After defining or affirming the vision, mission, activities and values, the next stage is identifying strategic issues. To accomplish this task, the board must look at conditions and trends in the physical, social, economic and political environments that may have a positive or negative impact on your organisation's ability to achieve the vision and carry out its mission. The board must also assess internal strengths and weaknesses.

This type of assessment is referred to in the industry as a SWOT analysis. SWOT stands for strengths, weaknesses, opportunities and threats. A SWOT analysis can consist of a combination of individual interviews, surveys, focus groups, research of relevant socioeconomic trends, and an internal organisational assessment of the administrative and programme-related capacities of the organisation. The methods used by the organisation to gather the information required for the SWOT analysis will be based on the financial and human resources available.

The overall scope of the SWOT analysis will be based on your mission. For example, a nonprofit community development organisation with the mission of developing affordable housing might examine the external environment to identify trends in federal or state housing policy, future funding availability for housing related activities, in addition to local and regional housing market forecasts. It might also examine trends in the construction industry regarding costs and building technologies, capital market conditions and changes in bank lending practices, demographic and socioeconomic trends, and future planned activities that may have a positive or negative impact on the condition of its target area or neighbourhood.

The overall goal of the SWOT analysis is to identify factors or conditions to which the organisation can build strategic responses. The internal analysis of the organisation should review and assess your organisation's capacity and performance in the areas of:

— Administrative policies and procedures
— Composition, capacity and performance of the board of directors
— Staff capacity
— Fund-raising capacity
— Financial status
— Financial management systems
— Volunteer resources
— Facilities
— Programme performance and effectiveness
— Public image

In conducting the SWOT analysis, you may wish to approach all or a combination of the following sources:

— Clients and constituents
— Community leaders
— Private and public funding sources
— Legislators, government officials and government agencies at the federal, state, county and local level
— Local and regional planning agencies
— Research departments of local universities
— Local organisations engaged in similar activities
— Advocacy or public interest groups focusing on related issues
— Neighbourhood institutions
— Other key stakeholders

In collecting information for the SWOT analysis, it is important that a consistent format be used, especially if multiple researchers and data collectors are used. A consistent format must also be used for conducting interviews. Draft a set of interview questions for use by all the interviewers who will be conducting individual or focus group sessions. Make the questions open-ended, such as:

— What activities does the organisation do especially well? How do you explain this?
— What other needs of the customers are already served by the organisation?

— Are there other organisations or companies that provide even better service to our customers?

After collecting all the data from the various sources contributing to the SWOT analysis, try to categorise or group the findings under similar themes such as:

— Economic (status of and projected changes in local employment and other relevant markets)
— Legal and political
— Regional (important themes affecting the entire area)
— Technological (current and future impact of technology)
— Population (broad trends affecting the target market)
— Competition (current and projected future status of suppliers of similar products or services)
— Social (current and projected local social factors such as the presence of community groups and the level of community cohesiveness)
— Physical (current and projected factors impacting the built environment)

Further categorise the findings on population under such themes as:

— Demographics (age, gender, race, religion and family size)
— Needs, wants and interests (the specific consumer preferences of the target market)
— Values and lifestyles (broader choices that underlie the specific consumer preferences)
— Socioeconomic status (based on household size, income and wealth)

Within these categories, identify potential opportunities and possible barriers to achieving the organisation's mission. There are several worksheets provided at the end of this manual to assist organisations in collecting and grouping the findings of the SWOT analysis.

Identify Strategic Issues

After all the data from the SWOT analysis have been gathered and categorised, the full board of directors should convene to review the findings. Based on the identified opportunities and threats, the board should decide which of these conditions or situations are having the greatest impact on its ability to fulfil the vision of the organisation and which opportunities must be capitalised upon immediately to achieve the organisational vision.

To select strategic issues, the board should look at the estimated cost of not dealing with identified strategic issues in terms of financial resources or loss of public credibility and the ability of the organisation to successfully deal with each. It should also review the internal strengths of the organisation. Once established, the board should prioritise the identified strategic issues to more efficiently allocate limited resources to addressing the identified strategic issues. Use the following ground rules in selecting strategic issues:

— Choose no more than five. Keep your list short. There are countless issues that affect your organisation, but the more you have, the less you can focus on those that are most important.

— Select issues that you can affect. The lack of income in your community may have a strong impact on residents, but if your organisation does not create jobs or otherwise improve the local economic situation, lack of income is not your issue. Stick to what you can change, if change is needed, and be realistic in that assessment.

— Donor interests are relevant, but not over riding. Foundations, government agencies and other donors have their own agendas and priorities. It is important to know what those are, but only as input into the organisation's decisions.

— Each external issue will be mirrored internally. Internal capacities are needed for external effect. Whether the external issue involves communication or programme development, the internal issues will be current capability and future resource allocation.

— Come back to the mission. Each strategic issue should relate directly to the mission statement of the organisation. "Opportunities" have the possibility of enhancing the organisation's ability to fulfil the mission, while "Threats" have the possibility of detracting from the organisation's ability to fulfil the mission.

After identifying and prioritising strategic issues, the full board of directors may wish to form strategic issue subcommittees to analyse and further define each and develop strategic goals and objectives for the full board to review and approve. These committees can consist of board members, staff, constituents and outside specialists.

Implementation and Monitoring Schedule

The final element of the strategic plan is the implementation and monitoring schedule. This should describe the parties responsible for completing the tasks related to the strategic objectives and provide a timetable for completion. The implementation plan should describe the resources required to achieve the objectives, identifying existing organisational resources to be allocated. Strategies to obtain additional required resources should also be described.

Establish a schedule to periodically monitor and evaluate the progress of the organisation in implementing the various strategic objectives. If internal or external conditions have changed, it may be necessary to revisit the planning process and assess the validity of the strategic goals and objectives.

Plan Presentation

The strategic plan is primarily an internal document to be used for guidance and evaluation; however, many funding sources require organisations to submit them. Therefore, attention should be given to the presentation of the strategic plan. A well-organised plan will enable the reader to find and understand its most important elements. Whenever possible, avoid the use of industry-based jargon and describe acronyms that might confuse lay readers and future generations of leadership who may review it.

Before distribution, be sure your strategic plan includes:

— Cover Page: Make sure your cover page contains:
  - — The name of the organisation, division or programme that is the focus of the plan
  - — The words "strategic plan" in the title
  - — The date the plan was completed or revised

- Executive Summary: No more than two pages:
  - The most important elements of the plan
  - Its purpose
  - Its projected implementation period

It should also list the strategic goals and highlight the objectives.

- *Table of Contents:* Some readers may only be interested in certain sections. Number each page and make sure the table of contents is accurate.
- *Attachments:* Review the plan's attachments and make sure they are numbered or lettered and properly sequenced as they are referenced in the text.

REFERENCES

Barney, J., "Firm Resources and Sustainable Competitive Advantage", *Journal of Management*, vol 17, no 1, 1991.

Chaffee, E., "Three models of strategy", *Academy of Management Review*, vol 10, no. 1, 1985.

David, F., *Strategic Management*, Columbus:Merrill Publishing Company, 1989.

Drucker, Peter., *The Practice of Management*, Harper and Row, New York, 1954.

Hamel, G. & Prahalad, C.K., "Strategic Intent", *Harvard Business Review*, May-June 1989.

Hammer, M. and Champy, J., *Reengineering the Corporation*, Harper Business, New York, 1993.

Lamb, Robert, *Boyden Competitive strategic management*, Englewood Cliffs, NJ: Prentice-Hall, 1984.

Levinson, J.C., *Guerrilla Marketing, Secrets for making big profits from your small business*, Houghton Muffin Co. New York, 1984.

Ohmae, K., *The Mind of the Strategist McGraw Hill*, New York, 1982.

Pascale, R. and Athos, A., *The Art of Japanese Management*, Penguin, London, 1981.

Peters, T. and Waterman, R., *In Search of Excellence*, HarperCollins, New york, 1982.

Rehfeld, J.E., *Alchemy of a Leader: Combining Western and Japanese Management skills to transform your company*, John Whily & Sons, New York, 1994.

Schonberger, R., *Japanese Manufacturing Techniques*, The Free Press, New York, 1982.

Woo, C. and Cooper, A., "The surprising case for low market share", *Harvard Business Review*, pg 106-113, November-December 1982.

8

Completing the Strategic Plan

The term was first used in the 1970's, and it meant that a staff of strategic planners more or less thought up "strategic programmes" and then tried to sell them to decision makers. In the 1990's, the view of strategic planning and strategic management is much different. Goodstein, Nolan, and Pfeiffer's definition of strategic planning takes us away from the notion that strategic planning is a staff job and focuses us more on a process that requires the senior leaders of an organisation to set its strategic direction.

The concept of strategic management builds on this definition of strategic planning, recognising that although "planning" is the prelude of strategic management, it is insufficient if not followed by the deployment and implementation of the plan and the evaluation of the plan in action.

Strategic management is a systems approach to identifying and making the necessary changes and measuring the organisation's performance as it moves toward its vision. It has been defined as a

> "... management... system... that links strategic planning and decision making with the day-to-day business of operational management."

The following model depicts the five processes of strategic management which are pre-planning, strategic planning, deployment, implementation, and measurement and evaluation. Strategic management goes beyond the development of a strategic plan, which included the pre-planning and strategic planning processes. Strategic management is the deployment and implementation of the strategic plan and measurement and evaluation of the results.

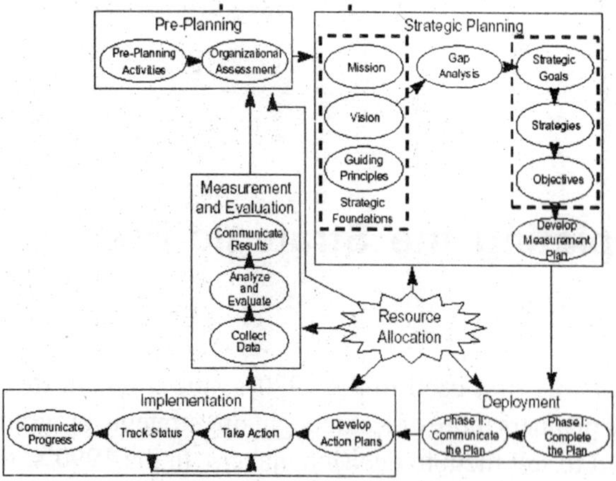

The Strategic Management Model

Deployment involves completing the plan and communicating it to all employees. Implementation involves resourcing the plan, putting it into action, and managing those actions. Measurement and evaluation consists not only of tracking implementation actions, but, more importantly, assessing how the organisation is changing as a result of those actions and using that information to update the plan.

It is the responsibility of senior leadership to strategically manage the organisation. Strategic management is a continuous process rather than a one-time event. Therefore, the senior leaders must become strategic thinkers and leaders of the organisation and its culture, changing it as necessary. To be the most successful, leaders need to be facilitators, coaches, consultants, and consensus-builders.

Transformational leadership is described by Bernard Bass as, "superior leadership performance that occurs when leaders broaden and elevate the interests of their employees, when they generate awareness and acceptance of the purposes and mission of the group, and when they stir their employees to look beyond their own self-interest for the good of the group."

Acquiring transformational leadership traits requires hard work and dedication, willingness to take some risks, and internalising the organisation's vision and guiding principles. When an organisation is practising strategic management, thinking becomes more visionary, which is characterised by:

— Breakthrough thinking about the future; organisational boundaries are more flexible

— A shift in focus from the inputs that are used to run the business to the outputs and outcomes the organisation desires to achieve

— A focus on optimising organisational performance and process quality as keys to delivering quality products and services

— A move toward an organisational culture that adapts easily to change

With practice, patience, dedication, and hard work, the organisational learning that takes place through the application of strategic management will bring the organisation closer to realising its goals and vision. With each update of the strategic plan, senior leaders will become better able to deploy the plan, implement changes, and measure organisational performance.

The pre-planning activities are typically conducted by strategic planning facilitators, assisted by an organisation's TQL coordinator. After the completion of the pre-planning activities, the senior leadership team can begin the strategic planning process.

This typically occurs at an initial strategic planning workshop. During the workshop, the senior leadership team, in facilitated sessions, establishes the foundation for its organisational improvement efforts by:

— Creating a vision of the organisation's future

— Developing a set of guiding principles (behavioural norms necessary to achieve that vision)

— Clarifying the mission, or core purpose, of the organisation

— Developing strategic goals (what must change to achieve the vision)

In the process of developing the goals, the team may also begin to develop some of the strategies and objectives for achieving the goals.

At the end of the workshop, the team identifies the steps needed to complete its planning and prepare for deployment and implementation. It takes about one month to complete the pre-planning activities.

The strategic planning facilitator will typically need about 20 days of effort, the TQL coordinator about 4 days of effort, the senior leader about 4 days of effort, and the other members of the senior leadership team about 2 days of effort to engage in these pre-planning activities.

The initial strategic planning workshop requires an investment of 3 days by the senior leadership team, the strategic planning facilitator, and the TQL coordinator.

The length of time required to complete, deploy, and implement a strategic plan differs by organisation because of each one's unique circumstances and culture. Some of the factors are the:

— Degree of commitment to the effort by the senior leaders, strategic planning facilitators, and TQL coordinator
— Level of Total Quality (TQ) knowledge among the senior leadership team
— Level of employee involvement in plan completion
— Deployment methodology
— Organisation's readiness for change

It usually takes about 6 months for an organisation to complete its first strategic plan and be ready to publish it. During this period, the organisation can expect the senior leadership team and TQL coordinator, with some support effort, to spend at least 20 days completing the plan and preparing to deploy it.

The process to this point is fairly structured and facilitated. However, after the initial strategic planning workshop, the process is much more flexible and is dependent on the choices made by the senior leadership team.

Phase I Deployment

Deployment has two phases. In Phase I, the plan is completed and published; in Phase II, it is formally communicated. Following are actions that are key to successfully completing Phase I and actions that guarantee failure.

Keys to Success	Facts of Failure
Assign roles and responsibilities	No accountability for deployment
Establish priorities	Too many goals, strategies, or objectives on apparent priority
Involve mid-level management as active participants	Plan in a vacuum of unfctional focus
Think it through decide how to manage implementation	No overall strategy to implement
Charge mid-level management with aligning lower-level plans	Make no attempt to link with day-to-day operations
Make careful choices about the contents of the plan and form it will take	Not being thorough glossing over the details

Roles and Responsibilities

The following are suggested roles and responsibilities:

- Reaches consensus on final strategic plan
- Strategies deployment and implementation methods
- Chooses what gets published
- Complete development of strategies and objectives
- Share draft plan with mid-level managers
- Accept and incorporate appropriate feedback from mid-level managers
- Brief senior leadership team on changes
- Share draft plan with employees
- Provide feedback to senior leadership team during facilitated feedback sessions
- Plans ways to incorporate strategic plan resource requirements into the budgeting process
- Assists the goal groups in their independent work by facilitating their strategy and objective development meetings

— Assists the senior leadership team by being the central point of contact for the strategic planning effort

— Handles the logistics associated with senior leadership team meetings

The organisation's senior leadership team is responsible for completing, deploying, and developing the implementation mechanisms for the strategic plan. They are responsible for involving employees in these steps and for committing the time and resources necessary to achieve success. As they outline roles and responsibilities for others, they must clearly articulate the decision making process that will be used. The TQL coordinator can assist the senior leadership team with the next phases of the strategic planning process. The strategic planning facilitator, who conducted the initial strategic planning workshop, may also be available to help.

Since assisting the senior leaders in developing a strategic plan is probably a new undertaking for the TQL coordinator, the senior leaders should ensure that this individual has attended the DON's Team Skills and Concepts, Fundamentals of Total Quality Leadership, and Methods for Managing Quality courses.

Forming Goal Groups

Goal groups are cross-functional teams established to work on the development and implementation of the goals and their associated strategies and objectives. They are cross-functional because each strategic goal touches on many aspects of the organisation. Goal groups are subgroups of the senior leadership team. As we move into implementation, these goal groups may link with existing teams such as Quality Management Boards (QMBs) and Integrated Product/ Process Teams (IPPTs), etc.

The goals developed at the initial offsite should be cross-functional. Therefore, cross-functional teams are needed to work on developing the strategies and objectives for accomplishing the goals. If subgroups of the planning team were formed to work on the goals at the workshop, then those goal groups may continue their work as intact teams. If goal groups were not formed at the workshop, they should be established at this time.

Goal groups help the senior leadership team develop the strategies and objectives needed to accomplish the strategic goals. Their job is to develop ideas and alternatives about how the strategic goals can be achieved and to brief those recommendations to the senior leadership team. At this point, they are neither solving problems nor implementing the strategies.

A strategy explains how the goal will be attained. An objective is a specific, measurable, short- to midterm action necessary to make a strategy work. An objective describes who will do what by when. A goal group may need the assistance of others when the senior leadership team is small in size or the members need to obtain the assistance of subject-matter experts and process owners to further develop the strategies and objectives. For example, if a strategy is being written to revamp the rewards and recognition system, a personnel specialist might be a subject-matter expert.

The goal groups can meet independently. When that work is done, the senior leadership team reconvenes so the goal groups can brief them on the strategies and objectives they have developed, incorporate feedback, and present their work for consensus. The term "cross-briefing" is used to describe the process whereby the goal groups report to the senior leadership team on the progress they're making on developing the strategic goals, strategies, and objectives.

In the cross-briefing process, the goal group leader presents the goal group's work and then fields questions and comments from the senior leadership team. The recorder takes notes on the senior leadership team's comments for use by the goal group to improve what it has developed. The cross-briefing process is used as a way to build consensus among the senior leadership team members on the strategies and objectives developed by the goal groups. Therefore, those giving the crossbriefings need to guard against responding defensively to the feedback received from the senior leadership team.

This is future-focused thinking that is best accomplished by having the senior leadership team get away from the office and dedicate one to two days to completing this phase of its strategic planning work. By looking at all the goals, strategies, and objectives together, suboptimisation of any one goal can be avoided.

Cross-briefings should be run by a strategic planning facilitator. It is during this process of reaching consensus on the strategies and objectives that unresolved issues and hidden agendas may surface. Development of the strategic goals was a rather "lofty" undertaking; development of the strategies and objectives brings the strategic plan into reality. All of those involved are now presented with a clear picture of the changes required of the organisation.

When these elements of the plan take shape, the impact of the plan on current organisational systems, processes, functions, rules and regulations, and the power structure becomes evident. A strategic planning facilitator can keep the senior leadership team focused, help raise hidden issues, assist in not retreating on the strategic plan, facilitate resolution of those issues, and assist the group in making quality decisions.

Sometimes the strategies and objectives needed to accomplish a goal are evolutionary. Goal groups don't always have all the solutions or all the answers about how to accomplish the goal. Sometimes more study or research is needed. The first step may be to put together a team to do this research or to conduct additional study.

The results of the research or study effort will determine what strategies and objectives will be needed to meet the goal. To determine whether their efforts are properly focused toward achieving the organisation's stated vision, goal groups should consider whether the strategies and objectives they develop adequately address the following:

— Does achieving the strategic goal require design of new processes or redesign of existing processes? Strategic Management for Senior Leaders: A Handbook for Implementation

— Do internal and external rules, regulations, policies, or standards need to be changed to successfully implement the strategy and achieve the goal?

— What needs more study before a strategy can be developed?

If the answers to these questions are inadequate, then the goal groups need to consider additional alternatives or ideas in developing the strategies and objectives. It is usually best not to invite other people to attend the cross-briefing sessions. Since the senior leadership team has not yet reached consensus on the strategies and objectives, the presence of people who are not part of that team may inhibit the process of surfacing and resolving issues, and it may discourage a candid dialogue among the team members.

Customers and stakeholders should not participate in the strategic planning sessions at this point in the strategic planning process. Their participation should be delayed until the senior leadership team is comfortable with the planned direction of organisation.

Establish Priorities

Prioritisation should not occur at the strategic goal or strategy level. All of the goals must be achieved to reach the vision. Singling out a few might suboptimize the effort. The objectives should be prioritised. Since all of the objectives cannot be worked at once, the senior leadership team needs to determine which objectives can be accomplished based on money, people, time, and current workload.

The senior leadership team needs to do an initial schedule of all of the objectives based on what it thinks is most important. Keep in mind that this is an iterative process, so the schedule may need adjustments. In establishing the schedule, consider whether or not implementation of one objective needs to occur before others can begin, and if and when resources will be available.

By creating a schedule, the senior leadership team can get a picture of the overall implementation effort, where adjustments are needed, and which objectives will require implementation first. This schedule provides a view of a vision-directed effort that can be used in the annual budgeting process.

Involve Mid-level Management

At this point, it is important to ensure that mid-level managers get involved in the planning process for two reasons. Getting feedback benefits the senior leadership team because they may discover that they have left out an important issue that the feedback will highlight. By making them participants in the plan's development, they are more likely to support implementation actions. Their perspectives and insights can make a better, more executable plan.

Their involvement will also dispel the perception that the strategic plan is a document created by "those in charge" and thrust upon the organisation. For this reason, it is vitally important for the senior leadership team to establish a process for obtaining feedback from mid-level managers. The strategic plan should not be finalised until their input has been considered.

Many senior leadership teams identify key objectives and let the employees complete the action plans because they tend to be more knowledgeable about their processes. The senior leadership team should ask for indepth feedback on the strategies and objectives because they lay out how the organisation intends to achieve the vision. It is within the strategies and objectives and particularly the objectives that the changes required of the organisation are explicitly expressed.

Senior leaders should choose an approach that fits with how the organisation best deals with new information.

— Hold an offsite to present the plan to the mid-level managers and solicit their feedback. If possible, use the same strategic planning facilitator who conducted the strategic planning team offsite to ensure continuity.
— Hold facilitated focus groups.
— Use the chain-of-command. Have each member of the senior leadership team share the draft plan with their respective mid-level managers, asking them to review the plan, get input from their employees, and provide feedback to the senior leadership team in a facilitated session.

The senior leadership team may want to solicit feedback from all employees on the strategic plan. Feedback can be collected by:

— Mid-level managers holding sessions with their employees
— Holding an all-hands meeting followed by a question and answer session
— Distributing the draft plan via e-mail and requesting comments

It is important to get employees involved early in the process so that they are informed of the new direction of the organisation and to help them understand how they can contribute to the organisation's success.

In some organisations, union members sit on the Executive Steering Committee or on a Partnership Council and, therefore, participate in the planning process.

If not, union leaders can participate in the planning process by providing feedback on the plan along with the mid-level managers. When asked what encouraged the union leaders to get involved in quality and process improvement, one recent winner of the Malcolm Baldrige National Quality Award said: "We could continue to fight management and see the company disappear or join with management in fighting the competitors. We chose the latter!"

Probably not. It is the sole responsibility of the senior leadership team to set the strategic direction of the organisation and map out how the organisation will get there. While the senior leadership team must be in tune with the needs and desires of the organisation's customers to address them adequately, being customer-driven does not mean that customers dictate the strategic direction of the organisation.

Customers' input should be gathered at the beginning of the strategic planning process during the pre-planning and assessment phases. Customer interviews and other types of surveys can be used to gather customer input and reveal customers' desires and expectations. The key is to focus on what the customers expect as a result of using your products and services. Share the plan with your customers after it is completed.

The senior leadership team is responsible for considering all of the feedback and incorporating what is appropriate. The senior leadership team as a whole should carefully consider the comments on the vision, guiding principles, and mission. The goal groups should address goal-specific comments. After the senior leadership team has reached consensus on any updates, it should let the employees know how their input was used.

Explaining why some feedback was not incorporated may be helpful, especially if a key issue had been raised by many. This helps employees understand why some actions can occur and why others cannot. Think it through—decide how to manage implementation The senior leadership team should begin developing implementation strategies before publishing the plan. The following implementation issues should be considered:

— Do lower-level plans need to be created?
— How do we establish oversight and accountability for implementation actions?
— Do the current process improvement teams, working groups, committees, etc., link with the plan? Do they need to be refocused to align with the plan? Do they need to be eliminated?
— How does the plan link with the budgeting process?
— How will we measure and evaluate progress?

The senior leadership team should outline who is going to be responsible for implementation efforts, i.e., who is the point of contact for the plan, who manages the implementation actions, who manages the resources. The senior leadership team should not establish a special budget for implementing the strategic plan. Because most organisations operate under budgets that are developed one to two years in advance, the budgeting process is always one step ahead of current work. The strategic plan needs to become an integrated part of the budget development and resource allocation process.

For information on resourcing the plan. The senior leadership team should decide which key top-level performance indicators will be used to measure progress. Part of measurement and evaluation comes from tracking the goals, strategies, and objectives. The other part of measurement and evaluation is the more formal system of data collection and analysis.

Mid-level Management and Lower-level Plans

The corporate senior leadership team should encourage suborganisations to create lower-level strategic plans if:

— The corporation's size is large enough to support suborganisations that act as separate business entities
— There is a diverse product or service line among the suborganisations
— The creation of a strategic plan at the lower level will not perpetuate a stovepipe culture that the senior leadership team is trying to change

Suborganisations that are smaller and whose products and services result in the same output as the corporate organisation should have a plan that includes strategies and objectives that contribute to the corporate vision, mission, guiding principles, and goals.

In this case, representatives from the lower organisations should have been included in the original strategic planning process. If the senior leadership team decides that lowerlevel plans are needed, strategic planning guidance should be developed for the leaders of the suborganisations. Training and facilitation support is also needed.

Typically the published strategic plan includes the vision, guiding principles, mission, strategic goals, strategies, and objectives. By publishing to the objective level, the intent of the strategic plan is explicitly laid out for everyone in the organisation. Sometimes organisations choose to publish only to the strategy level since objectives change over time, outdating the published plan.

The weakness in this approach is that the implications for action are not readily apparent and the plan may be perceived as a lofty document with no real application to the organisation. If the senior leadership team chooses not to include the objectives, it should consider publishing them as an accompanying tactical plan.

In addition to sharing the plan within the organisation, consider sharing the plan outside of the organisation. For external audiences, a separate plan may be needed that displays only the vision, guiding principles, mission, goals, and strategies. The amount of detail chosen to be included in the plan for external purposes needs to be tailored to each audience.

The senior leadership team might consider including:

- The rationale for creating the plan
- The process used to create the plan
- A glossary of terms
- Strategic planning team membership
- Implementation roles and responsibilities
- An overview on how current TQ efforts tie into the plan
- An overview on how progress will be measured and evaluated

There is no standard format. How the final document looks is not as important as what it says, how it says it, and how it influences and motivates people. For example, it may be necessary to publish the plan organisation's formal policy system to foster credibility.

References

Ackoff, R. L., *Creating the Corporate Future*, New York, NY: Wiley & Sons, 1981.

Bass, B. M. (n.d.)., *From transactional to transformational leadership: Learning to share the vision*, Organizational Dynamics 19-31.

Deming, W. E., *Out of the Crisis*, Cambridge, MA: Massachusetts Institute of Technology, 1982.

Floyd, S. W., & Wooldridge, B., "Managing strategic consensus: the foundation of effective implementation", *Academy of Management Executive*, 6(4) 27-39, 1992.

Gluck, F. W., Kaufman, S., & Walleck, A. S., "The four phases of strategic management", *Journal of Business Strategy*, 2(3), 9-21, 1982.

9

Implementing the Strategic Plan

The strategic planning process that was used to create the plan is inverted in the implementation phase. Completion of the objectives impacts completion of the strategies, then the goals, and leads toward accomplishing the vision.

To implement the strategic plan successfully, it is necessary for the organisation to have a formal implementation plan with actions assigned to either teams or individuals who are responsible for their accomplishment. If the organisation has been practising process improvement using the TQ model, managers and leaders will be familiar with the TQ team structure.

If the organisation has realised successes using this structure, they will probably want to continue it and will call their senior leadership team an Executive Steering Committee or Group (ESC/G) and their implementation teams Quality Management Board (QMBs) and Process Action Teams (PATs). However, in some organisations, the strategic planning process has led the senior leaders to the conclusion that current QMBs and PATs need to be rechartered, restructured, or realigned with the new strategic direction.

For this reason, the senior leaders have sometimes chosen to call the new teams—those that are dealing with implementation issues—Goal Groups, Strategy Teams and Objective Teams. What they are called is not as important as what they accomplish—implementation of the strategic plan.

Assign Roles and Responsibilities

The following are suggested roles and responsibilities:

— Leads the implementation effort

— Establishes clear roles and responsibilities

— Allocates resources for action items

— Holds monthly strategic plan meetings with the senior leadership team to monitor the status of the plan

— Leads by consensus, but makes key decisions when necessary

— Incorporates brief status updates at weekly staff meetings

— Communicates plan status, accomplishments, and lessons learned with the workforce

— Communicates results as appropriate to customers, stakeholders, parent organisation

— Support the strategic plan and incorporate in to day-to-day business and processes

— Prioritise objectives

— Allocate resources for action items

— Define measures for progress and mission performance

— Sponsor assessment surveys (e.g., internal employee climate surveys, customer surveys, etc.)

— Provide training resources

— Attend monthly strategic plan meetings

— Give brief status updates at weekly staff meetings

— Lead goal groups

— Serve as linking pins on strategy-level teams

— ChAssign roles and responsibilities arter teams

— Guide the workforce through implementation issues

— Remove organisational barriers to goal accomplishment

— Create or revise policies and procedures to achieve goals

— Communicate plan status, accomplishments, and lessons learned with their employees

— Create lower-level plans to support the corporate plan
— Serves on senior leadership team
— Identifies resource issues related to effective implementation
— Distributes and monitors use of allocated resources
— Ensures that budget reflects strategic plan implementation funding needs
— Determines how to reflect mission performance with budget
— Serves as point of contact for the plan with the senior leadership team
— Provides TQ guidance and consultation to senior leaders
— Assesses and coordinates training needs
— Conducts assessment surveys
— Tracks strategic plan action items
— Handles logistics for updating the plan
— Facilitates senior leadership team meetings and offers facilitation to other team meetings
— Works with senior leader to develop meeting agendas
— Works with linking pin to choose team membership
— Establishes team meeting schedule
— Leads team meetings
— Coordinates with strategic planning facilitator/quality advisor on meeting agendas
— Monitors plan of action and milestones
— Briefs status to higher level teams
— Requests necessary resources
— Asks subject matter experts to attend certain meetings
— Ensures distribution of meeting minutes
— Create plan of action and milestones
— Attend meetings
— Implement tasks
— Define measures
— Develop data collection plan

— Collect data

— Identify implementation problem areas

Many people are familiar with the team structure for implementing TQ. The same rationale used for establishing the team structure in a TQ organisation is valid for establishing implementation teams. Goals should be related to current and future business processes cutting across the major functions in the organisation. Therefore, strategic plan implementation teams are similar to TQ teams.

Generally, the differences between current QMBs and new goal groups are that existing QMBs are working on improving/re-engineering current significant mission processes; goal groups will be working on designing new products or developing new mission areas.

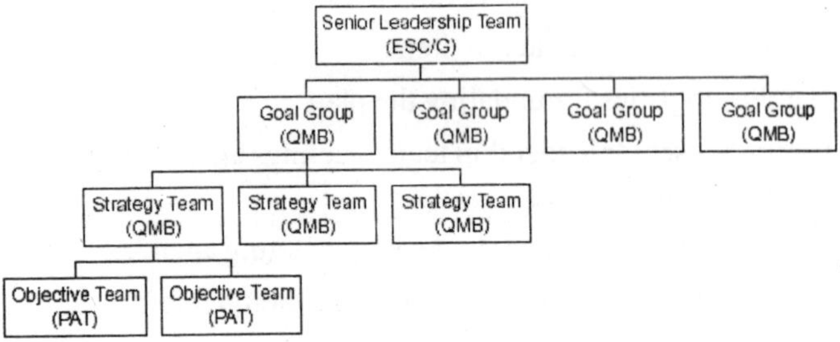

Team Hierarchy

— *ESC/G:* Team made up of the senior leadership of an organisation.

— *QMB:* Cross-functional team that works the strategic goal (also called Strategic Goal Groups)

— *QMB:* Team that works the strategies (also called Strategy Teams)

— *PAT:* Team that gathers data needed to work the objectives, develops implementation action plans, examines processes that are targeted for change, makes recommendations for implementation, and takes action (also called Objective Teams)

Goal groups, consisting of members of the senior leadership team, can be used to lead and monitor implementation within the goal area assigned to them. The goal groups may charter strategy teams (QMBs) or charter objectives teams (PATs), if needed, or assign an individual to work an objective if it does not require a team effort. Chartering of teams depends on the priorities laid out in the strategic plan.

Involve Senior Leaders

The senior leadership team is responsible for overseeing implementation. The team continues to scan the environment to identify any additional strategies or objectives, and discusses implications of changes. It is responsible for making crucial decisions about the direction of the organisation, adjusting the plan as necessary, and chartering teams to help it accomplish the strategies and objectives. By keeping a customer and mission focus and promoting communication between departments, the senior leadership team consciously tries to combat suboptimisation.

How often the senior leadership team meets varies by organisation, but during the implementation phase, periodic meetings, which may be facilitated, are required to focus solely on the strategic plan. Senior leadership teams find that by establishing a regular review schedule, they are able to keep the organisation focused on implementation. Some organisations have established a process whereby one or two of their strategic initiatives are briefed at each staff meeting on a rotating basis, providing a status tracking of all the initiatives each month.

Define an Infrastructure

The organisation needs to define the way it is going to act on the objectives targeted for implementation. Determining what type of infrastructure is best depends on the objectives themselves and the way the organisation is currently organised. For example:

— If the objective addresses changes to a process that cut across the organisation (the most likely case), then a cross-functional team should be established to work on its implementation. A crossfunctional team is one whose membership includes those from more than one organisational function. Each of the members has responsibility for some portion of an identified process.

- — If the objective addresses a major change within a functional area with no impact on another area, then the leader of that area should be tasked to implement the objective either by assembling a team or tasking an individual.
- — If the objective deals with a single, functionally-focused action, then it could probably be tasked to an individual who works in that function. If this is true, this objective may be too low a level to be part of the formal planning process.

In any case, the infrastructure needs to be defined to ensure accountability and responsibility for action. Some organisations have tried to reorganise and then do strategic planning for the "new" organisation. Oftentimes, organisational restructuring is thought to be the way to improve the organisation's performance. Historically, reorganisations have focused on structure, who reports to whom and who is responsible for what. Reorganisations have not focused on the way work gets done. Only after working on the work systems will the most logical structure become apparent.

Teams should be cross-functional if the goal, strategy, objective, or task extends across organisational boundaries. However, if the goal, strategy, objective, or task does not cross over functional boundaries, the team should consist solely of members from that one functional area. Questions leaders might ask before establishing a team include:

- — How does the team support the strategic direction?
- — What are the specific boundaries?
- — What resources will be needed?
- — Do we have the right people on the team to analyse/design a process and accomplish our objective?
- — What people not on the team are critical to its success?
- — Who will probably support the team's efforts, and who may be opposed?
- — What measures will be used to indicate success?

Detailed charters outline the purpose of the team, the expectations, and the resources committed to do the task. The charter tells the team why they have come together and what they are to accomplish. Time limits should also be incorporated. Charter guidelines and a sample charter for strategic plan implementation are provided in the Naval Air Facility Washington Case Study in Section II: Case Studies.

Particularly when getting started. If a strategic planning facilitator is not available, then the organisation's quality advisor is a good source for facilitation of teams. Their role is to work with the team leader to create meeting agendas, help with charters, and provide facilitation during team meetings primarily with the aim to train the group to become self-sufficient. It is important for the team to achieve consensus, to get all members of the team to speak their opinions, and to help the team leader develop and execute a productive agenda.

Link Goal Groups

It is important for higher level teams to review findings and suggestions from lower-level teams and make needed decisions in a timely manner. Organisations that have had team members trained in group dynamics found that their teams were very effective.

If formal training cannot be conducted before teams begin their work, the quality advisor or strategic planning facilitator should promote an understanding of group dynamics, teach the team about active listening, and provide the Department of the Navy's training courses—Team Skills and Concepts, Methods for Managing Quality, Systems Approach to Process Improvement, and Implementing TQL, all of which contain team-related topics. TQL Coordinators should be familiar with these courses.

Phase Integration of Implementation Actions

Implementation teams should develop implementation plans to address how they will carry out their charters. A plan of action and milestones (POA&M) to develop implementation plans and, subsequently, to manage implementation can be used.

It can provide a description of the tasks that need to be accomplished, show responsibility and resource requirements, expected outcomes, measures to be used, and status. For implementation to occur smoothly, consideration must be paid to the priority and sequencing of tasks and steps. To assess what action to take, the senior leadership team should:

- Identify current committees, working groups, QMBs, and PATs— both internal and external—that the organisation is involved with
- Identify team membership and purpose/charter
- Map current team taskings to strategic goals
- Assess team accomplishments to determine if they should be disbanded
- Determine which teams can take on additional actions consistent with implementing the organisation's strategic plan
- Redirect/recharter existing teams to implement the strategic plan or abolish teams that no longer contribute to the vision

Many corporate organisations encourage suborganisations to create lower-level plans. The implementation actions in these plans need to align with the corporate plan. The suborganisations can use the same planning methodology that was used by the corporate organisation but they need to tailor it to the level of planning required. For example, the same pre-planning process can be used that entails interviewing the planning team members of the suborganisation; however, the interview questions will need to be tailored to address the suborganisation's planning outcomes.

The suborganisation's plan may be targeted at one of the strategic goals in the corporate level plan or it may include several strategic, corporatelevel initiatives that the suborganisation needs to carry out. Whether or not the suborganisation needs to develop its own vision, mission, and/or guiding principles depends on the size, complexity, and product line of that suborganisation as compared to that of the corporate level.

Involve Everyone Within the Organisation

But it is actually more important to link the day-to-day business to the tenets of the strategic plan. It is a subtle but important distinction. The focus is on moving the current business towards a more strategic future business rather than make the future business fit today's business structure.

The greater the extent to which the plan sets a new and challenging strategic direction for the organisation, the harder it will be to align the day-to-day business since the extent of change required to be successful will also be that much greater. Said another way, the less strategic the plan, the easier the strategic management. However, the results may be negligible.

As the organisation begins to work on implementing its priority objectives, the actions may translate into additional work. The organisation needs to effectively manage "getting the product out" and "responding to fires" while acting on the organisation's strategic priorities. It will take time to institute new processes, to think and act on ways to do things differently in daily work. Implementing the strategic plan must take on the importance of a "fire drill" for the future.

The organisation exists in a world that is constantly changing, applying pressures from all sides. In order to survive and succeed, leaders need to be aware of these external forces and anticipate the changes they bring. Examples of these forces are higher authority strategic plans, emerging technologies, demographic changes, social forces, economic issues, the federal budget, changing customers, and the changing needs of existing customers.

The degree to which decisions are linked to the plan depends to a large extent on the usefulness and specificity of the plan. If the plan is truly strategic, it provides direction for the organisation. Everyone in the organisation can see where he or she fits into the organisation and can align both their day-to-day and strategic decisions on how they will conduct business with the plan's goals and strategies. In this scenario, decisions are closely tied to the tenets of the plan.

Remember that the plan is the means for communicating and achieving alignment and direction in the organisation. However, while it is important to link decisions with the intended outcomes, the plan should not be prescriptive.

Decision-makers must be flexible so they can respond appropriately but in a coordinated way to changes in the environment. The plan needs to become an outline for decision making because business decisions are related to allocation of resources. If those decisions are made in the context of the strategic plan, then resource allocation becomes aligned with the plan.

Allocate Resources for Implementation

Resourcing a strategic plan involves providing the people, money, and materials to ensure successful implementation. Many organisations link the strategic plan with the budgeting process at the initial strategic planning session or soon afterward when they create implementation teams.

Some choose to have implementation teams identify resources and present them to the senior leadership team for approval. This helps the senior leadership team prioritise implementation actions and allot resources to move the organisation toward achieving its strategic goals. There are at least four resources that are critical: the support of the comptroller, the support of the human resources manager, support for the implementation teams, and a viable programme for achieving the strategic initiatives.

One way to ensure the support and commitment of both the comptroller and the human resources manager is to include them on the senior leadership team and, therefore, in the strategic planning process. Too often, these very important people are relegated to adjudicating the competing plans of others and are not included in the planning process itself.

This is an opportunity to ensure their understanding of the vision and goals and solicit their ideas about how to develop strategies that will succeed. If not done during the development of the strategic plan, they should be involved as soon as possible in the deployment phase.

Too often, implementation actions flounder because implementation teams are not given adequate support. Earlier in this section, requirements for team training, tools, time to meet, and charters were described. Because the teams are often cross-functional, there may be no single person in the organisation who is responsible for providing them with these resources.

This is where the comptroller and the human resources manager can intervene. If they have a thorough understanding and are committed to accomplishing the goals of the strategic plan, they can assist in providing the resources for the implementation teams.

Without a programme for achieving the strategic initiatives, departments will spend their programme dollars on achieving short-term departmental results. And why not? If they don't spend the money, they will lose it—not only this year, but probably in the future as well. With a strategic focus, however, some departments have found that they can combine allocated monies and thereby achieve a synergistic effect for the dollars spent while accomplishing the organisation's strategic initiatives.

New budget requirements can become an issue if the plan calls for training, equipment, etc., to support development and implementation of a new way of doing business or perhaps a new mission area. A plan that is truly strategic represents changes to how the organisation executes its current business.

Some successful organisations have chosen to integrate their planning and budgeting processes by timing strategic planning events so that they will feed into budgeting events such as Programme Objective Memorandum (POM) development and the mid-year review process. In fact, strategic planning is an excellent way to make the planning process explicit in the Department of Defence's Planning, Programming, and Budgeting System (PPBS).

This question, although frequently asked, is too simplistic. In the beginning, the strategic plan drives budget formulation. Strategic plans help the organisation's leaders know their requirements so they can budget for the people, the programmes, the equipment, etc., they need to carry out their strategic direction.

If the budget is not fully funded for those people, programmes, equipment, etc., it is in the budget execution phase that the budget drives the strategic plan. However, if the strategic planning process has included prioritisation of the objectives, it is easier for the organisation to act on their highest priorities even when the budget is not fully funded.

Sometimes the availability and use of resources is not readily apparent, but strategic planning can make them more visible. For example, when the organisation establishes what is really important, it also makes explicit those actions or tasks which are not important. Eliminating redundancies in assignments or organisations can free up the use of resources, making them available for strategic actions. Sometimes resources are not readily available. The following actions are often successful in obtaining needed resources:

— Redirect current resources
— Reprioritise implementation actions
— Partner with another division or organisation to combine funding levels
— Ask the parent organisation or sponsor for more resources

Manage the Change Process

Transitions can cause major upheaval in the group dynamics of the senior leadership team and the direction in which the organisation is moving. However, if the plan is the product of the entire leadership team, it has a much better chance of surviving leadership transitions. The plan needs to be owned by the leadership team, not dependent on a single leader. Getting acceptance and input to the plan from new members of the senior leadership team is crucial to the plan's success.

During the turnover, it is important for the former senior leader to explain the strategic plan and the direction of the organisation to the new leader. The senior leadership team members can explain the history involved in making decisions, share with the new senior leader the progress that the organisation has made, and show results that have occurred.

The greater the extent the planning implementation process is in place, the greater likelihood that the strategic initiatives will survive. The new leader of the organisation may want to update the strategic plan to incorporate personal vision elements.

It is important that new members of the senior leadership team understand the importance of the plan and of their role in achieving the vision. The departing member of the team should brief the new member on the strategic plan and the strategic management efforts thus far. The departing member should show the new member how the responsibilities of the position impact the plan and what role the individual plays on the planning team. The senior leader should also brief new members on expectations regarding the plan.

It is critical to give the new leader or member all of the background information such as:

— Why the plan was created (drivers)

— The process that was used to create the plan
— Any environmental conditions that existed at the time of its creation
— The impact the plan has had on the organisation
— How the plan is being implemented (goal groups, cross-functional teams, etc.)
— How progress is being monitored and measured (monthly senior team meetings, measures being used)
— Roles and responsibilities
— Lessons learned
— Results that have been achieved
— Plans for formally revisiting the plan

For example, the senior leadership team might want to align the formal reward systems with the strategic plan. In so doing, the team might evaluate what factors need to change in the current reward systems and may decide to establish criteria in the system to reflect team participation and process improvement results. Performance appraisal criteria may also have to change for purposes of alignment with the strategic plan.

Evaluate Results

Use the POA&M format to help track status. Team leaders track the status of action plans. The group leader uses the status update to brief the senior leadership team on progress. Because there are two types of measurement systems that are necessary, different forms of evaluation occur. One type is the evaluation of activity, which involves looking at what implementation actions have occurred and evaluating the progress in implementing those actions.

Some implementation efforts may take longer than originally anticipated, requiring work on other implementation activities to be delayed. This is perfectly natural. The important thing is for the senior leadership team to keep up-to-date on implementation actions at regular review sessions, to make appropriate adjustments, and to remove organisational impediments. The other type of evaluation analyses the measurement data resulting from the strategic measurement system. This data is targeted at measuring outcomes of mission effectiveness now and into the future.

Typically, this type of measurement is new for organisations who are more than likely measuring at the product output level (number of parts produced, number of reports completed, or number of days to complete repairs). These types of measures are important to managing daily business, but it is in the strategic measures that a picture of the organisation's effectiveness is given. Through the strategic planning process, these outcomes become explicit and a strategic measurement system of the macro-level measurements can be created.

Ongoing communication is crucial for success. It is extremely important for the senior leadership team to share lessons learned, to share successes, and to show that work is being accomplished. The fact that senior leaders are paying attention to goal accomplishment will focus everyone's attention on the plan. The senior leadership team needs to choose formal communication methods that will reach the widest audience on a continual basis. Some organisations use their newsletters or magazines to provide status updates and lessons learned. Others post their POA&Ms on marquees or bulletin boards. In some large organisations, the leaders use video or electronic communications.

Many organisations include the strategic plan in their new employee indoctrination process. Some TQL coordinators send a copy of the strategic plan with the new employee's orders, outlining how his/her responsibilities impact the plan. If the senior leader addresses new employees in their orientation, a discussion about the strategic plan may be included. Newsletters or any formal written policy dealing with the plan can be distributed to the new employees. The new employee's immediate manager should explain how daily work processes impact the success of the organisation as reflected in the plan.

References

Gluck, F. W., Kaufman, S., & Walleck, A. S., "The four phases of strategic management", *Journal of Business Strategy*, 2(3), 9-21, 1982.

Hamel, G., & Prahalad, C. K., "Strategic intent", *Harvard Business Review*, 63-76, 1989, May-June.

10

Strategic Measurement

Strategic measurement is the identification, development, communication, collection, and assessment of selected outcome measures that are directly linked to the organization's performance of its mission and attainment of its vision. These measures should be outcome-focused, to assess the impact of the organization's strategic efforts.

Roles and Responsibilities

The following are suggested roles and responsibilities:

- Leads development of strategic measurement plan
- Incorporates measurement plan into deployment and implementation of the strategic plan
- Monitors and evaluates strategic measures
- Communicates measurement results to workforce
- Adjusts measurement plan as necessary
- Adjusts strategic plan as necessary
- Allocates resources to implement strategic measurement plan
- Support the strategic measurement plan
- Champion the need for strategic measures
- Define strategic measures and performance indicators
- Charter measurement team and identify members
- Provide guidance to measurement team

— Approve final strategic measurement plan
— Monitor and evaluate strategic measures
— Communicate measurement results to employees
— Adjust measurement plan as necessary
— Adjust strategic plan as necessary
— Allocate resources to implement the strategic measurement plan
— Individually, develop measures within their area of responsibility that link with strategic measures
— Individually, provide data associated with strategic measures
— Develops baselines, data collection and evaluation process, feedback system
— Develops resourcing plan
— Develops a plan of action and milestones for implementation
— Develops a deployment approach
— Disbands when strategic measurement plan is approved
— Serves on senior leadership team
— Distributes and monitors allocated resources
— Incorporates strategic measurement implementation funding needs into budget as part of strategic plan implementation
— Assists measurement team in understanding how budget relates to mission effectiveness
— Develops measures for determining cost-effectiveness of strategic measures
— Develops plan to reinvest savings
— Serves as a point of contact for strategic measurement plan
— Assesses and coordinates training needs
— Tracks strategic measurement plan action items
— Handles logistics for updating the strategic measurement plan

The senior leadership team charters a measurement team to complete the development of the measurement plan. The measurement team:

— Defines measurement administration responsibilities: Measurement administration responsibilities include who will collect, gather, store, and analyse the data needed to support the performance indicators.

— Gathers data to develop baselines for each performance indicator: The measurement team gathers the data to develop baseline performance and then presents these baselines to the senior leadership team so that it can establish the baselines.

— Develops a feedback system: A feedback system tells the senior leadership if it is measuring intended mission effectiveness, using the best indicator for those items, and if it is progressing toward the vision.

— Identifies resource requirements

— Develops a plan of action and milestones to implement the strategic measurement plan

— Creates a deployment strategy for the measurement plan: Deployment of the measurement plan needs to be integrated with the overall strategic plan deployment.

The senior leadership team chooses members who represent a cross section of the entire organisation, including at least one member of the senior leadership team to serve as a downward link. Membership is determined by the number of indicators the organisation develops and by subject matter expertise about the various processes for which data will be collected.

The purpose of this model is to depict the basic flow of work and information in any organisation. All organisations deal with internal and external suppliers who provide inputs to the organisation in the form of money, people, material, information, etc. The organisation then utilises people, methods, machines, material, processes, and its structure to transform that input into the products and services (outputs) it provides to its customers or end-users.

The customer then uses the products or services and experiences a result or outcome from that use. For those organisations with no clear end-users, such as operational units in the military, outcomes are defined as mission effectiveness. Measurement of any improvement or change initiative throughout the extended system is important in order to assess whether a change has had the intended effect.

When engaged in measurement at the process level, there are four opportunities for measuring and assessing the effects of process improvement activities, outcomes, outputs, processes, and inputs. At this level the outcomes are associated with satisfaction of that particular end-user's requirements or mission effectiveness. When engaged in a strategic management process, strategic measures must be identified and defined with the associated data collected and analysed to support those measures.

In strategic measurement, the strategic measures define the aggregated outcomes of mission effectiveness now and into the future as described in the organisation's vision and strategic goals. These aggregated outcomes are at a higher level than a single end-user for a single product or service line. Strategic measures define measurement at the organisational level to indicate overall organisational performance.

Once the strategic measure is determined, it is important to select measurements for the inputs, processes, and outputs which directly contribute to the outcome measure. In other words, it is best to start by determining the outcome measure first and then select input, process, and output measures that have a clear relationship to that outcome. For example, if ship readiness is the desired strategic measure, a process measure that measures the capacity of the ship's laundry or an input measure that measures the quality of its soap powder would have no bearing on the outcome.

They may be good indicators of another desired outcome, such as quality of life, but they are not good indicators of readiness. Where readiness is the desired outcome, a process measure might be maintenance of ships and an output measure might be number of ships available for sea duty. Typically, government organisations have a lot of measurement data around inputs, processes, and outputs, but lack the data to assess organisational outcomes. There are a couple of reasons for this.

The organisation may not have a strategic plan that explicitly states the outcomes; therefore, measures have never been developed to support them. Or the organisation may have the data to support the outcomes, but is not collecting, storing, and analysing that data so that it becomes useful information in determining mission effectiveness.

Many organisations collect customer satisfaction data but do not have a measurement system in place to effectively use that information to improve the organisation.

The main reason is that outcome data are difficult to define and collect, particularly for public sector organisations. This is not to say that one type of measurement is bad and one type is good. Measures are only useful when appropriately applied. For example, process measures are useful when undertaking process improvement activities, when monitoring the process to ensure it is stable, and to have a baseline for comparisons when making system changes.

Financial measures are useful for monitoring expenditures against obligation and to control organisational spending. They may be useful as an output measure when efficiencies and process improvements are applied. Input data, particularly quality data, are necessary to determine when to begin improvement efforts. As with any type of measurement it is important to understand what is being measured and why.

Any good measurement system should include outcome, output, process, and input measures. For example, if a strategic goal for a shipyard focuses on maintaining a cleaner environment, there are several possible measures that can be taken related to ships leaking oil. One measure might be the number of oil spills given the number of ships. The number of ships in this case is the input and the number of oil spills is the output. So if the data show that the number of oil spills has declined given an increase in the number of ships, this seems like a very good indicator of a cleaner environment. But looking closer, the number of oil spills does not indicate how much damage is being done to the environment.

Outcome measures may be related to fish contamination, decrease in wildlife, water pollution, etc. A good surrogate, or proxy, measure from the shipyard's point of view may be volume of oil spilled. Both the output and outcome measures are needed to provide a complete picture.

Use of Measurement

The selected measures must meet the needs of the organisation's leadership for assessing the progress of the organisation and still provide meaningful policy guidance to the lower echelons. There are eight basic measurement principles:

1. *Measures, to be useful, must be linked*: Measures at one level in an organisation should result in measurements at the next lower level. Ackoff writes that there are two types of links—coordination and integration. Coordination means that "no part of an organisation can be planned for effectively if it is planned for independently of any other unit at the same level." Integration means that "effective planning needs to be carried out interdependently at all levels." Links to address both these issues must be addressed by the team structure and measures used to tie them together.
2. *Measures are experimental*: A performance measure selected for a process or system can only be the organisation's best guess as to the most appropriate indicator particularly as it relates to changing missions for the organisation. It may be necessary to modify the measurement if a relationship between what is measured and the goal to be achieved cannot be established.
3. *Measures may be incomplete:* Measurements may provide only a partial picture of what is being measured, particularly when first getting started. As a first step, operational definitions of measures are critical to understanding whether a measure is adequate. Sometimes outcome data are nearly impossible to obtain; or, they occur so infrequently as not to be practical. What may be needed are surrogate measures that are closely tied to the outcome to approximate—or be a surrogate for—the desired measures. For example, success in winning a battle is the intended mission effectiveness outcome of a military operation, but not a practical measure.

   Mission readiness, or preparedness to fight and win, becomes the surrogate. This is why it is important to carry out the second step, which is the identification of factors that make up the outcome measure. These factors form the performance indicators for the measures around which data will be collected. When surrogates are used, it is important to do a validity check to make sure they do relate to intended outcomes. Experts in the subject matter and historical data may need to be consulted. The more future-oriented the measure, the harder and more critical it is to define and measure the related factors.

4. *People at the appropriate level need to be involved in developing the measurement*: The senior leadership team defines the strategic measures to be used for the same reasons that strategic planning must be done by the senior leadership: they are responsible for establishing the strategic direction of the organisation. Others will define supporting measures, such as process measures and output, for the strategic measures.
5. *A family of measures is necessary to adequately describe the organisation, process, or system:* Traditional measures are generally financial in nature—which only covers one aspect of the organisation. Multiple measures, describing different aspects of the organisation, are better than singular measures for providing a comprehensive picture of the organisation. This refers to the need to link measures and to ensure that the data collected are necessary and sufficient to support the family of measures.
6. *Measures over time show trends*; additional information is required to determine the causes of success or failure. While a performance indicator can show that something is being done better over time, the measurement will not provide the reason for this improvement. Teams with process knowledge are necessary to analyse the data.
7. *Measure only what is important:* Organisational resources must be expended to collect, store, and analyse measures. Therefore, measurement activities should not be conducted solely as an exercise in measuring. The purpose of measurement must be clear. Understanding how measures are to be used is critical.
8. *The measures selected must support decision making:* Measurement data requires analysis to provide information to be useful to decision makers. Considerable time and effort must be given to assess how the data would improve decisions and what would be done with the data. Information that has no bearing on the decision has no value at the time of the decision. Collection of data that is not used should be discontinued.

Strategic measures focus on vision attainment. Hold a workshop, similar to the strategic planning workshop, with the senior leadership team to develop strategic measures. Following are steps that the senior leadership team should follow to develop a strategic measurement system:

— *Operationally define the strategic measures:* Strategic measures are operational definitions of the outcomes of mission effectiveness now and into the future. If the organisation has a comprehensive vision supported by strategic goals that operationally define the outcomes expressed in the vision, then the senior leadership team can derive performance indicators from the strategic goals. If the vision and strategic goals are very broad, then it may be necessary for the senior leadership team to further discuss the outcomes and goals and operationally define what they are trying to achieve.

— *Define performance indicators:* Performance indicators are derived from the strategic measures. They are the key evidence with which to measure performance. Because the operational definitions of the key concepts are on a macro-level, the performance indicators will be similarly broad.

— *Charter a strategic measurement team:* The strategic measures are the foundation of a strategic measurement plan. They are given to a measurement team who completes the measurement plan.

— *Establish baselines:* Baselines are the current performance levels for the performance indicators selected. If data that support a performance indicator are currently being collected, then a historical baseline exists. If the data are not currently being collected, a baseline needs to be established. The measurement team will determine the baselines for the performance indicators from current data or by collecting data over a short period of time to provide an approximate baseline as a starting point. Their strategic measurement plan will include these recommended baselines for approval by the senior leadership team.

— *Approve the strategic measurement plan:* The senior leadership team will review the recommendations made by the measurement team, including the baselines and the data collection methodology, and approve them when agreement is reached.

— *Inform the workforce:* The senior leadership team needs to communicate to the workforce the new strategic measurement system that will be put into place and how they can contribute to the success of that system.

— *Implement the measurement plan:* Take the actions necessary to put the strategic measurement system into place. Clarify important roles in measurement development and data collection and analysis.

Five to seven strategic measures are recommended. Too many measures can lead to collecting data that is meaningless. Try to collect a slate of measures that cover the breadth and indicate the health of the organisation. The measurement team determines what data are necessary to collect. To determine what data need to be collected, the team needs to:

— Define the indicators

— Determine what data are needed to measure the indicators

— Determine if that data are already being collected

— If not, figure out how to collect the data

— Define data collection rules that outline how the data apply to the indicators

If the data collected supports the performance indicators chosen for the strategic measurement system. A review of current measures needs to be done by the measurement team to determine if they support the indicators; if it does, then that data needs to be organised into the strategic measures. However, if the review reveals measures that do not support the strategic measures and aren't required by law, statutory requirements, or higher echelon requirements; aren't being used for management control purposes; or aren't being used for process improvement efforts, then stop using them and expending the effort to collect the associated data.

It is important to collect data on all of the strategic measures because, even though concerted work may be focused only on one or two goal areas, the results of that work may impact all of the measures. Until there is enough data to understand relationships among the goals, there is no basis to know how much benefit directed focus will have on overall achievement of outcomes.

Although most people are unable to focus on more than a few things at one time, leaders sometimes allow measurement systems to capture everything, the useful and the not-so-useful. Such actions can distract the organisation from reaching its vision. Valuable resources may be expended on efforts that do not support the strategic plan. The use of strategic measurement, on the other hand, strengthens the organisation's focus on the future by filtering out information not required to achieve the strategic goals. It limits the number of measures to approximately six, forcing the organisation to concentrate on the vital outcomes.

In a traditional measurement scheme, each function has its own set of measures. These specialised measurement systems segregate functions and isolate suborganisations from the larger organisation. Once these measures are compartmentalised by function, they cannot simply be aggregated as a means of assessing overall corporate performance.

Organisational measures have traditionally been a mixture of regulatory requirements, error corrections, leaders' information needs, and sometimes data on process performance. While some of these may be valid and useful, they are not strategic measures. In general, these systems are used to control present activities. In contrast, a strategic measurement system communicates to all echelons of an organisation what is vital to achieving its vision of the future. The strategic plan has established a vision of the future for the organisation.

The strategic measurements reinforce the strategic plan by helping to focus everyone's attention on attaining those goals that will lead to that future. When two key projects, programmes, or activities are competing for resources, the focus of the measures can help leaders determine which of the competing actions should receive immediate support. When measurements are understood, decision making can be pushed down to a level where action can be initiated close to the problem, situation, or opportunity.

Using strategic measurement, those making decisions can propel the organisation forward toward the vision without having to elevate each decision to the highest level. It is fundamental that anything the organisation chooses to expend resources on should be measured. It is important to track all actions related to the implementation of the strategic plan. Leaders must know the status of progress taken on the objectives, strategies, and goals so they can assess individual, team, and organisational performance. But they must also be able to assess the effectiveness of mission accomplishment and the changes (those strategic goals) which were established in order to attain the vision.

Suborganisations should create lower-level measurement plans that link with the corporate strategic measurement plan. If the suborganisation has a separate strategic plan, then it will also need a separate strategic measurement plan. If the suborganisation's strategic plan starts at the strategy or objective level, it needs to have measures that link directly to the corporate strategic measurements. In the event that only a few measures can be linked, the suborganisation should create additional strategic measurements that better describe its outcomes.

Update the Measurement System

In some instances, a strategic measure selected by the organisation might not be the correct one. The expected relationship between the measure and performance might not materialise. Periodic reviews to determine whether there is a relationship between the measure and what is being measured can ensure that the "right" measures are selected. If the relationship is weak, analysis must be done to determine the cause.

Strategic measurement helps leaders continually establish and evaluate progress toward goals, targets, and policy over a long period of time. The strategic plan itself is usually written from a 5, 10, or 15-year perspective. Similarly, measuring the attainment of the goals is a long-term endeavour. The organisation looks for performance improvements by watching the strategic measurements. The causes for any changes in performance should be determined by investigating system, subsystem, and process measurement data.

Some strategies devised to achieve goals might not work. The measures will show that the relationship between the strategy and the expected outcome does not exist. By using graphic tools, this lack of relationship will become apparent. Further investigation will reveal the causes. By using the feedback from the strategic measures to validate or adjust the strategic direction of the organisation the feedback data becomes input that the leaders can use to make decisions in their daily business. It is the decisions that are made today that impact the future of the organisation.

Most people want to know how the results impact the organisation and themselves. Sharing results should be part of the formal communication mechanism established for the strategic plan. Measurement can be threatening. The senior leadership team needs to anticipate people's possible reaction to measurement. Below are some reasons why people may dislike measurement:

— Poor performance may be found
— The value of measurement is not understood
— People don't understand how to use measures
— People's contribution to the organisation and the measures is not evident
— It places accountability on individuals
— Measurement has typically been used as a means of punishment
— Measurement takes time and effort

The results from the strategic measures become inputs to updating the strategic plan. Sometimes the results may reveal areas where goals, strategies, or objectives are inadequate. Therefore, the goal, strategy, or objective may need to be adjusted. It may also show that the attainment of the goal, strategy, or objective is complete. The senior leadership team needs to adjust the plan as needed.

References

Metz, E., "Managing change: Implementing productivity and quality improvements", *National Productivity Review*, 3(3), 303-314, 1984.

Paine, L. S., "Managing for organizational integrity", *Harvard Business Review*, 106-117, 1994, March-April.

Regents of the University of California, "The pitfalls of strategic planning", *California Management Review*, 1-15, 1993, Fall.

11

External Market Analysis

The purpose of an external analysis should be to consistently improve the choices a company makes and enhance the company's competitive standing. According to David Aaker, author of Strategic Market Management, the role of external analysis evaluates investment decisions on where to compete, should existing businesses be liquidated, milked, maintained or invested in for growth? Questions of what growth directions should receive investment, should there be market penetration product expansion or market expansion are also investigated.

Aaker also suggests that questioning the functional area strategies for implementation, position strategy, segmentation strategy, distribution strategy, manufacturing strategy should also be of concern. Finally, the questions what are the key success factors and what assets and competencies should be created, enhanced, or maintained should be asked too. Strategic uncertainties are often difficult to assess when doing an analysis of external analysis. When questions are explored relating to uncertainties, very often more questions will appear.

Future levels of demand are often the centre of questions of uncertainty. These questions are fuelled by performance improvements, competitive technological development and financial uncertainties in the industry. David Aaker suggests that external analyses are often conducted annually. However, he recommends that they need not be done as in-depth from year-to-year, but only done with a focus on a particular product or segment of the business.

Aaker tells readers that, "The need for strategic review and change is often continuous. Information sensing and analysis therefore also need to be continuous." And "The framework and concepts of external analysis can still play a key role in providing structure even when the analysis is continuous and addresses only a portion of the whole." Customers of the business may be the most determining factor of change requirements and can be the most-powerful source of information for creating a strategic plan that addresses operational opportunities, threats and uncertainties.

SEGMENTATION PROCESS

Segmentation, according to David Aaker is the key to developing a sustainable competitive advantage. Being able to identify customer groups defines the process of segmentation and allows the company to focus on competitive needs. In order to identify each segment, questions of who are the biggest customers, most profitable, most attractive potential customer should be asked.

There are of course subgroups of every segment that should also be assessed. Subgroups of each major segment could be identified through benefits sought, usage level, application, organisation type, geographic location, loyalty and price sensitivity. Market strategist David Aaker suggests that for each subgroup, questions of determining what elements of the product or service the customer values most, customers' objectives, how segments differ in motivation priorities and what changes are occurring customer motivation and priorities should be addressed.

Customers may also have needs that are unmet and should also be addressed when assessing customer segments. Perhaps there may be customers who are dissatisfied and are changing to other brands or suppliers. If so, they should be interviewed, if possible and adaptations products and services should be considered to win customers back. Reasons behind the customers' problems associated with the product or service need to be assessed consistently, as well as possible future problems that customers are not yet aware of.

Also, questions of whether competitors are using weakness from your company as leverage should be researched and addressed. Customers can be defined through common characteristics, which include geographic areas, lifestyle, sex, age, occupation, organisational type or firm. Also, identification of customer type may be broken into groupings of how they use the product or service, benefits sought, price sensitivity and how and if they use competitor's products and services.

An example of customers who use a product for benefit may be the product is quick-to-fix or has health benefits. People may also benefit from pricing reasons. They may perceive the product or service to be of value because it is lower priced in comparison to competitor's products or services. Perhaps the product/service is of a greater perceived value because it is priced higher and represents a superior product or service. Whatever the reason the customer may continue to purchase a product or service, it should lead to developing a sense of brand loyalty, another type of segment identification.

Brand Loyalty

Brand loyalty may be the greatest asset a company has. Therefore, it should be consistently sought after and evaluated. Customers who become loyal to a company's brand may do so based upon quality, price, consistency, service or other such competitive reasons associated with the product or service. Whatever the reason customers become loyal to a product or service, it should be maintained and consistently evaluated.

In the 1980's Coke changed the recipe for its primary product that customers were very loyal to. This led to a customer revolt that eventually caused the company to revert back to the original recipe and admitting it made a mistake. Part of assessing customer loyalty also includes what motivates the customer to purchase a product or service.

Marketing analysts should ask the questions what lies behind the purchasing decision of the customer and how dies that differ by segment? Any unmet needs of the customer truly represent opportunities for the company that should be addressed, because they truly are threats to the company's share of the market or potential share. If your company does not address these issues, they may be addressed by a competitor's company, which could give them a marketing edge to build a strategy around.

Evaluating the Competitors

It is important to evaluate the competition on a regular basis. Identifying who it is that you compete with, who is the most intense and least intense can give strength in developing a marketing strategy. Marketing strategists should evaluate also who are the makers of substitute products and who, potentially could become potential competitive entrants. Evaluating the competitors means analysing competitors' objectives, strategies, level of commitment, costs, image, advantages and disadvantages.

In doing so, it will give a view of possible leverage areas, strategic weaknesses, customer problems and unmet needs. This process could be done effectively by identifying and placing competitors in strategic groupings. Groupings may include similar competitive strategies, distribution channel, communication strategies, price, position, aggressiveness, assets, and competencies, including brand associations, logistics, capability, global presence, or research and development.

Areas of particular interest for doing a competitor analysis should be done in sections pertaining to innovation, manufacturing, finance, management, marketing and customer base. Using interviews from customers of competitors, information found on competitor websites and other such media may assist in categorising and evaluating the level of strength and weakness of each of these areas.

References

Aaker, D. A., *Strategic market management 6th edition*, New York, NY: Wiley & Sons, 2001.

Metz, E., "Managing change: Implementing productivity and quality improvements", *National Productivity Review*, 3(3), 303-314, 1984.

Paine, L. S., "Managing for organizational integrity", *Harvard Business Review*, 106-117, 1994, March-April.

Regents of the University of California, "The pitfalls of strategic planning", *California Management Review*, 1-15, 1993, Fall.

12

Strategic Management for Improving Performance

Financial Performance

Strategy textbooks, which are largely devoted to commercial business situations, generally take some indicator of financial performance as the measure of concern. The large financial values involved in the commercial sector create an understandable incentive for academics, consultants and executives to develop strategy tools for such cases. However, as a result, the strategy concerns of public sector, voluntary, and other not-for-profit organisations are somewhat neglected. Ideally, we need tools and frameworks that are helpful to management in all cases, not just for business.

Furthermore, many strategic issues in corporate situations, while they will ultimately affect financial performance, primarily concern nonfinancial issues: poor marketplace reputation, rapid loss of staff, business lost to competitors, and so on. Nevertheless, since the financial performance of firms is helpfully clear, as well as highly valued, we will start with these concerns before widening the question to encompass other kinds of objectives.

A wide range of financial measures are featured in firms' reporting, controls and objectives, but the overriding concern with the interests of investors has led to the choice of one specific measure-economic profit-as the basis for assessing performance for any particular time period. Two elements of profit must be distinguished. First is the "normal" profit that investors would expect to receive for the use of their capital, given the level of risk they are taking on by investing in a particular type of business. This leaves a second element, the "economic profit", which is the surplus that remains after the costs of all inputs (including the cost of capital) have been paid out, so:

Economic profit = operating profit minus taxes minus cost of capital

This has become more than just a theoretical concept, with economic profit or the closely related "economic value added" (EVA) being adopted as a management tool by many large corporations. An exclusive focus on current profit poses a rather obvious problem. We can nearly always boost profits now, by simple changes such as pushing up prices or cutting expenditure, although shareholders will not thank us for these actions if we damage future profits.

Historical and current profits are therefore only relevant insofar as they provide important clues to what profits will likely be in the coming years. This severely limits the value of any strategy approaches or frameworks based on explanations for profitability in a single period, no matter how persuasive the statistical significance of those explanations.

The money available to distribute to shareholders in future years will be the cash flow generated by the company's operations, minus any additional capital input required to make that operating cash flow possible. So another measure that receives attention is "free cash flow." Current period profits include an allowance for writing off the past expenditure on fixed assets, known as depreciation. This depreciation needs to be added back and replaced by the actual expenditures on fixed and working capital. This results in the following measure of a firm's free cash flow:

Free cash flow = operating profit + depreciation - taxes - change in fixed and working capital

The value of a firm to its investors reflects the expected stream of all future free cash flows, but is not simply the sum of these amounts. Cash received today and in the near term is valued more highly than the cash that may be received far in the future, due to the increasing uncertainty involved and the fact that the money invested has alternative uses. Each period's cash flow is therefore discounted by the firm's cost of capital to arrive at its "present value" (Figure 1), and the firm's total value is the sum of all those values out into the future.

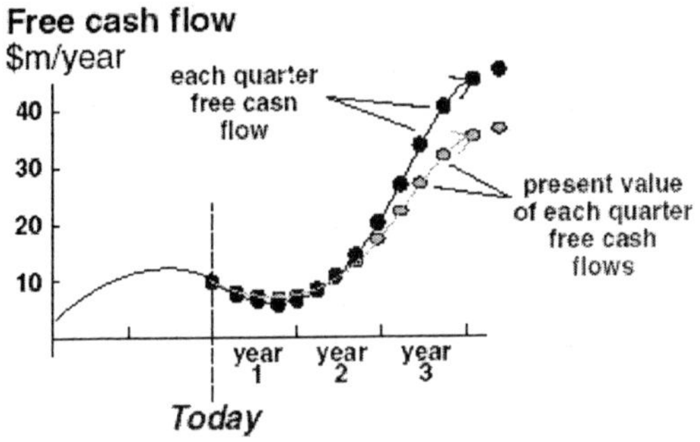

Figure 1. Future free cash flows and their present value.

To evaluate a firm's strategy, we therefore need a way to estimate the future trajectory of cash flows, not just a single period. Furthermore, since strategic management concerns improvements in performance, we need a way to estimate what impact on that cash flow trajectory may arise from any actions or decisions we may be considering.

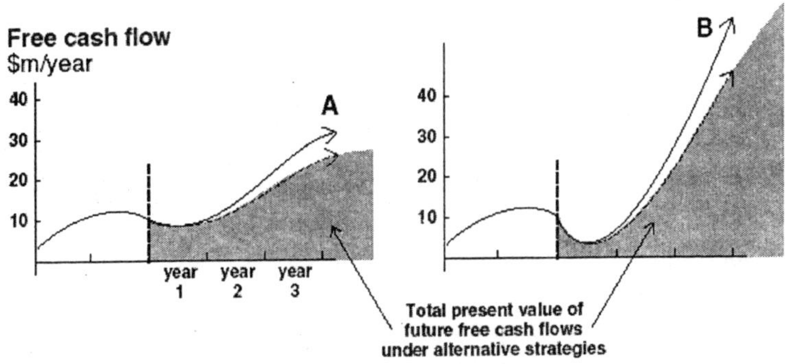

Figure 2. Total value of a firm under alternative strategies.

Such changes may be relatively minor, such as a price reduction intended to accelerate sales growth, or major, such as the acquisition of another substantial business. In Figure 2, Strategy B should be preferred because it delivers a greater total discounted present value than Strategy A, even though it involves lower cash flows in year one. Outcome B could, for example, arise from entering a new market or launching a new product, either of which would incur short-term costs but with the prospect of enabling additional growth thereafter. Management will, of course, face the challenge of convincing investors to share their confidence in option B!

Strategic management is about building and sustaining performance into the future: This is not a novel idea in the strategy field, but goes back to seminal work in the 1950s by Edith Penrose, who pointed out that superior profitability is neither interesting in itself, nor sustainable in any but the most exceptional circumstances. Rather, management should be concerned with growing future economic profit. To illustrate the idea that shareholders value future cash flows, even if money has to be invested in the short term, Figure 3 shows the profit history for Amason.com.

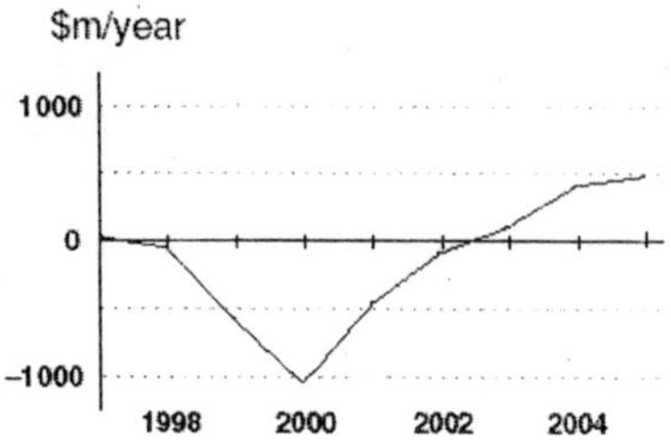

Figure 3. Profit history at Amazon. com.

In the years up to 2001, the company repeatedly delivered only losses. Investors nevertheless ascribed value to the firm because of the prospects that profits would arise in due course. Indeed, those early losses were often greater than investors had previously expected, yet they still valued the company positively since each new level of loss arose from additional spending to develop ever more sources of sales and thus future cash flows.

NONFINANCIAL PERFORMANCE

The purely financial view implied by this approach to valuing firms need not be inconsistent with other objectives, or with concerns for wider issues, such as social responsibility. Indeed, lack of attention to such issues can easily create problems that ultimately damage long-term profits and business value. Management often sets targets for measures that are not expressed in financial terms-customer growth, market share, staff numbers, and so on.

Some companies even set aims for intangible measures, such as reputation. This is not to say that they ignore bottom-line financial performance. Rather, they focus on these other factors because they drive financial performance. Investors, analysts and other outside commentators also pay attention to firms' performance on such measures, so nonfinancial aims and progress towards them are often made quite public. Airlines report passenger volumes, cellphone operators report on subscriber numbers, fast-moving consumer goods (FMCG) firms report market shares, and so on.

Skype, the voice-over Internet protocol (VoIP) telephony service, is a well known situation where management and outsiders alike watched progress with keen interest. As Figure 4 shows, attention focused on the quarterly growth in the number of registered users. Having registered subscribers is not especially useful, however, unless they are using the service, so a secondary indicator is actual usage.

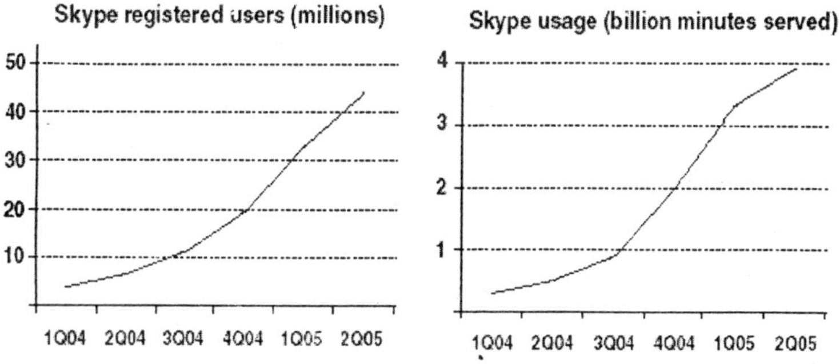

Figure 4. Early growth in registered users of Skype VoIP, and usage of the service.

As at the end of the second quarter, 2005, management might have been somewhat disappointed to see that usage growth had dipped below growth in user numbers. However, it is possible that VoIP, like other new technologies, won the keenest users first, so this was not necessarily a cause for concern. These nonfinancial indicators do not make financial performance unimportant, of course, and Skype seeks to earn revenues from add-on services, such as "Skypein" and "Skype-out", which connect calls in from, and out to, normal phones.

NONCOMMERCIAL SETTINGS

Nonfinancial performance aims are understandably common in public sector, voluntary, and nongovernmental organisations (NGOs). One such case concerns the increasing prevalence and cost of diabetes in affluent societies. In the United States, for example, the number of people with diabetes more than doubled between 1980 and 2003, from 5.8 million to 13.8 million (Figure 5).

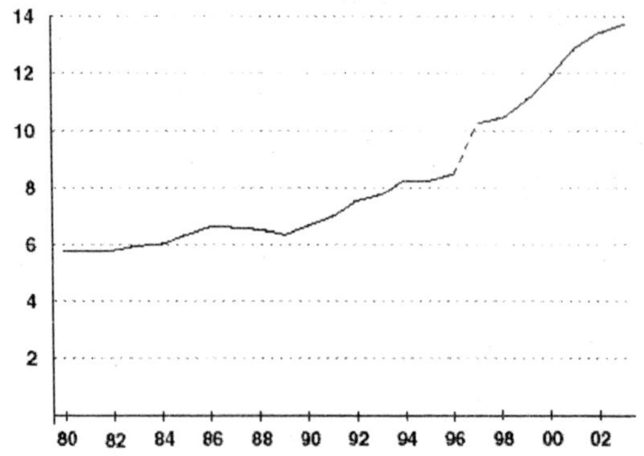

Figure 5. Prevalence of diabetes in the United States (millions).

Now there is a financial objective in this case: to limit the cost of treating diabetes and the various unpleasant illnesses that it can cause. The total costs of diabetes in the United States in 2002 were estimated at $132 billion, with $92 billion of that amount in direct medical expenditures and the other $40 billion in indirect costs due to disability and premature mortality. But since those costs flow strongly from the number of people with the complaint, it is entirely reasonable that attention should focus on this nonfinancial indicator.

MANAGEMENT CHALLENGE

We have established that the time path of future performance is central to the concerns of investors in commercial firms, as well as to stakeholders in public policy and nongovernmental organisations. Disappointment with strategic performance defined in these terms is widespread, so it is important to examine the issue in more detail. There are three distinct, but related questions lying behind the issue of how businesses and other organisations perform through time:

— Why has our historical performance followed the time path that it has?

— Where will the path of future performance take us if we carry on as we are?

— How can we improve that future performance?

The first question may not be relevant in every case-a new venture start-up has no history, for example. However, in most cases, history is highly relevant to the likely trajectory of future performance. To see why these three questions are important, and how widely they vary in character between different situations, consider the example of Amazon.com in more detail.

Amazon.com is an outstanding growth story, as the company expanded from the online sale of books by offering an increasingly wide range of other high-value/small-size consumer goods. Since its founding in 1994, the company has promised and delivered growth in its business although, it took until 2002 to translate increasing sales volume and revenue into profitability. So how do our three questions apply to Amazon.com?

Why has our historical performance followed the time-path that it has? Sales have grown strongly as consumer uptake of online purchasing has spread and as Amazon.com has extended its product range and entered new geographic markets. Earnings have bounced back from heavy losses into positive profitability, as early expenditure generated the sales growth and gross profits to more than cover the continuing costs of serving customers' demand.

However, the company's development need not have followed the same path, even if it ended up at the same point in 2005. Figure 6 compares the company's actual record with an alternative, fictional history. In this other world, the answers to the first question would be quite different.

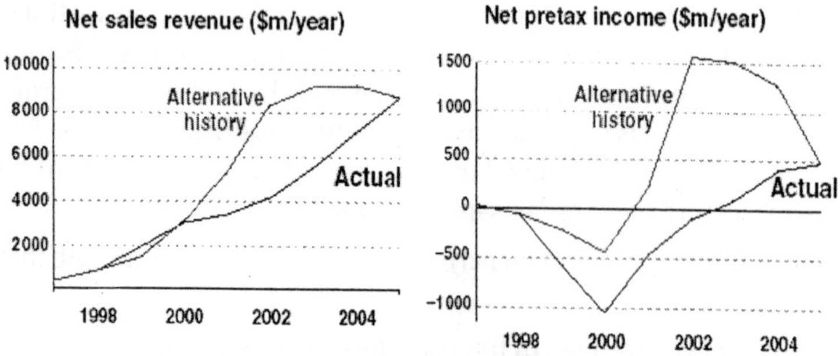

Figure 6. A hypothetical alternative sales and profit history of Amazon. com.

The company might conceivably have grown its revenues still more strongly between 1999 and 2002 than it actually did, due to an even faster penetration of online shopping by consumers or extension of its product range and services. From 2002 to 2005, sales growth could have slowed and reversed, perhaps due to saturation of the potential market, the emergence of strong competitors, or a slowdown in the company's expansion of its offerings.

The alternative income line is more worrying still, and explanations might include reduced margins due to competitive activity, poor cost control, or deliberate increases in spending in an effort to restart growth. Where will the path of future performance take us if we carry on as we are? This second question shows the importance of answering the first. The two alternative histories must imply very different prospects for the future, even though the 2005 endpoint is identical.

Figure 7 extends the time horizon beyond 2005, and offers a plausible future for Amazon.com's sales and profits, given the company's actual history. Sales continue to grow for much the same reasons they have in the past-more consumer use of online shopping and extended coverage by the company of product and geographic markets. As a result, profits continue to grow.

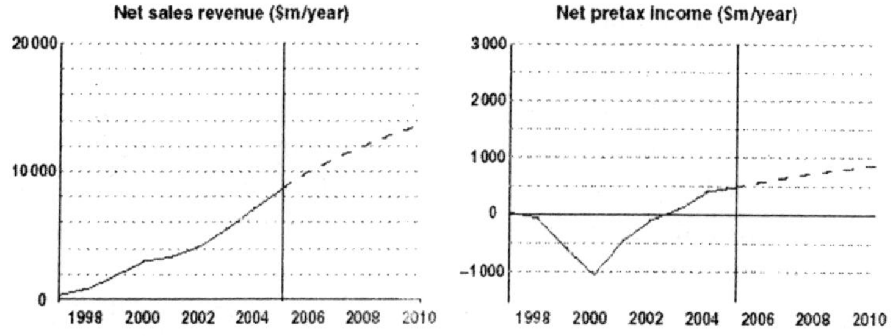

Figure 7. Plausible sales and profit prospects for Amazon. com, reflecting its actual history to 2005.

But the answer to "where might we be heading?" would likely be very different, had the alternative history occurred. Now we are worried that the slowdown in sales could become a serious downturn, especially if the recent history had reflected progress by powerful rivals. If this were to come about, the profit forecast could be very disappointing, with the company slipping into losses as it struggles to contain costs that it has built up to support a growing sales rate.

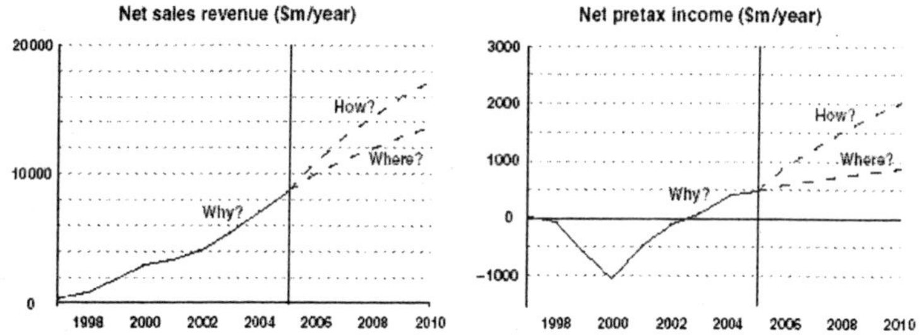

Figure 8. Plausible improvements to sales and profit prospects for Amazon. c om, given its actual performance history.

How can we improve that future performance? Amazon.com's actual history to 2005 offers encouraging prospects for sales and profit growth thereafter, so in reality, answers to this third question focus on pushing growth just a little faster, while not risking damage to the business system that supported its performance to date. Perhaps further product and service development would drive additional growth, and this could plausibly lead to still higher profits (Figure 8).

The answers to this third question would have appeared very different if the company had reached 2005 by the alternative path. Instead of asking how the firm might safely push for even faster growth, it would instead be worrying about how to stop sales revenue slipping backwards, and then how to restart growth. Such a turn-round would likely be costly, so the time path of recovery might well show an even worse profit performance in the next year or two than the "do nothing" projection.

Setting Appropriate Objectives

Failing to understand these three questions of performance through time can make it difficult for management to determine an appropriate performance goal. Two types of errors are common. Objectives may be set that are completely beyond the scope of the business to accomplish. Alternatively, management may significantly underestimate performance that might be possible, if it were to pursue policies that would allow the business to fulfil its potential.

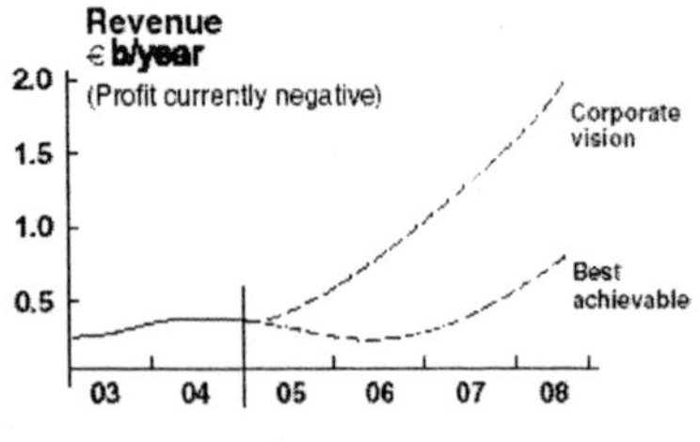

Figure 9. Revenue growth aims in a new market for an IT / communications firm.

Figure 9 shows overlay ambitious targets for an international group in the IT and communications industry that was intent on capitalising on the emerging opportunity for integrating mobile communications with corporate information systems. The opportunity was genuine, very large, and developing rapidly, driven by new technology and the efforts of some large competitors. Top management set a target of multiplying the business fourfold in four years.

Unfortunately, this required three times the number of technical specialists that the company had in its sales and customer support teams. Very few such people existed in the industry and they were in high demand. It would take at least two years to develop existing staff, and the business was declining rather than growing. The goal was entirely unrealistic. It is important not to confuse this error with the setting of "stretching" goals, which can energise an organisation toward what may appear a daunting ambition.

Companies frequently establish a future vision and most standard strategy texts offer examples of vision or mission statements that set the tone for an organisation's progress toward outstanding achievements. However, that is not what is being described here, which is a specific financial target that clearly cannot be hit due to the basic physics of the business system. Setting targets like this destroys credibility in any vision that management may articulate, undermining, rather than assisting in its achievement.

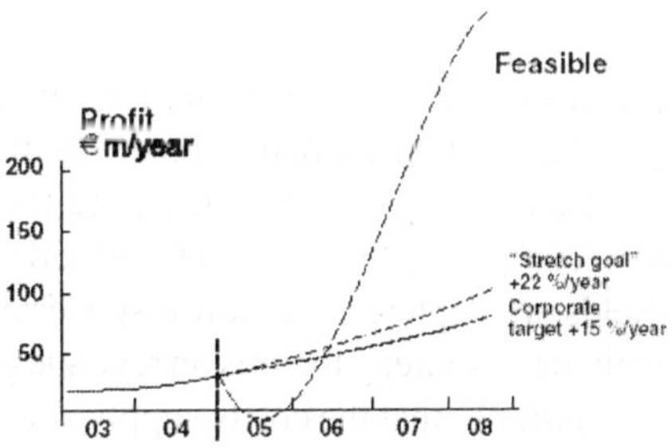

Figure 10. Profit growth opportunity for the East European credit card business of a major bank.

The contrasting case in Figure 10 concerns the credit card business of an East European bank. The firm had an overall corporate goal to achieve 15 % annual growth in profits. Given the attractive opportunity in the market, it set a "stretch goal" of 22 % growth. On examination, it became clear that the opportunity was already many times greater than this bank or its rivals had appreciated. None had assembled the resources or capacity to develop the opportunity nor had they undertaken the necessary marketing to capture the potential. This division could readily multiply profits by many times over the next few years, provided that it immediately committed sufficient resources.

Measurement of Financial Ratios

It also pointed out that financial ratios can be easily manipulated in the short term, to the detriment of future profits. In general, then, when looking at strategy, management should be giving higher priority to how profits will grow over time, rather than to these ratios. This is not to say that financial ratios are unimportant. If they are not healthy, or cannot be expected to move to healthy levels, then management will not be able to deliver on its strategy goals.

Nevertheless, we argue strongly that management should switch from being driven by financial ratios to taking control of the absolute scale of financial results. This implies that profit margin, return on capital or any other financial ratio should never be chosen as the metric on these performance-over-time charts. Instead, the charts should be populated with absolute values of profits or revenues, or with absolute values of business activity, such as sales volume or factors that drive that activity.

In many businesses, customer numbers are an obvious choice. Certain sectors have rather particular business drivers. Construction companies, for example, need to anticipate the number of future projects and oil companies focus on how their oil reserves will change as existing fields are depleted and new discoveries are made. Care is needed, though, if the strategy focus is on revenue growth or its drivers. This implicitly assumes that the costly supply side of the business will be fine-that it will be soundly developed to be affordable and sufficient to win and support revenue aspirations.

If this might not be the case then attention should probably be moved to the revenue and cost prospects, i.e. to likely profit results. In nonbusiness cases, too, a natural starting place is with likely future activity rate, or with the factor that drives that activity-e.g. the number of diabetes sufferers mentioned above, which drives activity rates for various medical services. Voluntary organisations supporting disadvantaged groups will focus on the likely future rate of demand for their services, driven by the number of people served.

Police and armed forces will be concerned with the likely rates of criminal or hostile activity and therefore with the numbers of criminals or enemy forces driving those rates. Again, this is not to say that financial viability is unimportant or that financial ratios should not be tracked to ensure an organisation's viability. However, this is not the strategic focus-an organisation's financial health should serve its purpose, rather than being its master.

Market Share

In some industries, management is focused-sometimes seemingly obsessed-with market share. There are a number of problems with this measure as a basis for strategy.

- First there is the rather simple point that you will enjoy larger sales with 25 % of a $100 million/year market than with 50 % of a market that is only $ 20million/year in total.
- Secondly, market share is merely a coincidental ratio between sales and the total market, so a company has no decision levers that connect directly to this ratio. It is sales that any decisions or policies will affect-by winning customers and persuading them to buy more. The same applies to your competitors, so when you track market share, you are mixing up the consequences of both your own choices and those of your rivals.
- Thirdly, seemingly small movements in market share can disguise big underlying changes. This may delude management into thinking nothing much is happening and that nothing much can happen.

In the case of a mature pain-relief product, market shares were changing very little while, in relation to the company's sales rate, many new customers were acquired and others lost. A new focus on reducing customer loss rates highlighted the potential for real sales growth that the company had not seen for years. Market share did increase as a result of developing a clear picture of how sales might grow, but no amount of attention to this ratio, or the tiny fractions by which it had changed from year to year, revealed anything useful about what the company should do.

A competitor's achievements or failings also contain important information-such as successful acquisition of new customers or the failure of a marketing campaign to boost customer purchases. Your market share may have gone up or down by a percentage point or two during a particular year, while a large competitor has lost 20 % and a new rival has won a significant share. Both those changes contain much more useful information than the marginal shift in your own situation. Your strategy should incorporate learning from the things that the new rival is doing and avoiding whatever difficulties the loser experienced.

Percentage Growth Rates

The growth rate for a market or business is another common indicator that can be highly misleading. Again there is the simple observation that 10 % growth in a $100 m market is more actual business than 50 % growth in a $10 m market. The limited relevance of this percentage measure is highlighted particularly as new markets emerge or new businesses develop.

At some point in their history, Skype and Amazon.com alike probably hit a level for their customer base that was three times the previous year, so their growth rates were 200 % per year. However, this percentage contains no useful information.

Absolute numbers, on the other hand, are critical-specifically, the number of new customers and their future revenue potential. When markets are developing, market growth rates and market share measures both mislead management into ignoring the potential customers, sales and profits that will become available as this potential develops. This has led to the sound suggestion that "opportunity share" is a better issue to track. Skype's market share of the 2005 VoIP telephony demand was much less significant to its future prospects than was the fraction of potential demand that it had captured.

The importance of opportunity share is not limited to new technology industries. In 2004, the Chinese insurance market was worth 150 bn yuan ($18 bn) and growing at a reasonable, if not spectacular, rate. As China opens its markets to foreign participation, large insurance companies are scrambling to grab a share, often by acquiring local distributors.

The real prize, however, lies with the vast numbers of customers who are currently uninsured but likely to become available as income levels rise. Ill-advised attention to current market share is leading some to sign up poor quality business, where salespeople move from firm to firm, taking their clients' business with them.

Benchmarking

Something of an industry has grown up for research organisations that survey firms in a sector and sell back to them anonymous performance rankings for all the firms on various measures. Individual companies can then compare their performance on a specific issue with "benchmarks"-the best performance to be found among their competitors.

Benchmarking may help to ensure firms are with the pace on key measures of operating performance, like quality levels and productivity. This may be fine when you are comparing like with like, for example car makers with similar product ranges, but it can be dangerous when firms are operating with significant differences.

One oil company participated in a benchmarking study that included comparisons of maintenance spending. This company's expenditure per unit of production was somewhat greater than the "best in class", and the gap represented huge potential savings. Sure enough, by pursuing this benchmark, costs were reduced and profits boosted-for a while. Five years later, the company's equipment was in such a poor state that breakdowns and emergency repairs soared.

There were even worries about safety being compromised. Spending had to be raised far above the original rates just to stop things from continuing to decline. Even if you are comparing yourself with similar competitors, the danger is that the allegedly best-in-class competitor may itself be making a mistake.

Multiple and Conflicting Objectives

Most organisations discover that it can be risky to focus on one performance measure alone. Pursuing profit growth might be achieved at the expense of losing sales and market share, if it is achieved by raising prices, which could lead to losing customers. Consequently, many companies have an eye on both profits and sales volume (or less advisedly, market share). Conversely, some companies focus on market share believing that profitability will follow.

This assumption received strong support from research in the 1960s and 1970s, which seemed to show that firms with higher market shares were typically more profitable than firms with less. This encouraged many companies to pursue increased share at almost any cost, neglecting the true reasons why larger firms were more profitable. While the correlation may have been statistically significant, it did not follow that market share caused profitability.

More successful firms generally had better strategies and management of their operations, resulting in both growing sales volume and profitability. Few firms today pursue profitability or sales growth alone-or any other single measure. Most pursue a balance between these two items, and often more, recognising that it would be foolish to ignore the factors necessary for the sustained health of the business. Those factors often include "soft" issues, such as reputation, service quality or product appeal.

The observation that firms need to track and manage performance on multiple dimensions has led to the widespread adoption of "balanced scorecard" systems, which lay out a range of mutually consistent performance measures covering customer-related, organisational, financial and operational factors.

In practice, organisations cannot avoid simultaneously tracking several measures. Therefore, the analysis of strategy dynamics will always track multiple measures, even when it starts from a single primary indicator of how performance is changing into the future. This will enable management to see how conflicting aims are changing in relation to each other, and to make appropriate trade-offs continually as the future unfolds.

Strategic Timescales

Most examples of performance challenges discussed so far have played out over recognisably strategic timescales-several years at least. However, not all strategic situations have such long-term horizons. The example of Skype already illustrates a situation that is evolving rapidly. For the organisation to simply watch progress from year to year would be far too casual. "Strategic" does not equal "slow!" Even though concern is with future performance, short-term conditions and events can have a big impact on longer term outcomes.

Take the case of a pharmaceuticals company facing an attack by its largest competitor. The general manager of this 250 m/year business unit discovered he had four weeks to prepare for a major competitive onslaught. Why the urgency, and why is this short episode strategically important?

The market in question is travel vaccines, so sales build strongly during the prevacation period of May through June. There are five to six major diseases covered by the available vaccines, such as hepatitis A and B and typhoid. The market in the region where this attack is about to break out is worth approximately 500 m/year and is growing. This company has 50 % of the market, and the major rival has about one-third, with the rest being served by smaller firms.

Both of the large companies have an almost complete range of vaccines, except that this firm has the only vaccine approved for one major disease, a product that generates 50 m/year of the company's revenue and one-third of its profits. The threat arises as the major rival announces its own alternative-a near-identical molecule that has just been approved. Doctors are delighted, because the competitor has a track record of undercutting on price by at least 15 %.

The competitor's salesforce of 50 is excited, because they have long suffered resistance from doctors due to this gap in their product range. Their company inundates the medical journals and doctors' surgeries with advertising and promotional literature. One year ago, this same rival successfully stole 40 % of the company's sales on another product within three months of a similar launch.

While this situation will play out over a few months, it is still a strategic issue. Losing a substantial fraction of this critical market threatens the cash flow that supports the salesforce, R&D and marketing expenditure. Failure will demoralise the company's salesforce, and encourage many to leave-most likely to the competitor! The company has historically sustained higher prices by offering better customer support, but this is costly, and the price premium that funds this service is threatened by the competitor's low-price positioning. Overall, this single episode could be the start of an unstoppable decline for the whole division.

As things turned out, this company was able to fend off the attack by its competitor without even having to reduce prices. The defence included exploiting inaccuracies in the competitor's claims for its product, loading the doctors' inventory with their own product, and undermining the morale of the competitor's salesforce and their commitment to the new product.

Even though many organisations operate in environments that move quickly, senior management is still surprisingly committed to annual planning systems that have no capacity to respond to such rapid changes. Budgets are set, say, in December for the coming 12 months and managers are held to those numbers regardless of unforeseen events. This results in errors of two kinds.

As the year progresses, unforeseen difficulties arise-a competitor launches a better product for example-but the company still carries on as though the original sales target for the year was correct. Alternatively, things may turn out better than expected-perhaps customer adoption accelerates well ahead of forecast-but sales and marketing budgets that were chosen on much more cautious assumptions are immovable.

Aim of Performance

The Amason.com example features the pleasant challenge of sustaining growth that is already strong. Not all organisations are so fortunate as to be concerned only with how quickly they can keep growing.

Stability

Many firms, particularly in developed economies, operate in markets that long ago went "ex-growth", with every customer who might be interested in taking the product or service already doing so. Examples include utilities such as power or water supply, fast-moving consumer goods (FMCG) such as cleaning materials or food and drink products, and well-established services such as hairdressing. There i a difficult balance to achieve in such cases.

On the one hand, operating in a low-growth or no-growth market is not sufficient reason to assume that no growth is possible. On the other hand, efforts to pursue growth that are not realistically attainable can be badly damaging. One pcssibility for driving growth in mature markets is to challenge the reasons that are assumed to be preventing growth. This occurred in the cinema industry in the 1970s. Until then, it had been widely assumed that movie going was doomed by the growth of TV and other home entertainment.

Investment by film studios led to a stream of new, big-budget movies, and cinema operators developed much improved cinemas, which brought the industry back into growth. Even if the industry is irretrievably mature, growth in sales and profits can often be taken from competitors or substitutes. Firms in such markets are often satisfied to take small points of market share from their competitors and, if sustained over a long enough period, such creeping progress can indeed lead to a significant change.

However, more substantial performance may be possible, as the earlier example of the pain-relief product shows. For this brand, simply slowing the churn rate among consumers would allow sales to grow, which could be achieved with a more focused marketing strategy than previously employed. As a result, the renewed sales growth could be initiated with a reduced marketing budget, leading to a disproportionate increase in profits.

While it is important to seek opportunities for profitable growth in low growth industries, it is also essential to avoid pursuing growth that will damage the business. One company that encountered this danger at least once in its history is McDonald's. In spite of declaring a lower target for earnings growth, the net income of McDonald's actually rose from $893 m in 2002 to $1 471 m in 2003 and $2 279 in 2004. Nor did it take long for investors to recognise the realism of this new strategic focus.

The stock price, which had fallen from over $29 to $15 by the end of 2002, recovered to $24 by the end of 2003 and climbed to $34 by late 2005. All of these activities occurred during a time of immense pressure on the company from public concern with the health effects of its products. Blockbuster Inc., the global rental store chain for in-home movies and games, also has to sustain performance in mature markets.

The company boasts more than 9 000 stores throughout the Americas, Europe, Asia and Australia. It built its business by renting videos during the boom in consumer purchases of video recorders in the 1990s. Although it has since moved on to renting out DVD films and video games, it is constantly threatened by substitutes for its service, such as the increasingly wide range of movie transmissions by cable and satellite TV, or postal distribution of rental DVDs from the likes of Netflix and Amazon.com.

Growth-to-Maturity Transition

The contrast between the strategic imperative facing firms in high-growth markets and those in more mature sectors comes into sharp focus when industries move rapidly from growth to maturity. Management has to switch from driving exploitation of the emerging opportunity to conserving what has been accomplished and extracting sustainable value into the future. The cellphone industry exhibits this transition clearly.

As markets developed, cellphone operating companies engaged in a race to sign up new subscribers, offering generous handset subsidies and reseller incentives. However, as penetration of cellphone ownership approached 100 %, marketing strategies began to demonstrate a significant shift.

First, operating companies tried to persuade subscribers to switch from competitors' services to their own. It did not take long, though, for cellphone operators to realise that stealing each others' customers was ultimately a zero-sum game. With the costs of signing up a new subscriber often more than the full-year income that each might generate, with usage charges falling and with churn rates (the fraction of customers leaving each year) hitting 25 % or more, the financial case for such ferocious competitive efforts quickly became marginal.

Most recently, then, the marketing efforts of major operators such as Vodafone and Verizon Wireless have changed once again. They now focus on raising usage by existing subscribers, both for phone calls and for additional services, rather than on enticing subscribers to switch. Not all companies recognise this need to change strategy as growth slows. The dotcom boom of the late 1990s saw many casualties of this error, one example being Exodus Inc., a provider of Web site hosting and related services.

The company persisted in employing large numbers of people and spending large amounts of money despite industry research showing that the remaining potential for its services was approaching zero. The cooling love affair with everything e-based in 2000 saw the demise of some of its main customers and this, combined with the company's relative inattention to supporting its existing customers, raised customer churn to a rate that matched its win rate.

The cost of pursuing unachievable growth quickly overwhelmed the company's revenues, leading to a collapse in earnings, and the bankruptcy that ended its existence as an independent entity. The United Kingdom satellite broadcasting company, British Sky Broadcasting PLC, is another firm facing the challenge of this growth to-maturity transition. As its name implies, the company broadcasts digital TV from satellite, and offers a very wide range of channels for viewers who subscribe to its service.

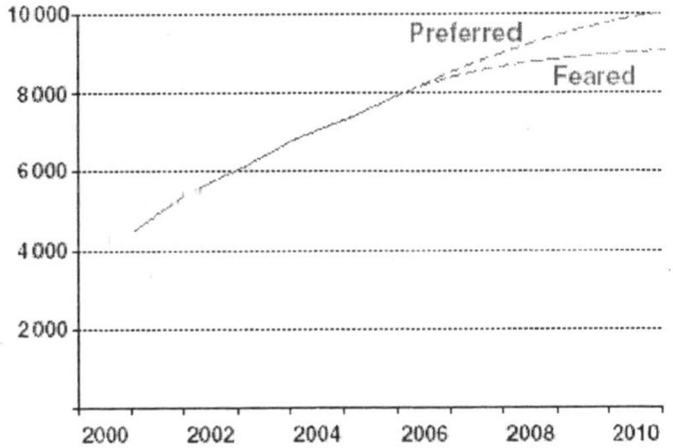

Figure 11. Subscribers to BSkyB at year end.

The uptake of this service grew strongly from 4.5 million at the end of 2000 to 8 million at the end of 2005 (Figure 11). With a total of 26 million homes, the market appeared still to offer ample opportunity for further growth, especially since, unlike in the United States, penetration of cable TV was low (3.8 million) and showing little growth. The company therefore committed to still higher penetration, promising investors that it would acquire 10 million subscribers by 2010.

Unfortunately, reaching this objective presented a number of challenges. First, 2005 saw the strongest growth yet in penetration of "Freeview" services-digital TV broadcast direct-to-home (DTH) from terrestrial transmitters, provided free of charge, though with a limited range of channels. Viewers of this service hit 4.6 million in 2005, an increase of over 1.5 million from the previous year. At the same time, churn rates amongst Sky's own subscribers continued rising, exceeding 11 % or nearly 0.9 million per year. Nevertheless, the company persisted in its growth efforts, with costly increases in marketing spend and discounting of its services. The curious feature of this situation is that no one actually asked the company to make the promise in the first place.

Notice that Figure 11, like the chart for the vaccine's sales above, shows two alternative outcomes-a "preferred" projection, which reflects how management would like to see the future turn out, and a "feared" view of what might happen if things do not work out. This pair of projections is not simply a comparison between high and low growth. Notice, for example, that the feared future starts out on much the same trajectory as the preferred.

Rather, each projection depicts a coherent story of plausible events. In this case, the preferred forecast arises if viewers are slow to take-up the Freeview alternative, leaving plenty of potential for Sky to win new subscribers. In the feared alternative, take-up of Freeview is rapid, so although Sky initially keeps winning new subscribers who really want the full range of channels, the remaining potential quickly drops, so that the rate of new subscribers soon approaches zero.

Decline

Other firms find themselves facing conditions that are still more challenging than mere maturity in their industry-some sectors experience inexorable decline. The people who head such organisations are rarely recognised with the heroic status accorded to leaders of exciting growth businesses. Yet any success they achieve is no less important to their investors, and often requires considerable skill and determination. A current example concerns the switch from photo-film to digital cameras.

According to PMA Marketing Research, consumer photographic print volumes in the United States fell from about 30 billion in 2000 to less than 19 billion by 2005, as uptake of digital cameras made the use of traditional photo film increasingly obsolete.

Retail travel stores face a tough time as travellers switch to the online purchase of holidays and other travel, and newspapers face declining advertising revenues as advertisers switch marketing budgets to online channels. Not all such challenges are driven by changes in technology, however.

Firms in the European defence industry faced dramatic falls in demand for military hardware following the collapse of the former Soviet Union. The pain of industry decline need not, however, be equally shared by all. Strong strategic management enables businesses to thrive at the expense of their competitors. Even as the switch to digital photography began to bite between 2000 and 2003, Kodak's arch rival Fuji captured market share, worsening Kodak's difficulties.

In the European defence industry, BAE Systems PLC saw revenues rise between 2000 and 2004 from £12.2bn to £13.5bn as its strategy took business away from weaker rivals. In many cases industries see widespread rationalisation as those weaker participants close down or sell out to the stronger survivors. This is further evidence that there can be substantial strategic opportunity in apparently difficult industry conditions

We should not leave the issue of performance in declining situations without a word about organisations whose purpose is in effective to accelerate decline, even to the point of putting themselves out of business. Many voluntary organisations aim to eliminate some hardship or problem, such as reducing homelessness, drug use or domestic violence. "Success" for such organisations would mean achieving zero rates for their key indicators of harm, at which point the organisation's purpose would cease.

Many public sector and nongovernmental organisations also recognise success in terms of eliminating the need for their work. In December 2005, the United Nations (UN) was able to announce the conclusion of one of its largest missions ever to eliminate civil conflict, as it planned the withdrawal from Sierra Leone of the last of its peacekeepers-a force that had once numbered 17 500. The force had been deployed in 1999 to restore government control and to disarm and demobilise fighters.

The UN's intervention was prompted by a further escalation in an eight-year conflict that had killed 20 000 and left thousands more badly injured. Essentially, the "performance objective" was to reduce to zero the rate of deaths and injuries (Figure 12). Note that this chart again makes explicit both a preferred and feared future from the point in time at which the situation is being assessed, each of which reflects plausible story of how the future may develop.

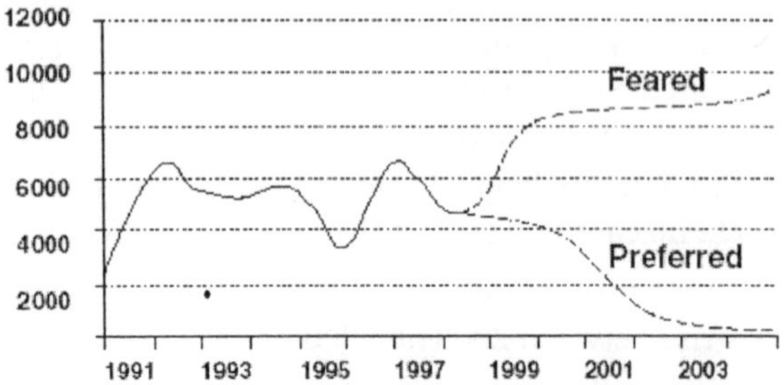

Figure 12. The estimated number of deaths and serious injuries from civil conflict in Sierra Leone.

Fulfilling those aims had not been without difficulties. In early 2000, more than 700 UN peacekeepers were abducted and later that year 11 British troops were taken hostage by the militia group, the West Side Boys. This event, however, prompted a sweeping rescue operation that all but eliminated that militia, sending a powerful signal that the UN force was serious about its intent. Over the subsequent five years, 72 000 combatants were disarmed and demobilised, and over 30 000 arms were destroyed. By 2002, the major conflict was effectively over, with virtually no casualties being reported.

Functional Performance Objectives

Concern with improving performance over time is not limited to organisations' overall strategic aims, but may also arise on issues concerning just a part of the organisation-staffing, marketing, product development, information systems, etc. Success in these specific functional areas may support a wider improvement in overall performance, but they often deserve attention in their own right.

Among the cases we have already discussed are some that naturally present challenges for the sales and marketing functions-growth in subscribers for BSkyB and sales for the painkiller, for example. In others, sales and marketing clearly have a major role to play, such as McDonald's recovery in earnings. Time charts for sales volume and revenue are an essential starting point for any strategy intended to improve these performance indicators.

In many cases, this may be the major focus for improving profits, provided we can be confident that the cost elements are well managed. Sales growth is not always an appropriate aim, and in some cases can even be a major error.

As the Exodus Inc. case illustrates, many organisations may be better advised to hold on to good quality business-larger, high-value customers who generate high rates of gross profit, while being readily supported by affordable sales and service capacity-rather than scavenging for any growth they can find, regardless of whether it can be translated into profitable business.

Even when sales growth is the correct objective, it can be a mistake to leave all such problems at the door of the salesforce or marketing department. A number of failings in other functional areas of the business can compromise sales success-poor product quality or lack of capacity in production and distribution can undermine otherwise successful sales effort.

It is also important to remember that sales growth is not only the result of what has been won, but reflects what has been lost too. Poor service quality can cause customers to leave, including even such apparently trivial issues as poor management of cash receivables in the accounting function.

Staffing Difficulties

The earlier telecom company example has already shown how staffing difficulties alone can undermine achievement of otherwise quite plausible objectives. That company needed to develop a strategy to initiate and sustain rapid growth in the specialist staff it required. Staffing challenges are common sources of difficulty, and can be quite difficult to solve.

A sound strategy for staff development can be particularly tough when business relies on highly skilled people, such as in consulting companies, law firms and other professional service organisations. One mid-size law firm had grown successfully, providing specialist services to medium- to large-sized companies. Its reputation with the clients it had won over previous years was such that it was constantly being asked to do more for those clients, so had little need to seek new ones.

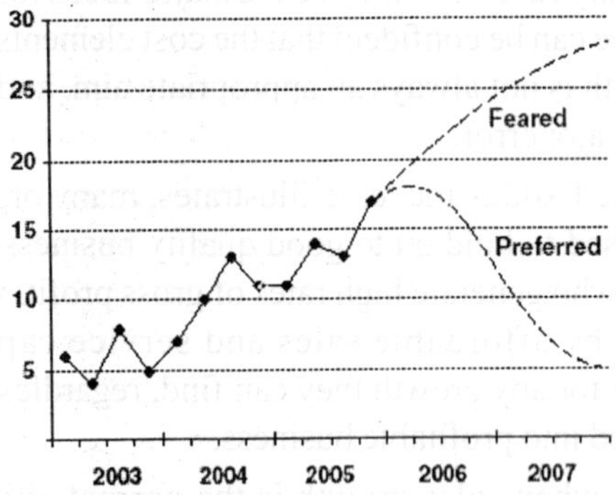

Figure 13. Quarterly staff losses at a mid-size law firm.

The firm found itself losing talented people, which made it increasingly difficult to serve its clients' rising demands (Figure 13). Staff losses were concentrated amongst lawyers with 5-10 years' experience. This amplified the problem, since this group carried the burden of leading the work for client projects. Shortages at this level threatened the firm's ability to undertake work that had been sold by partners, or to complete that work to a high standard.

This risked damaging established client relationships, ultimately threatening a fall in the firm's revenues, rather than furthering the growth it sought. Ironically, the cause of this trouble was the firm's growth in the four to five years before 2003. A large number of young lawyers joined during this time and quickly progressed through to senior partner positions by winning new client relationships. They were well rewarded, so had no reason to move on at that time.

Exit interviews with the lawyers who were leaving suggested two problems. First, they were overburdened with the increasing volume of work coming from clients. Normally, such professionals put up with this pressure for the promise of substantial rewards when they achieve partner level. However, the second reason given was that they faced the prospect of being stuck at their grade, with limited opportunities to progress to partnership themselves.

With little chance of progress, these talented people were choosing to pursue their careers elsewhere, leaving those who had joined the firm earlier and had reached more senior positions to cope with the client work themselves, which increased further the work pressure. To take a more positive example, progressive improvements in staffing issues can be powerful drivers of performance. Not many people may know of Yum! Brands Inc., but they do know of the Kentucky Fried Chicken, Pizza Hut, and Taco Bell chains the company owns.

Spun off from PepsiCo in 1997, Yum!'s management appreciated that treating its franchisees and staff well was vital if those people were to keep customers happy. By 2005, US restaurant employees were on average staying 12 months with the company, far longer than is typical for the industry. Not all staff challenges are about obtaining the resources needed to drive growth. It is not often appreciated that a management hierarchy is a powerful system for "breeding" growth. As young people are brought in at junior ranks, others expect to be promoted to middle management.

Existing middle managers hope for senior positions and ambitious senior people want the top jobs. Since there can be many times more people at any level than at the level above, only a small fraction can expect a promotion in any year. For example, if there are 1 000 juniors and 100 middle managers, of which only 20 per year are leaving or being promoted, then only 2 % of juniors can hope for promotion in any year.

There are only two solutions to this problem-either the organisation must be growing (just 5 % growth per year means that 7 % of juniors can be promoted in this example), or else senior people must be moved out to make space for juniors. The flatter the organisation, and the wider the span of control from one level of seniority to the next level, the more serious this issue becomes. Certain additional factors can worsen this need to speed up the turnover of staff.

In 2004, one large United States financial institution had the laudable aim to increase the proportion of people-of-colour and disadvantaged staff amongst its senior management from 60, or 6 % of that rank, to 200 by 2008. Turnover amongst senior people was running at less than 5 % per annum, and there were few experienced minority staff in the pipeline, so unless something else could be changed, the entirely well-intentioned objective could not possibly be met.

This would be very serious for the company's reputation, causing potentially considerable damage to its future hiring needs, and even to its business revenues. Incidentally, this challenge is dwarfed by that facing some South African businesses, where regulations require representation among all management grades for people-of-colour to reach levels representative of the population as a whole within just a few years.

Product Development

Major drugs companies provide a good example of how serious time-based challenges can be in research and development programmes (R&D). These firms have grown to their present scale over several decades, on the back of a stream of major drug discoveries-highly effective treatments for widespread and costly ailments, such as heart disease, stomach ulcers, and depression. These so-called "blockbuster" drugs, with annual sales of $1bn, are so critical that firms pursue enormous R&D investments in an effort to discover more such drugs.

The imperative to discover big revenue products is intensified by the limited patent life for drugs, which means that high prices and revenues can only be sustained for a limited number of years before sales are decimated by low-price generic products-essentially the same product, but without the brand name. For these firms, the performance over time of concern is the rate of new product introductions that offer a high potential revenue stream.

Unfortunately, having successfully developed drugs to treat the most widespread complaints through the 1980s and 1990s, companies are left only with complaints that are suffered by fewer people in developed economies, or more complex complaints for which wonder drugs are harder to find. Controversially, the last large-scale opportunities for disease treatment are concentrated among the population of the world's poorest countries.

This has led to accusations that drug firms are ignoring the needs of the poor due to their inability to pay the high prices needed to justify the large R&D costs involved. In other industries, firms have found ways of serving the poor profitably, an aim that many pharmaceuticals firms also pursue.

Capacity

Time-based challenges frequently arise in the building of capacity, whether for production, distribution or service. Retailers of all kinds face this challenge-"capacity" in their case consisting of retail stores. We have already seen in McDonald's an example of such a company running out of good quality locations where they can expect strong incremental sales.

Supermarket chains such as Wal-Mart in the United States, Tesco in the United Kingdom or Japan's Daiei also used up the best locations long ago and must work hard for new opportunities, either developing novel retail formats that can reach smaller markets, or else switching to emerging markets.

Manufacturing capacity can also pose strategic challenges. Roche Diagnostics is a major global producer of blood test meters for diabetics, under the Accu-Chek brand. Numbers of people with this disease are very large and growing quickly, although only a fraction of these are severe enough to need blood meters. During 2004-5, the company introduced two new products, which it hoped would extend the brand's uptake amongst meter users.

In addition, the company's existing meter users would likely want the new products, since machines typically last just three years, and users are naturally interested in having the latest model. Since nothing exactly similar had occurred in the market before, at least on such a scale, the company faced great uncertainty regarding the likely rate of uptake for the meters, and therefore the capacity required to fulfil that demand.

Neither the replacement rate amongst existing Accu-Chek users nor the penetration rate among new users could be known exactly before the launch. The problem was exacerbated by uncertainty as to whether the two new products should be launched simultaneously and at the same time in many countries, or staggered over several quarters and different geographic markets. This uncertainty posed a tricky question about how much production capacity to build for the new products-should initial capacity be sufficient to fulfil the highest likely rate of uptake, or be limited, leaving further expansion to be deferred until uptake rates became clear?

If the latter course were adopted, what might be the value of potential sales that would be lost through inability to supply? Furthermore, what competitive risk might this pose that sales might be taken by the company's arch-rival, Johnson & Johnson, and other competitors? Firms facing similar decisions risk making a subtle, but important strategic error.

The business case for building higher or lower levels of capacity may take reasonable account of the medium-term trade-off between the higher cost of building plenty of capacity versus the loss of sales and profits from building too little.

However, this is not the end of the story, since underprovision creates a serious strategic threat-in this case, the risk of medical advisors, retailers and end users all switching their allegiance to rival products. This would threaten not only immediate sales, but longer term business too. Yet such consequences are rarely factored adequately into such decisions for fear of missing quarterly earnings targets.

Another example requiring a strategy for capacity growth, this time from a public policy perspective, concerns the provision of biodiesel-an environmentally attractive alternative to diesel produced from petroleum. Although diesel is not a popular fuel for cars in the United States, it is widely used in Europe and elsewhere, and could potentially switch a large fraction of overall fuel consumption onto renewable sources.

Oil from crops, such as rape seed, and even old cooking oil, can easily be converted to motor diesel. It is already technically feasible for mid-scale diesel users, such as taxi firms, to operate their own small conversion plants. Since the technology is feasible and environmental benefits are so clear, why has this system of biodiesel production not swept the industry? Unfortunately, powerful forces are holding back growth in capacity. First, whilst purchase and use of a conversion plant may make economic sense at a particular point in time, fuel prices are volatile, driven both by the global supply-demand for petroleum and the short-term supply-demand balance for particular fuels. Unless tax policy is heavily skewed in favour of the new product, this uncertainty will likely continue, which makes investment in conversion facilities risky.

The constraint on capacity is worsened by the impact of the same uncertainties for farmers who may be considering switching acreage on their farms to oil-producing crops. While they might see a good price for such crops in one particular year, these farmers cannot be sure when they are sowing crops that the same conditions will apply when it comes to harvest time. This adds further to the uncertainty facing firms wondering whether to install conversion capacity.

Equivalent issues apply to the addition of crop-based ethanol to gasoline in the United States and other markets. For a government committed to raising the adoption of biofuel, a time chart of "the issue" would feature the historic growth in capacity, the likely future of capacity growth under current policies, and an alternative higher growth aspiration.

Functional challenges often need to be examined over short timescales. In fashion retailing, for example, the success of new product introductions is fundamental to the appeal of a store's overall product range. One such company operated a fast-test policy, in which it would test new product lines in selected stores for just two to three weeks before deciding whether to order large quantities for the whole chain.

The company took on a new senior executive with much experience in the sector, who made a number of changes, such as reallocating floor space amongst product categories, and switching key product ranges to new suppliers because of better supply prices. Within weeks of these changes, the fraction of test products making the transition from trial to the core product range had fallen from 0.8 to 0.6.

The company faced a tough decision. It could try to reverse the changes, although it could not be certain which were most harmful, or whether some might, on their own, have been successful. They could also not be certain that all the original suppliers would be able to respond. Again, though, why is such a short-term issue "strategic"?

This seemingly isolated error hits several parts of the business. First, in addition to failing in the eyes of consumers, the changes led to the loss of other staff in the buying and merchandising group. Without these people, the company could not be certain of reestablishing good performance on this important issue.

The reduced appeal of products sourced under the new arrangements also meant that those items that did make it to the core range suffered a faster fall-off in sales. Consequently, while discounted products previously featured little in the company's stores, these came to represent a large fraction of both floor space and sales. Having previously been known for its highappeal clothing, on which it could sustain high margins, consumers quickly came to associate the company with cheap goods at discount prices, making it difficult to reverse the changes.

The particular market segment this company served is viciously competitive, with several similar chains fighting it out in most shopping areas. This company's loss of position was quickly captured by rivals. Finally, if these problems were to continue for any length of time, they would make many of the stores uneconomic, resulting in closure and further loss of revenue and profit.

Support Functions

A focus on performance over time is also a good starting point for functional departments whose primary role is to support other groups. Common examples arise in departments that provide information systems and finance/accounting services. Sometimes such groups are run as profit centers-"selling" their services to other departments, to generate revenue, and managing their resources (largely people and equipment) to deliver adequate service at sufficiently low cost to make a "profit."

In other cases, these services are outsourced to independent firms, such as EDS Inc., CSC Inc. or providers from low-cost economies such as India, China or Eastern Europe. When these functions are operated wholly or partly in house, their leadership is concerned with future levels of activity and providing the necessary resources to serve that activity. A starting point for establishing and running their strategy will be a time chart of projected activity rates and capacity, measured perhaps in full-time equivalent people, or person-hours per month.

Simply running the service for their customers is not the whole story for internal service functions. Such groups have the equivalent of a company's "product range." This means they have to be concerned with product development, i.e. creating new services that the business may require. They may also offer project-based services to other parts of the business, creating the equivalent of an internal consultancy group.

All such tasks add to the "demand" on their capacity, and ensuring that these tasks will be well implemented requires a time chart of expected future project numbers and the labour requirement these will bring.

Customer satisfaction is another factor that internal service functions share with businesses. In the case of business customers, poor service can lead to such customers deciding to switch to competitors. This is not necessarily so easy for internal users of service functions, but service department management is nonetheless keen to keep service quality high.

Any drop can result in removal of support by their users for any spending they may need to make, and in extreme cases, poor service quality can drive internal customers to seek service from third-party suppliers-the equivalent of "losing customers." It is therefore vital for management of these service departments to track service quality over time.

References

Collins, J. and Porras, J., "Building your company's vision", *Harvard Business Review*, **75**(5), 65–72, 1996.

Hamel, G. and Prahalad, C.K., *Competing for the Future*, Harvard Business School Press, Boston MA, Chapter 2, 1994.

Jones, A.P., Homer, J.B., Murphy, D.L., *et al.*, "Understanding diabetes: population dynamics through simulation modeling and experimentation", *American Journal of Public Health*, 96(3), 488–494, 2006.

Kaplan, R. and Norton, D., *The Balanced Scorecard*, Harvard Business School Press, Boston MA, 1996.

Mankins, M.C. and Steele, R., "Stop making plans: start making decisions", *Harvard Business Review*, 84(1), 76–84, 2006.

Martin, J.D. and Petty, J.W., *Value-based Management*, Harvard Business School Press, Boston MA, 2000.

Penrose, E.T., *The Theory of the Growth of the Firm*, Oxford University Press, Oxford, 1959.

Prahalad, C.K. and Hammond, A., "Serving the World's poor", profi tably. *Harvard Business Review*, 80(9), 48–57, 2002.

Rappaport, A., "Ten ways to create shareholder value", *Harvard Business Review*, 84(9), 66–77, 2006.

13

Strategic Planning and Corporate Evolution

The long-range planning activities pursued since the mid-1990s represent a departure from the Air Force's routines for visioning and planning in two major respects. First, earlier planning usually focused on the development of technical systems, mostly connected with military operational issues and research and development, and downplayed other dimensions of the organization's technological capability, such as human knowledge and skills, managerial systems, and norms and values.

Second, the recent long-range planning activities have opened up issues that were previously regarded as settled matters, in particular whether the core technological capability of the Air Force should continue to be the application of military force by landbased fixed-wing aircraft flown by Air Force pilots. Raising this question brought into open discussion what some participants called gut issues. These struck at the heart of how the Air Force defines itself and its core activities, and they prompted myriad questions associated with long-range adaptation to new opportunities and challenges.

A central facet of these gut issues was whether the Air Force would be abandoning its birthright if it broadened its core technological capability to include greater use of unmanned aerial vehicles (UAVs) or space-based platforms for weapons and command-and-control systems. Taking the focus off the application of military force by fixed-wing piloted aircraft could conceivably intensify interservice rivalries over what has been the Air Force's turf since 1947.

It might also weaken conventional arguments for maintaining four military services, including the Air Force, if space emerges as a separate domain of national defence. Just as a shift in core technological capabilities could unsettle the division of labour among military services, so too could it upset the status quo within the Air Force itself. Since its creation, the Air Force has construed its core technological capability as applying military force using aircraft flown by highly trained pilots selected from the creme de la creme of a large pool of prospective candidates.

The resulting bias toward aeronautical acuity reached the highest ranks in the service, such that few "nonrated" airmen become generals, much less gain four stars. Even among pilots, a pecking order operates on the basis of the type of aircraft flown. This reflects the old saw that brain surgeons are the fighter pilots of medicine. That is, pilots who fly fighter jets advance to the upper echelons of the Air Force's leadership much more frequently than do those who fly bombers or transports.

In light of these realities, redefining the core technological capabilities of the Air Force could easily transform career expectations and the internal power structure of the institution. After deliberating on these matters in the initial round under General Fogleman's guidance, senior leaders agreed to alter the Air Force's technological capabilities. The ratification of this commitment took the form of a "vision" entitled Global Engagement.

The document identified an array of core competencies, namely, air and space superiority, global attack, rapid global mobility, precision engagement, information superiority, and agile combat support. It also directly addressed the question of institutional identity: specifically, the document stated the intention to become an Air and Space Force enroute to becoming a Space and Air Force.

The subsequent visioning process under General Ryan wrestled with three persistent issues: how to go about reconfiguring programmatic commitments and resources to coincide with intent; how to garner the resources for future programmes while keeping personnel and equipment from breaking down as a result of the punishing tempo of activity necessary to meet demand for real-world operations; and whether the terminology of space and air, whatever the order of the words, simply perpetuates separatist views of the two domains.

Degree of Departure from Previous Approaches

Corporate strategic planning, as pursued by the Air Force since the mid- 1990s, fits broadly within the spectrum of executive entrepreneurship. It emerged at a time in which leaders in government agencies-both political appointees and career officials-had come under the influence of a spirit of reinvention. This movement, which originated in the private sector and was expanded to encompass public service management, sought to foster organisational excellence by encouraging innovation.

It received exceptionally strong backing during the Clinton administration through the leadership of the vice president, Al Gore. He masterminded and guided the National Performance Review (NPR) that became the umbrella for the administrative reform movement in the federal government. Not with standing its kinship with the reinvention movement, the Air Force approach clearly went beyond entrepreneurship in a strictly managerial sense. Joel D. Aberbach and Bert A. Rockman assert that NPR focused on efficiency to the almost total exclusion of questions regarding programmatic effectiveness.

The distinction boils down to whether government entrepreneurship is limited to producing better goods and services more cheaply or whether it should consider how such goods and services contribute to public goals such as national security. The Air Force woke up one morning in the mid-1990s to the realisation that it maintained a lot of programmes that contributed little to national security, that things would get worse unless it dramatically shifted resources from activities with poor marginal utility to those showing great promise, and that in any case, it needed a bigger share of the federal budget to fulfil its growing obligations toward national security.

This realisation led to a process of reinvention that exploded the boundaries of managerial entrepreneurship and took the form of a very robust variant of policy entrepreneurship. To be sure, General Fogleman led the ranks in the innovative movement of the mid-1990s.

As chief, he enjoyed an excellent position from which to refine and advocate his view of the future. General Ryan is less a futurist by temperament than Fogleman, but he still considered the process of adaptation initiated by Fogleman as a key Air Force commitment. When he took over as chief of staff, he made a point of stating that he-along with the other four-star generals-had embraced the visioning process that resulted in the Air Force's new vision of its future. However, styling this case study as an examination of individual entrepreneurship-Fogleman's and Ryan's-would miss the point.

The case represents an instance in which an initiative pressed forcefully by a key player took on an organisational reality that transcended the vagaries of personalities. One well-placed and highly regarded respondent whom we interviewed maintains that survival of strategic visioning through the Ryan years provides prima facie evidence of institutionalisation on the grounds that "two points define a line."

The Fogleman-led visioning process that culminated in the fall 1996 Corona conference-a session of the tri-annual meeting of all Air Force four-star generals-was based on having first conceptualised important questions of identity and technological capabilities. The process of strategic planning began with the identification of issues.

The explicit subject matter even at this early stage was the future of the Air Force, not the future of its technical systems, which stood in marked contrast to past planning efforts. That the focus concerned broad service capabilities rather than narrow technical systems became clear when the sixteen issues were released: they included contentious and potentially intractable matters such as integrating air and space, future space operations, battle management and command and-control operations, unmanned aerial vehicles, and career patterns.

With respect to the latter issue, for example, the 1997 Long-Range Plan affirmed that in the future, "any military or civilian member experienced in the employment and doctrine of air and space power will be considered an operator," whereas previously only pilots were considered "operators" and all others "support." Strictly speaking, the outcome of the Fogleman strategy-formulation process was a declaration of intent, rather than a plan.

The 1997 Long-Range Plan defined the desired future in terms of forty-two "end states" to be attained within the time frame of the 2000-25 planning horizon. For instance, integrating air and space involved four end states: education and training in exploitation of air and space assets in an integrated manner, organisation of the Air Force for integrated operations, harmonising air and space assets in a seamless manner, and establishing the Air Force as the leader in stewardship of the space domain.

The Long-Range Plan stopped short, however, of specifying the exact paths for reaching these end states. Clark Murdock, a key civilian player in the planning process, pressed the view that an end state would prove "sufficiently granular to be actionable." That is, it would make it possible to delineate more or less preferred actions in the near and midterm. It would also exert normative force in decisionmaking processes that have a more direct impact on the evolution of the Air Force's technical systems than does long-range planning.

Murdock frequently incanted the mantra of Air Force programmers regarding planning: "If it ain't in the programme, it ain't." This pithy one-liner became very long-winded indeed in the implementation of the plan-growing more into a book than a single sentence. At the time, however, it captured the determination of many key players to improve the connection between planning and programming.

If one thinks of a plan in terms of a point of origin, a path, and a destination, the 1997 product proved more precise than most plans in its specification of destinations. It was relatively vague, however, on the paths to be travelled from the point of origin to those destinations, especially considering that it was developed by the armed services. Military planners typically thrive on laying out the details of a journey from point A to point B.

The issue of whether the 1997 document actually constitutes a plan may be debatable, but the interviews conducted for this project strongly suggest that the participants in the process believed that they were planning strategically. Rather than engage in a lengthy semantic diversion, we choose here to briefly outline a few of the terms that credibly describe what participants in the Air Force's corporate process thought they were doing. To begin, adjoining strategic to planning adds to the latter's difficulty.

According to Webster's, a plan is "a detailed formulation of a programme of action." The same source characterises a strategy as "an adaptation or complex of adaptations... that serves or appears to serve an important function in achieving evolutionary success." Striving for evolutionary success undoubtedly motivated the Air Force's substantial investment in long-range planning. We therefore see little room to contest the issue of whether the Air Force has been engaged in strategic planning.

A futuristic projection to the year 2025 served as the preamble for the first Long-Range Plan; this was an express departure from the service's convention for such exercises. Visioning, which is what the participants were encouraged to undertake, required vision. Webster's defines vision as "unusual discernment or foresight." These definitional bearings reveal a huge difference between visioning and vision. The former gazes boldly into the future, but the latter is ascribed only when events prove the futurist right.

Strategic planning as pursued by the Air Force during both the Fogleman and Ryan eras involved quintessentially a pooling of the senior leadership's perceptions of the future. These participants devised agreed visions of the opportunities and challenges that the Air Force would face over a long horizon. Only then did the Air Force leadership "backcast" from the visions to their current competencies and capabilities in order to assess the necessary adjustments for the service to prepare for the envisioned future. Third, the Air Force leadership then attempted to distil and gain consensus on the programmatic commitments required for achieving desired adaptations in a timely fashion.

We view this approach, as positioning for opportunities. Writers such as Martha Derthick and Theda Skocpol identify a fairly robust specimen of the same practice in domestic agencies. They identify it most clearly in the manoeuvres of the Social Security Administration (SSA) during the gradual expansion of the contributory social security system from its inception in 1935 to the inclusion of medical provision for the aged in 1965 and the indexation of Social Security pensions in 1972.

Skocpol characterises the SSA leadership as a spearhead for ending poverty among the aged; in particular, programme coordinators seized auspicious contexts such as President Lyndon Johnson's War on Poverty as occasions "to institute long-planned extensions of universal provision for the elderly." Derthick attributes the SSA's success over the years to a mix of restrained specificity in communicating its vision and pragmatism:

> In explaining and appraising the executive planners' success... it is important to keep the scope of their goals in perspective. They defined their objectives largely in instrumental terms.... They were successful in this. A big programme exists today that conforms to the first principles laid down in the founding years. Had goals been defined in terms that stipulated ultimate social outcomes with some precision, success would surely have been much harder to achieve.

The SSA track record stands in opposition to the permanent officials of an organisation becoming so strongly associated with specific options that other players in the policy arena immediately discount the agency's contribution to discourse. At the same time, the agency's permanent officials must have already done the internal spadework if they are to influence deliberations once an issue comes to the fore.

Major adaptations in political systems and governmental organisations often stem from an intuitive grasp of epochal shifts in challenges and opportunities. When such renderings of epochal shifts gain currency, leaders find fertile ground for relatively substantial policy innovation. Their actual progress will depend on their persuasive powers, the cogency of their case, and, crucially, the degree to which unfolding events sustain or call into question their lines of argument.

Fogleman's persuasive powers far exceeded Ryan's, but Ryan compensated through his reputation as a pragmatist-if he made the case, the Air Force leaders would more readily suspend their disbelief. Finally, events in Bosnia, Kosovo, and Afghanistan added credibility to the Air Force's view of its future. For instance, the tremendous success of drones in the Afghanistan campaign certainly made a visionary out of General Fogleman, who had pressed the case for unmanned aerial vehicles (UAVs) against some opposition during his stewardship of the Air Force.

In the mid-1980s Colin Campbell and Bert A. Rockman independently employed the term metacycles to describe epochal shifts that seem to call for departures from business as usual. Both authors apply the term to the plight of chief executives in advanced democracies at that time. It seems, however, to pertain as readily to executives within government organisations—be they political appointees or career officials-who conclude that incremental approaches to evolutionary adaptation will fail to rise to new challenges and exploit new opportunities.

The political context for the U.S. Air Force in the mid-1990s similarly evoked a period of grappling with inchoate metacycles. These took the form of challenges that went far beyond the usual temporal horizons of Air Force planners. They spun off from a host of emergent issues. What was the role of the U.S. military going to be in the post-cold war era? How were the services going to adapt to the related expectation that they now contribute toward deficit reduction? And, most critically for the Air Force, what would happen if the U.S. military did considerably less of its fighting from fixedwing aircraft with human pilots?

The Air Force elected to address new challenges and canvass new opportunities by pursuing its future through strategic visioning. This evolved under General Fogleman into an effort to radically realign operations and programmes on the basis of bold projections of what an envisioned Space and Air Force might look like in 2025. General Ryan's retreat to the more integrative concept of an Aerospace Force did not diminish the degree to which the Air Force engaged in strategic visioning of significantly stretched horizons.

We employ the term positioning for opportunities to describe the Air Force's investment in visioning. This nomenclature deliberately differentiates between what we have observed and opportunism. We agree with John Kingdon that the policy entrepreneur's connection to events often parallels the surfer in relation to the perfect wave. Surfers are "ready to paddle, and their readiness combined with their sense for riding the wave and using the forces beyond their control contribute to success." However, two factors play heavily on the degree to which opportunities are successfully exploited.

The first of these concerns the cogency of the policy entrepreneur's case in relation to those of other claimants to resources. Theda Skocpol notes that one underpinning of the Social Security Administration's success in gradually expanding its services was that the agency's proposals would fit with what was "actuarially sound." An armed service can similarly trump other contenders by invoking the potential contribution of a proposed programme to national security.

The second factor rests on the degree to which policy entrepreneurs in an organisation extrapolate from experience to press their case and realise that garnering such evidence often requires up-front investments. Surfers do not have the time to discuss with their colleagues whether a wave presents a perfect opportunity (and challenge) and if so why. The policy entrepreneur, however, must justify the timeliness of committing.

Furthermore, arguments extrapolated from agreed renderings of experience often tip the scale toward one programmatic investment over others. Consider, for example, the extra funds the second Bush administration sought for drones and satellite surveillance in the aftermath of their demonstrated effectiveness in Afghanistan. Marshalling such cases, to be sure, involves luck, but it also requires that an agency has adequately prepared the evidence in order to be able to present a plausible story line.

The agency must also maintain links to others in the policy arena so that they will allow it to repeat and refine its case each time an opportunity presents itself. More fundamentally, positioning for the wave often requires up-front commitments such as research and development and preliminary investments in hardware or infrastructure. We certainly can imagine policy sectors in which entrepreneurship remains cerebral. This condition, however, rarely pertains in an armed service. Such contexts confront us with the fact that even surfers require a state-of-the-art surfboard if they are to ride that perfect wave with optimal results.

Role of Organisational Characteristics

We have personally met General Fogleman, who launched the Air Force on its prolonged episode of strategic visioning, and he did not strike us as being a Don Quixote. This raises the question of whether there is something peculiar about the Air Force that made it amenable to the process that we chronicle and analyse here. Alternatively, are there lessons that might apply to other organisations in the U.S. federal government? Are they missing something that the Air Force grasped?

In some respects, the Air Force is not a typical federal agency. One finds relatively few political appointees in its top positions, and Air Force personnel, rather than civilians, occupy most of the top positions in the service's executive leadership. To be sure, the generals who masterminded much of the process do not fit the image of a government of strangers-that is, the split in many agencies between political appointees and career officials-that Hugh Heclo evoked in his famous characterisation of the divisions among key executives in most federal agencies.

The so-called bluesuiters ultimately did have to contend with civilian supervision of their quest for evolutionary success. Indeed, civilian engagement seemed to rise exponentially as the blue-suit strategic visioning began to raise issues of major political significance, such as whether the weaponisation of space was inevitable. Even apart from such dynamics, the Air Force operates within the same political-governmental system as other federal agencies and, therefore, faces similar institutional constraints.

Within the executive branch, bluesuiters must first win over the secretary of the Air Force, along with other political appointees vying for influence within the department. They must then make their case with the Joint Chiefs of Staff, the other services, the secretary of defence, and the White House and the Executive Office of the President. The latter two include officials in the National Security Council and the Office of Management and Budget.

These players ostensibly should take an interest in long-range issues, but in fact they tend to get caught up in fighting brush fires for the administration, to the extent that they can devote little time to strategic visioning-especially if it concerns matters far in the future. As the bluesuiters work through this maze, they often find it difficult to get other players' attention. Paradoxically, when they do get a response, they often encounter deep antagonism both from close competitors who have followed their manoeuvres too keenly and from relatively distant parties who are convinced that the bluesuiters' agenda clashes with their own.

The web of interconnections between parts of the executive branch and supporters and opponents in Congress further exacerbates the difficulty of devising and pressing a coherent strategic vision for any organisation in the U.S. government, much less a highly visible one such as the Air Force. Issues such as how many C-130s a state's Air National Guard maintains, whether the Air Force should have more F-

22s and fewer Joint Strike Fighters, and whether it can reduce the number of B-1s in service generate passionate debate in Congress.

Bluesuiters aspiring to bring a strategic vision to the national agenda must first learn how to keep their eye on the big picture. They must also develop ways of using specific instances of tension in Congress as opportunities to educate players about the costs of deferring investments in the future in order to serve interests vested in the status quo. The "uniformed patriot" culture of a military service perhaps explains why the Air Force remains persistent in bringing its perception of future needs to the public forum.

After all, members of the military see not only matters of life and death embedded in responses to the future, but also questions of national survival. Nonetheless, we can certainly conceive of civilian agencies-operating entirely in the realm of domestic policy-in which officials similarly see themselves as responsible for plotting the long-term consequences of the status quo and recommending changes in course on the grounds of public and national interest.

However, they have to play much more of an inside game than do bluesuiters. Joel D. Aberbach and Bert A. Rockman, who compare executive-bureaucratic political gamesmanship during the Nixon, Reagan, and Bush Sr. administrations, find sharp drops in career officials' interactions with congressmen and Hill staffers from the former to the latter two administrations. They attribute these to the Reagan administration's strategy of severely constricting direct contact between senior career officials and those outside the executive branch as a means of curtailing the policy entrepreneurship of the former.

The study raises the question of whether closing career officials out of direct participation in decisionmaking might prove a self-denying ordinance: "Why staff a public service with highly qualified individuals if they will not be given some latitude in figuring out how to do things and advising superiors as to the options?" However, one of the respondents, whom the authors quote to support their claim that career officials view themselves as motivated by issues of public good, conveys a deep appreciation of the ambiguity surrounding such an assertion from the standpoint of executive-bureaucratic politics: "The one thing that keeps us still here... is that we do have a hell of a dedication to the mission of whatever it is that we are doing, and we seem to be willing to cope with all of these frustrations. We do it because we believe so deeply in these bigger things."

The respondent's phraseology suggests an underlying skepticism about ultimately making a difference, which we did not encounter with the Air Force respondents. Aberbach and Rockman argue that the nation cannot expect creativity from its standing bureaucracy until it checks the competition between the political executive, Congress, and the federal judiciary over policy, which, in turn, has led to micromanagement of career officials. The scope of this problematic suggests the need to look more closely at just how encumbered agencies have become and what types of strategies they might pursue, in collaboration with their political leaders, to function more creatively with regard to evolutionary adaptation.

Contending with Constricted Latitude

Institutional constraints have become increasingly important for federal agencies in the past thirty years. In the mid-1960s, conventional wisdom among political scientists accepted that changes under American-style "polyarchy" would occur almost exclusively in "incremental" forms. In other words, the system-with, for instance, separation of powers, federalism, and the malleability of the state apparatus to special interests-would usually serve up relatively modest responses to policy challenges. The past thirty years have seen a deterioration even of the system's capacity for incremental change.

As described by Mancur Olson in the early 1980s, institutional stances have ossified to the point where change becomes ponderous, at best. For example, deadlock between the White House and Congress used to be ascribed to divided government, that is, control of the former by one party and one or both chambers of the latter by another. However, the Herculean struggles faced by Jimmy Carter and Bill Clinton under a united government suggest that the separation of powers combined with the ossification of special-interest perspectives has transformed deadlock into gridlock, recurrent even when the same party controls both the executive and legislative branches.

If we move away from Olson's ossification image into a different realm of anatomy, it would appear that the system has developed fairly significant arterial sclerosis. No matter how deeply committed they may be, those trying to pursue policies with greater strategic cogency will still face very constricted parameters. In cardiology, surgeons can achieve revascularisation of blocked arteries through bypass surgery or, less invasively but potentially less successfully, angioplasty.

The intractability faced by any reform-oriented federal agency usually precludes anything as dramatic and definitive as the institutional equivalent of bypass surgery. The Air Force's corporate strategic planning process might thus comport with revascularisation through angioplasty. Alternatively, cardiorevascularisation can also occur naturally through the formation of collateral vessels that give blood an alternate route to the heart. In the case at hand, this would mean that the Air Force, despite its institutional constraints, reinvented itself through internal resourcefulness and ingenuity. If so, any positive lessons learned from this study will find a ready audience among similarly limited federal agencies.

All federal agencies are now required to undertake some form of strategic planning under the 1993 Government Performance and Results Act (GPRA). What constitutes strategic planning in the federal government has thus taken on new meaning. The Air Force presents itself as an especially appealing research site for a case study in this emerging approach to achieving greater direction and coherence in federal agencies. The Air Force's strategic planning activities since the mid-1990s appear to be an exceptionally robust specimen of the generic practice. This owes to the energy with which the Air Force based its approach to strategic planning on futuristic visioning about how it might best pursue evolutionary adaptation.

More important, perhaps, the type of visioning pursued in the Air Force takes us beyond the objectives of GPRA. It is one thing for the National Park Service to work more rigorously at establishing its medium-term objectives and then tracking performance toward fulfilling them. It is quite another for it to fast-forward to the year 2025, gaze at what National Parks will look like if current policies remain fundamentally unchanged, envision desirable alternatives to the status quo projected twenty-five years into the future, and then backcast to the present to see which course corrections suggest themselves as desirable and feasible.

Expanding the Horizons for Strategic Planning

Evolutionary adaptation proves exceptionally difficult for organisations within the U.S. federal government. When we look at other countries, we find higher capacities for longer-range thinking and action associated with evolutionary adaptation. Although significantly driven by the need to renew their mandates, governments in parliamentary systems frequently commit considerable energy to strategic thinking that goes beyond the current legislative calendar.

In these systems, political appointees play only limited roles, so career civil servants often serve as the architects of innovative ways in which departments and agencies might face future challenges. Critically, two key elements of these systems are missing in the United States.

— First, the government-of-the-day often exerts sufficient control over the legislative branch to take initial steps toward a long-range strategic commitment once a consensus builds around it in the executive branch. This provides an incentive for career officials and a way for them to contribute to a legacy.

— Second, a strong, systemwide esprit de corps often prevails within these countries, which allows officials to detach themselves to some extent from the short-term interests within their units and departments.

Getting the innovative juices flowing among career officials within U.S. governmental organisations usually proves a much tougher sell. Officials seldom see that their political masters can deliver on commitments to take the first steps toward change. Moreover, units within agencies that float ideas for innovation can do a lot of damage to themselves by giving away hostages to opponents.

In the fragmented U.S. bureaucracy, these might belong to the same organisation-even wear the same uniform-yet maintain competing loyalties. In this regard, R. Kent Weaver and Bert A. Rockman's seminal inventory of the costs and benefits of the separation of powers offers pertinent guidance. Efforts to achieve innovation in the United States more frequently end in stalemate than is the case in other systems. However, in contrast to responsible party government as found in many parliamentary systems, the separation of powers can sometimes provide circumstances in which departments and agencies can play administration and congressional patrons off one another.

Obviously, engaging key players in the policy domain requires promoting innovation as serving the national interest or fostering electoral approval. Under some circumstances, U.S. agencies can ride the crest of a bidding-up process to achieve relatively comprehensive policy change. Positioning for such opportunities-that is, being ready to spring forward with highly developed options when auspicious circumstances emerge-suggests itself here as a worthwhile strategy for innovators.

In this regard, Martha Feldman's work on the crazy-quilt world of energy policymaking under Carter and Reagan demonstrates that while the process may not be coherent, it provides for myriad opportunities in which highly trained specialists can thoroughly examine their options. In particular, bureaucratic analysts develop and maintain inventories of "policy positions and reports that policymakers may request when needed." In this regard, agencies play exceedingly important roles in what John Kingdon argues gets the innovative ball rolling-the predecisional process of alternative specification.

The United States is not the only country in which engaging interest in corporate strategic planning faces serious difficulties; the conditions for the approach ebb and flow in other systems, as well. The United Kingdom, Canada, and Australia, for instance, all made considerable efforts at comprehensive strategic direction in the mid-1970s that ran a foul of departmental intransigence.

Broadly, the initiatives sought to prioritise demands for continued expansion of the welfare state, notwithstanding the exceedingly daunting fiscal pressures associated with the economics of decline. Fiscal realities won out in the end, and a politics of constraint emerged in which bold images of the future gave way to narrow-gauged concerns about the efficiency and effectiveness of existing government programmes. The former focus spawned a very strong corporate-some call it managerial-mind-set in many non-American public services.

In the 1980s, many public sector organisations of English-speaking countries other than the United States guided themselves through management boards or direct contractual agreements between the heads of operational units and ministers. In both circumstances, the career executives of the principal "businesses" of government organisations would have to outline and justify their objectives and submit to reviews of their performance in terms of outputs and outcomes.

Even with very substantial organisational commitments to such collective guidance, however, management boards and performance agreements inevitably encountered difficulty in installing and operating a feedback loop between corporate strategy and budgeting. The relation between the 1993 Government Performance and Results Act (GPRA) and what the Air Force has pursued proves somewhat tenuous. The Air Force effort has far exceeded the legal requirements of the act, and in many respects it reflects its own leaders' distillation of smart practices in the private sector.

Despite its more limited scope, however, the GPRA has significantly increased discussion of strategic planning in the federal government. It attempts to graft onto the U.S. departments and agencies something roughly akin to the corporate approaches that emerged in the 1980s in other English-speaking systems. Paul Light has correctly categorised GPRA as liberation management. It seeks to improve performance through the carrot of increased managerial discretion over the use of resources and the stick of greater individual and organisational accountability to achieve specific goals.

In this regard, GPRA fits within the general framework of new public management. However, as Peter Aucoin pointed out very early on, new public management clashes with the overarching conception among politicians that government has grown too large and must be put under tighter scrutiny. In 1997, the General Accounting Office (GAO) recognised the relevance of this dynamic for GPRA-especially given that departmental compliance with the act is a congressional mandate.

The GAO noted that the legislative staffers who do the bulk of reviewing of GPRA reports concentrate on their "oversight roles and stress near-term performance," whereas agency officials emphasize "long-term goals, adaptability to changing needs, and flexibility in execution." In some respects, GPRA can trace its lineage to the Planning, Programming, and Budgeting System (PPBS) that emerged in the Department of Defence under Robert McNamara and ultimately won the imprimatur of Lyndon Johnson for implementation throughout the U.S. government.

The fact that the Pentagon still follows a PPBS approach makes this point especially pertinent to the case. However, GPRA's architecture concerns itself much more with the need for coordination between agencies and Congress on corporate strategy than with the primary focus of PPBS-namely, prioritisation of long-range objectives so that decisionmakers might align budgetary commitments more cogently.

The Air Force strategic visioning commitment thus fits the PPBS template more closely than the GPRA one-with the important caveat that planning, programming, and budgeting will never link sufficiently unless Congress grasps and supports how a service seeks to connect the three. Indeed, the Air Force encountered a sharp learning curve in this area, at first attempting to run an in-house process and eventually recognising that it had to work much more intensively in educating Congress about the long-range consequences of budgetary choices.

This comports with Aaron Wildavsky's view of how PPBS might have worked had the proper conditions prevailed in the 1960s. He saw a strong analytic culture as the sine qua non for PPBS and, in fact, viewed this as a strength of the Pentagon not often shared by domestic agencies. Wildavsky held a very high standard for policy analysis. He viewed it as a capacity to transcend "the fire-house environment of day-to-day administration" and trace out "the consequences of innovative ideas" rather than "projecting the status quo" into the future.

In words that could easily apply to the principal rationale behind the Fogleman and Ryan planning efforts, Wildavsky noted that the originators of PPBS wanted to close the gap between planning and budgeting: "They wanted to stop blue-sky planning and integrate planning and budgeting.... They wanted to use the programme budget to bridge the gap between military planners, who cared about requirements but not about resources, and budget people, who were narrowly concerned with financial costs but not necessarily with effective policies."

Since GPRA does not encompass strategic visioning in this sense, we find ourselves looking beyond agencies' efforts to comply with the act in order to relate the case to dialogue about smart practices for corporate strategic planning in the federal government. While the literature still has a considerable way to go, it can provide some guidance for the case at hand.

For instance, Sandford Borins aims to distil best practices for innovators in bureaucratic agencies at the federal, state, and local levels. In particular, he concedes that the best innovation in large organisations most frequently arises "through the efforts of mavericks at 'skunkworks' far from central offices, operating without a clear mandate from above and using bootlegged resources."

Borins's characterisation of innovation might strike the reader as the furthest thing conceivable from the situation of the U.S. Air Force. Not only does the Air Force run an exceedingly diverse and complex bureaucratic system, but it gobbles up nearly 4 percent of the annual budget of the federal government.

The U.S. Air Force case thus presents a daunting challenge, as the magnitude of corporate strategic planning in an organisation of this size far exceeds the scale of any existing benchmarks. However, it provides a unique and timely opportunity to establish a benchmark for exercises of similar scale that other sizable agencies have begun to pursue under GPRA and other auspices.

Effective Implementation

Not with standing the difference in scale between the Air Force's strategic visioning efforts and those undertaken in other public service organisations, the latter initiatives do bring important themes to the discussion.

— First, the agency must devise a feasible and convincing framework for visioning and planning that nonetheless establishes true "stretch goals" that challenge the organisation profoundly.

— Second, processes focused on adaptation to possible events far in the future rely extensively on scenario building and war gaming.

— Third, the success of the process depends substantially on the personal qualities of the organisation's leaders and the extent to which they involve themselves in the strategic visioning and planning.

— Fourth, collective processes will greatly enhance the cooperation of both the barons and the rank and file of an organisation.

— Finally, factoring in the likely responses of stakeholders is crucial to both visioning and planning.

Devising stretch goals is one of the mechanisms through which strategic visioning takes an organisation beyond planning in the classic sense. It can make the planning process even more difficult and elusive than it normally is. Public sector organisations must grapple with government's inherent limitations in reconciling the standards of a plan-namely, a detailed formulation of a programme of action-with strategy.

Bureaucratic strategy usually falls short of detailed prescription because of uncertainties in both the identification of the future public good and the degree to which stakeholders will support the stated goals. In this respect, the concept of strategic visioning perhaps fits government agencies even better than private sector organisations. Though difficult to pursue, it takes into account the degree to which corporate strategic planners in the public sector find themselves discerning and targeting inchoate futures whose value ultimately lies in the extent to which they wrench stakeholders from incremental adaptations to the status quo.

Advocacy of strategic visioning implies two things. First, while organisations cannot discern their future with certitude, they can improve their performance by anticipating environmental changes that will require them to draw on capabilities that they would not develop by following the status quo. Second, incremental change based on piecemeal modifications of the status quo will inevitably result in the organisation falling short of requirements sometime in the future, and this failure to adapt will endanger its institutional viability.

In the case of a government organisation, the failure to adapt could appreciably harm the public good-for the Air Force, national security-just as a similar lapse in a key industrial concern could erode a country's competitiveness in the global economy. The available literature suggests that more often than not, organisations that have succeeded in corporate strategic planning were able to wean themselves off incrementalism and establish stretch goals.

For instance, Sandford Borins analyses submissions from 217 semifinalists for the Ford Foundation's state and local Innovations in American Government Awards programme between 1990 and 1994. He finds that only seven percent of the innovations emerged from organisation wide strategic planning. However, 59 percent of the reforms that were developed by discrete units of an umbrella organisation emerged from comprehensive efforts at redesign. Only 30 percent of the initiatives evolved from "groping" or incremental efforts to adapt to change.

Borins also finds that comprehensive planning occurs most frequently among organisations that require large capital investments, programmes that involve the coordination of a large number of organisations, and theory-driven programmes. Borins's findings comport with those of a 1997 Federal Benchmarking Consortium (FBC) study of best practices in the private and public sectors that might be appropriate for large federal government organisations.

The study promotes a view of corporate strategic planning that assumes a high degree of visioning-and even asserts that corporate strategic planning stands at the intersection of art and science. However, the study also emphasizes that visioning and planning far into the future most frequently occur in organisations with either complex processes or very long-range programmes (or both). The report highlights the importance of future thinking for devising stretch goals and for enabling the organisation "to recognise and capitalise on the events transpiring outside its span of control."

The Air Force's visioning acknowledges the profound bias toward incrementalism of its real-world context but anticipates circumstances in which it might, if adequately prepared, seise opportunities for substantial evolutionary adaptation. Its approach to unmanned aerial vehicles (UAVs) serves as an example of this phenomenon. Through what were initially relatively modest investments and deployments, the Air Force has, in just a few years, given life to a new concept-namely, that much of its work can be done with drones that do not endanger human resources.

The increase in the role of UAVs from Kosovo to Iraq probably exceeds even General Fogleman's expectations for this approach to surveillance and attack, which in the mid-1990s prompted skepticism in the Air Force's pilot-dominated culture. The FBC report also finds that scenario building and role playing can greatly assist an organisation in identifying its desired path into the future. Such approaches constitute the second key factor for connecting visioning and planning. The FBC study observes that private corporations use this approach extensively, often even employing the term war games.

Obviously, the military brings to such a task immense experience with war games. Such exercises serve little purpose in visioning, however, if they consist in applying existing methods of operation to the status quo projected x years out. In other words, stretch goals will not emerge unless the game itself forces thinking beyond conventional parameters.

In any case, role playing through scenarios that invite a realistic grasp of future challenges can have immense effects in organisations: the players develop an appreciation of the need to prepare for uncertain futures, and nonplayers similarly broaden their views of organisational challenges when the findings from the games are properly disseminated. War gaming not only adds cogency to organisational visions, but can also inject a sense of urgency into the process of planning for the future.

General Fogleman considered that visioning would be relevant only if the Air Force backcast, so that expectations for the future actually guided changes in current programmatic commitments. The FBC study finds that the private corporations that prove most successful at strategic planning have achieved a similar discipline: "After describing the vision of the future using standard techniques, the company leaders essentially move backward from the future state to identify how the company must look at a given point in time if the desired future is to materialise."

The third key factor for strategic planning, leadership, depends on the personal qualities of those in charge and their full engagement in the process. Borins describes what he calls a trichotomy of innovation: politicians usually lead innovation when an organisation faces a major crisis; agency heads normally assert themselves most clearly when they first assume their responsibilities; and middle-level and frontline officials most often probe creative options when faced with internal problems or technical opportunities.

In all three cases, the courage to lead agencies to innovation stems from the integrity of those in charge-meaning they have not allowed crises to arise or deepen through neglect of warning signs or paralysis in the face of gridlock. In Borins's words, they bring to their work "the ability to recognise problems or opportunities in a proactive manner." The FBC report highlights the important role of the chief executive in taking an active part in a strategic management group, together with the other top leaders of a corporation.

It also stresses the need for the chief executive to personally "explain and cascade" the resulting strategic vision throughout an organisation. Public service organisations do present ambiguity, however, along the lines identified by Borins. Who is the chief executive? The former British prime minister Margaret Thatcher, for instance, wanted her ministers to actively manage their departments. Some did. In fact, a few participated directly on their ministries' management boards.

Most ministers, however, remained aloof from managerial activities, notwithstanding Thatcher's preferences. In such cases, either the head career civil servant was given or assumed the managerial mantle, or the department shunned the corporate approach completely.

The best results with corporate approaches to management came from departments in which the ministers took a keen and direct interest in managing their departments. The nature of these organisations' activities played a role, as well.

If they broke down relatively neatly into comparatively free-standing "businesses," then the minister could gain a cogent view of each major unit's objectives and gauge its civil-service head's performance on the basis of whether the objectives were met. In other words, the department would operate as a conglomerate and the minister as chairman of the board and chief executive officer.

Ambiguity existed in the U.S. Air Force in three ways. In the first round, the political head of the Air Force-the secretary, Sheila Widnall-did not engage in the strategic planning process until issues with serious political dimensions emerged. General Fogleman was thus clear to act as a chief executive along the lines suggested by Borins and the FBC report. This fit the preference for having bluesuiters run the business end of the Air Force.

Ambiguity entered the equation, however, because governmental corporate strategic planning, by nature, takes an organisation into a stratum of policy commitments that ultimately require authoritative sanction by the political leaders. Dr. Widnall's successor, F. Whitten Peters, assumed an active role in the second round, led by General Ryan. This introduced a dynamic whereby the private sector model of principal executive authority being clearly vested in one individual did not pertain.

Although Peters essentially functioned as chief executive officer and Ryan as chief operating officer, the two often worked in tandem over matters pertaining to the former role. Even so, role ambiguity played a more important part during the first rather than second round. Restrained political leadership allowed General Fogleman to follow the prevailing stylistic preference of bluesuiters at the time, whereby secretaries played mainly symbolic and legitimising roles while chiefs got on with the business of running the Air Force.

The second ambiguity lies in the entrenched cultural tensions of the U.S. executive-bureaucratic system, and it is amplified by the high stakes connected with what the Air Force does and the perpetual disputes over the resources it receives.

The separation of powers makes it hard for federal government organisations to plan like private corporations. For the purposes of institutional survival, chief operating officers must weigh issues such as their departmental secretary's standing in the administration and the ability of the administration to get its positions through Congress.

Even in a symbiotic arrangement such as that enjoyed by Peters and Ryan, the relationship between a secretary and a chief of staff proves much less hierarchical than that between a chairman of the board and a chief operating officer or even a British cabinet minister and the permanent civil servant who heads the department. If departmental secretaries in the United States choose to engage in corporate strategic planning, they must enter a dialogue with permanent officials. Officials will thus find it hard to bring about authoritative corporate change if their political appointees have not participated in the process. Similarly, political appointees, who can change policies against the will of their permanent officials so long as the president and Congress approve, cannot change the corporate ethos of their organisations unless they have worked through the dialogue.

The third ambiguity stems from the fact that the Air Force's core businesses do not lend themselves to the tidy divisions found in a conglomerate. Two large operations-the so-called shooting commands of Air Combat and Space-differ in that the latter draws on considerably fewer resources than the former and faces huge political obstacles to developing space-based attack capabilities. In addition, much of its surveillance role operates in support of Air Combat operations.

A much smaller shooting command, Special Operations, participates extensively in joint operations with other services. The Air Mobility, Air Force Materiel, and Air Education and Training commands support the shooters, and Air Mobility also performs substantial functions for other services, especially the Army and the Marines.

Furthermore, Air Force Materiel and Air Education operate largely with pass-through funds expended in the service of other commands. Finally, the Air Force ultimately operates at the behest of five regional combatant commanders who are mandated to prepare for and preside over military operations in the European, Northern, Southern, Central, and Pacific geographic divisions established by the Pentagon. Coordinating plans and operations with combatant commanders greatly compounds the difficulty of corporate approaches to leadership in all of the services.

These three ambiguities make it exceedingly difficult to delineate businesses and their objectives within the Air Force or to achieve horizontal resolution of conflicts between the major corporate units. These and similar circumstances are commonplace in the federal bureaucracy. One might therefore expect to find a keen interest in collective mechanisms for developing strategies and coordinating units, but in fact convincing participants of the utility of such devices is a hard sell in the U.S. federal bureaucracy.

The separation of powers sustains an incentive system that encourages units to work alone in the search for political mandates and budget resources. Likewise, experience teaches them that corporate strategic approaches often fail even to gain the attention of the political leaders, much less negotiate the treacherous waters of executive-legislative relations.

Not with standing these counterindications, the literature suggests that collective processes are key to obtaining a consensus among leaders regarding future directions and ensuring that the rank and file understand and support the objectives.

The FBC report states emphatically that without a consensus, there is no plan. Moreover, chief executives cannot devise visions and plans on their own, but rather must work closely with other corporate leaders. Borins also makes a strong, empirically based case that holistic innovation in organisations most frequently takes place when the process has been supported by the central staff and the agency's leaders have interacted regularly through formal coordinative mechanisms. Borins concludes that "collaboration across organisational boundaries does not happen naturally; it must be made to happen."

General Fogleman did not stumble on this concept. He believed that the Air Force had functioned in a consultative way in other difficult phases of its development and that it should do so again when he became chief in 1994.

It took some time to formalise the exact contours of the process, but they were eventually clarified through the critical roles of Corona-the council of four-star generals who developed the 1996 vision-and the board of directors-the group of three-star generals who prepared issues for the Corona conference.

Fogleman subsequently created an Air Force Staff unit, XP, whose three-star head assumed responsibility for the integration of planning and programming. The two disciplines continued to operate independently, however, because XP served two separate sets of deliberative machinery, one for planning and another for programming. Moreover, the Corona council and, in particular, the board of directors did not function in the same way under General

Ryan's visioning round as they had under Fogleman's. These considerations present a number of issues surrounding the question of where exactly the Air Force's corporate persona is lodged.

For instance, should the Staff control the programming process despite inroads made by the major commands in the visioning and planning processes? The debate spawned an initiative focused on revamping the planning, programming, and budgeting systems along more inclusive corporate lines-namely, the Air Force Resource Allocation Process (AFRAP). Finally, the literature strongly prescribes external consultation with stakeholders as a key ingredient to successful corporate strategic planning.

While this presents problems for any federal government agency, the secrecy surrounding many of the weapons systems and concepts of operations envisioned for the future seriously limits the Air Force's ability to pursue external consultations. Space, for example, was a central concern in General Fogleman's planning process, but most of the related issues were classified as top secret throughout the period in which he was chief.

The adversarial politics associated with the separation of powers discourages the planner from cooperating with congressmen, congressional staff, and contractors, who are likely to betray confidences if they feel that their agendas and priorities will not prevail. The FBC report makes a strong plea for external consultation, although it frequently refers to the marketplace and customers, which suggests that it is mainly oriented to agencies that provide goods and services to specific individuals and groups.

Such commercial analogies do not apply to the Air Force because the market, even including other military services, does not offer substitutes for much of what it provides. Furthermore, it generally cannot discriminate among the citizens who receive its benefits. Liaison with Congress would certainly constitute the most important form of external consultation for the Air Force.

The two organisations are not likely to work in tandem, however, as indicated by the General Accounting Office's assessment of the likely dynamics for dialogue between agencies and Congress on strategic plans produced in compliance with the Government Performance and Results Act.

The cultural divide leaves agency heads "skeptical that consensus on strategic goals could be reached, especially given the often conflicting views among agencies' multiple congressional stakeholders." The Air Force ultimately developed a successful approach for bringing the results of its visioning and planning to bear on congressional budgeting decisions.

Rather than pressing a comprehensive transformation package, the Air Force chose a more gradual approach of focusing on fork-in-theroad issues: if Congress made the wrong choice on one of these critical decisions, the chance that it would be able to purchase a critical capability within the desired time frame would shrink to dangerous proportions from the standpoint of national security.

Such smart practice fits recent research on historical institutional adaptation in the federal government. For instance, Patrick J. Wolf, who analyses 170 cases of federal agency reform from 1890 to the present time, finds that organisations operating with a relatively high degree of autonomy from direct political control are the most innovative. This suggests that the Air Force was wise to incorporate administration appointees in its visioning and planning processes and to become increasingly judicious in the types of pleas it makes to Congress.

Daniel P. Carpenter's study of innovation in executive-branch agencies between 1862 and 1928 finds that the most effective organisations partook of state building by seizing opportunities to demonstrate to Congress and the public how they could make a difference in areas of great national concern. They gained relevance not by articulating grand designs, but by establishing symbiosis with sympathetic parties in the policy marketplace.

References

Jones, A.P., Homer, J.B., Murphy, D.L., *et al.*, "Understanding diabetes: population dynamics through simulation modeling and experimentation", *American Journal of Public Health*, 96(3), 488–494, 2006.

Kaplan, R. and Norton, D., *The Balanced Scorecard*, Harvard Business School Press, Boston MA, 1996.

Mankins, M.C. and Steele, R., "Stop making plans: start making decisions", *Harvard Business Review*, 84(1), 76–84, 2006.

Martin, J.D. and Petty, J.W., *Value-based Management*, Harvard Business School Press, Boston MA, 2000.

Penrose, E.T., *The Theory of the Growth of the Firm*, Oxford University Press, Oxford, 1959.

Prahalad, C.K. and Hammond, A., "Serving the World's poor", profi tably. *Harvard Business Review*, 80(9), 48–57, 2002.

Rappaport, A., "Ten ways to create shareholder value", *Harvard Business Review*, 84(9), 66–77, 2006.

Bibliography

Ackoff, R. L., *Creating the Corporate Future*, New York, NY: Wiley & Sons, 1981.

Barney, J., "Firm Resources and Sustainable Competitive Advantage", *Journal of Management*, vol 17, no 1, 1991.

Bass, B. M. (n.d.)., *From transactional to transformational leadership: Learning to share the vision*, Organizational Dynamics 19-31.

Bowers, C. A., *Education, Cultural Myths, and the Ecological Crisis: Toward deep changes*, New York: SUNY, 1993.

Capra, Fritjof, *The Web of Life: A new scientific understanding of living systems*, New York: Anchor books, 1996.

Chaffee, E., "Three models of strategy", *Academy of Management Review*, vol 10, no. 1, 1985.

David, F., *Strategic Management*, Columbus:Merrill Publishing Company, 1989.

Deming, W. E., *Out of the Crisis*, Cambridge, MA: Massachusetts Institute of Technology, 1982.

Drucker, Peter., *The Practice of Management*, Harper and Row, New York, 1954.

Floyd, S. W., & Wooldridge, B., "Managing strategic consensus: the foundation of effective implementation", *Academy of Management Executive*, 6(4) 27-39, 1992.

Gluck, F. W., Kaufman, S., & Walleck, A. S., "The four phases of strategic management", *Journal of Business Strategy*, 2(3), 9-21, 1982.

Hamel, G., & Prahalad, C. K., "Strategic intent", *Harvard Business Review*, 63-76, 1989, May-June.

Harrison, E. Frank, *The Managerial Decision-Making Process* (5th ed.), Boston: Houghton Mifflin, 1999.

Hawken, Paul; Lovins, Amory and Lovins, L., Hunter. *Natural Capitalism: Creating the next industrial revolution*, New York: Little, Brown, and Company.

Mankins, M.C. and Steele, R., "Stop making plans: start making decisions", *Harvard Business Review*, 84(1), 76–84, 2006.

Martin, J.D. and Petty, J.W., *Value-based Management*, Harvard Business School Press, Boston MA, 2000.

McCall, Morgan W., Jr., & Kaplan, Robert K., *Whatever it takes: The realities of managerial decision making* (2nd ed.), Englewood Cliffs, NJ: Prentice-Hall, 1990.

Penrose, E.T., *The Theory of the Growth of the Firm*, Oxford University Press, Oxford, 1959.

Porter, Michael E., *Competitive Strategy: Techniques for analyzing industries and competitors*, New York: Free Press, 1980.

Prahalad, C.K. and Hammond, A., "Serving the World's poor", profi tably. *Harvard Business Review*, 80(9), 48–57, 2002.

Williams, Steve W., *Making better business decisions: Understanding and improving critical thinking and problem solving skills*, Thousand Oaks, CA: Sage Publications, 2002.

Index